Marriages of

JOHNSTON COUNTY, NORTH CAROLINA

❧

1762-1868

96 - 1157

Marriages of

JOHNSTON COUNTY,

NORTH CAROLINA

1762-1868

Compiled by

BRENT H. HOLCOMB

Baltimore

GENEALOGICAL PUBLISHING CO., INC.

1985

INTRODUCTION

THIS VOLUME contains abstracts of all 3,946 extant marriage bonds issued in Johnston County, North Carolina from 1762 to 1868, when marriage bonds were discontinued. Although the county was formed in 1746, the earliest extant marriage bond is from the year 1762. The abstracts were made from a microfilm copy of the bonds and are arranged throughout in alphabetical order by the name of the groom, each entry further providing the name of the bride, the date of the bond, and the names of the bondsmen. To facilitate research, brides and bondsmen are also listed in the index. The reader should keep in mind that the name of the groom is spelled as the name was signed, or, in the case of a person who could not write, the way it was signed for him. The name of the bride appears as it was spelled by the clerk or the person making out the bond. Since the bride did not sign, the spellings may vary widely from the way the name would properly be spelled.

Marriage bonds are the only public records of marriage prior to 1851. Although the marriage bond law was enacted in 1741 and remained in force until 1868, the clerk of the county court was required only from 1851 to keep a register of all marriages performed by license (issued with the bond). In many cases from the year 1851 (and in a few before that year), the license with return by the officiant is extant. This return usually gives the exact date of the marriage, and occasionally the place of marriage, as well as the name of the officiant.

The researcher should bear in mind that bonds alone are not proof that a marriage took place, only that a marriage was intended. Also, not everyone who married in Johnston County between 1762 and 1868 is identified in this work, for some marriages were performed after publication of banns, and no bond, license, or other public record of marriage was required.

BRENT HOWARD HOLCOMB, C. G.
Columbia, South Carolina

JOHNSTON COUNTY, NORTH CAROLINA, MARRIAGES 1762-1868

Abell, James H. & Lucy J. Etheredge, 23 Jan 1856; m. 24 Jan 1856, by P. I. Carraway, M. G.

Acock, Daniel & Elizabeth Stansel, 25 Oct 1844; Willie Stansel, bm.

Acock, James & Charity Wilkerson, 29 Mar 1808; Charles Wilkerson, bm.

Adams, Alford & Zilpha Gatlin, 29 May 1827; John Dixon, bm.

Adams, Allen & Sally Ryals, 23 Dec 1805; Jacob Wood, bm.

Adams, Alsey & Nanny Baker, 9 Sept 1853; m 15 Sept 1853, by Right Ryals, J. P.

Adams, Bryan & Redly Johnson, 29 Sept 1813; Jesse Adams, bm.

Adams, David & Lucy Grimes, 30 Aug 1820; Charles Stevens, bm.

Adams, David B. & Rebecca Davis, 16 Oct 1848; W. F. S. Alston, bm.

Adams, Edwin & Maia Holland, 27 Jan 1844; Jesse Holland, bm.

Adams, Green & Olive Mainard, 20 Sept 1814; William Wilder, bm.

Adams, Howell & Elizabeth Lowell, 26 July 1799; Clayton Lowell, bm.

Adams, James & Edney Hobby, 21 Dec 1803; Martin Woodall, William Allen, bm.

Adams, Jesse & Harriet Dunn, 4 Dec 1843; Starling Massingill, bm.

Adams, Jesse & Mary Mitchell, 13 Dec 1862; m. 16 Dec 1862 by B. A. Wellons, J. P.

Adams, Jesse A. & Sarah Peacock, 1 Mar 1867; R. A. Adams, bm; m 7 Mar 1867 by B. Godawin, J. P.

Adams, John & Margaret Johnson, 20 Jan 1827; Allen Johnson Sr., bm.

Adams, John & Olief Bailey, 25 Aug 1842; Gray W. Thomas, bm.

Adams, John Q. & Civil L. Reaves, 28 Aug 1839; T. Bagley, bm.

Adams, Joseph & Elizabeth Lee, 26 Mar 1839; Josiah Adams, bm.

Adams, Joseph J. & Lucetta Ann Ogburn, 2 Jan 1854; m 12 Jan 1854 by J. T. Leech, J. P.

Adams, Josiah & Betsy George, 16 Nov 1813; Reuben Sanders, bm.

Adams, Lewis & Susanna Morgan, 3 Dec 1799; John Morgan, bm.

Adams, Nathan & Elizabeth S. Holt, 1 Apr 1853; m 3 Apr 1853 by Needham Ingram, J. P.

Adams, Redick & Polly Avera, 16 May 1833; Young Bridgers, bm.

Adams, Right A. & Theny Ingram, 25 Feb 1834; Right H. Adams, bm.

Adams, Sidney & Louiza Garland, 6 Apr 1826; Hinton Vinson, bm.

Adams, Vine H. & Luanna Johnson, 22 Feb 1836; Harry Johnson, bm.

Adams, William & Nancy Maclemore, 25 Jun 1836; Sidney Adams, bm.

Adams, William & Sally Blackmon, 27 Apr 1847; Benjamin Moor, bm.

Adams, William & Martha Green, m 7 Jul 1859 at Jordan Sanders, by Right Ryals, J. P.

Adams, Wm. M. & Winnifred Allen, 24 Nov 1840; David B. Adams, bm.

Adkerson, Micajah & Mary Adkerson, 7 Jun 1796; Benjamin Bryan, bm.

Alexander, Adams & Mary Ann Card, 1 Aug 1803; W. H. N. Arthur Bryant, bm.

Alferd, John & Polly Ann Avera, 27 Dec 1848; Joseph E. Barham, bm.

Alford, Bython B. & Joanna Barnes, 19 Aug 1843; William S. Ballinger, bm.

Alford, Peyton, of Wake County, & Lewcy Hinton, 28 May 1805; Blake Brady, bm.

Alford, Willey & Elizabeth Edwards, m 28 May 1855 by B. B. Alford, J. P.

Allen, Ahab & Redly Johnson, 4 Jul 1834; Elisha Harrison, bm.

Allen, Alexander & Emily Elizabeth Johnson, 27 Jan 1852; m 30 Jan 1853 by R. Masingill, J. P.

Allen, Alfred & Lewcy Johnson, 10 Sept 1839; Alfred Johnson, bm.

Allen, Ben (colored) & Jane Avera, 22 Nov 1866; Theophilus Whitfield, bm.

Allen, Bryan & Susanna Wood, 29 May 1821; John Morgan, bm.

Allen, Demsy & Betsy Byrd, 17 Sept 1807; Reding Byrd, bm.

Allen, Giddion & Mary Eason, 14 Dec 1771; John Smith, John Pope, bm.

Allen, Gideon & Esther Johnson, 25 Feb 1800; James Woodall, bm.

Allen, Gideon & Elizabeth Russel, 2 Mar 1807; Jno. Farmer, bm.

Allen, Gideon & Charity George, 4 Mar 1823; Barzella Blackman, bm.

Allen, Gideon & Redley Johnson, 12 Apr 1833; James Allen, bm.

Allen, Gideon & Aby Bryan, 24 Sept 1833; John Peacock, bm.

Allen, Gideon & Lucy Jane Massingill, 30 Jan 1855; m 1 Feb 1855 by Robt. Massingill, J. P.

Allen, James & Elizabeth Rhods, 28 Jun 1823; John Allen, bm.

Allen, James & Winefred Adams, 2 Nov 1829; Thomas Lee, bm.

Allen, James N. & Martha Massingill, 29 Aug 1866; Gideon Allen, bm; m 9 Sept 1866 at Marthw Massingills, by Jas. H. Adams, J. P.

Allen, James W. & Partheny H. Massingill, m 4 Mar 1857.

Allen, John & Sally Johnson, m 4 Jan 1854 by Robt. Massingill, J. P.

Allen, John B. & Candis Stallings, 2 Apr 1823; Nathan B. Allen, bm.

Allen, John E. & Elizabeth Avera, 22 Nov 1848; Wm. R. Lee, bm.

Allen, Joseph E. & Bedy Whittinton, 6 Apr 1844; Nicholas Lee, bm.

Allen, Josiah & Winnifred Ingram, 30 Oct 1821; James Allen, bm.

Allen, Josiah G. & Elizabeth Allen, 30 Dec 1852; m 4 Jan 1853 by R. Masingill, J. P.

Allen, Josiah G. & Nancy Jane Massingill, 26 Mar 1861; m 31 Mar 1861 at Robert Massingill, by Jas. H. Adams, J. P.

Allen, N. E. & Louenzy Adams, 17 Jul 1866; L. G. Allen, bm; m 19 Jul 1866 at W. M. Adams, by R. Massingill, J. P.

Allen, Nathan & Apsabeth Ballenger, 22 Mar 1791; William Ballenger, bm.

Allen, Nathan L. & Mary Jane Adams, 17 Mar 1832; Joseph John Adams, bm.

Allen, Sir William & Ridly Allen, 17 Jan 1841; Alfred Johnson, bm.

Allen, Sir William & Narcissa Allen, 4 Jun 1863; m 7 Jun 1863 at Mrs. M. Adams, by R. Massingill, J. P.

Allen, Thomas & Bedith Smith, 9 Apr 1797; Bryant Adams, bm.

Allen, Thomas & Esther Lee, 20 Nov 1821; William S. Whitenton, bm.

Allen, Thomas & Elizabeth Munds, 11 Oct 1853; m 16 Oct 1853 by C. Langdon, J. P.

Allen, Timothy & Easter Tomkins, 16 Aug 1866; H. E. Thain, bm; m 16 Aug 1866, by Jethro Thain, J. P.

Allen, William & Rachel Jones, 17 Nov 1794; Jack Woodall, bm.

Allen, William & Betsy Ricks, 12 Mar 1803; John Stevens, bm.

Alston, W. F. S. & Emily M. Clifton, 25 Aug 1847; Needham B. Stevens, bm.

Altford, Bryant & Mary Rose, m 21 Dec 1854, by Edwin Boykin, J. P.

Altman, Doctor (colored) & Charlotte Benton, 17 Aug 1866; Jno. C. Hood, Jr., bm; m 22 Sept 1866 at John Burtons, by Bryant Williams, J. P.

Altman, Joel & Nancy Blackman, 21 Mar 1797; John Lee, bm.

Altman, Wiley & Sarah C. Toler, 30 Jan 1849; Caler(?) R. Toler, bm.

Ammons, David & Louisa H. Lee, m 4 Jun 1861 by George Green, J. P.

Andrews, Green (colored) & Sylvia Ward, 12 May 1866; George W. Braswell, bm.

Applewhite, Jonathan & Lucretia A. Whitley, 30 Sept 1861; m 15 Oct 1861 at Mrs. Maria Whitley's, by James Mahoney.

Applewhite, William H. & Virginia Whitley, 24 Nov 1866; R. D. Whitley, bm; m 27 Nov 1866 at A. M. Whitley's, by A. J. Finlayson, M. G.

Arnold, William & Lucinda Massingill, 11 Oct 1832; Crawford Mitchell, bm.

Arp, Jonathan & Doruthe Wilder, 15 Feb 1797; Burrel Arp, bm.

Artes, Luke & Martilla Bell, 10 Oct 1815; Jacob Powell, bm.

Artis, Archibald & Nancy Hathcock, 14 Nov 1857; William H. Avera, bm; m 26 Nov 1857 by J. C. Hood, J. P.

Ashe, Thomas L. & Delilah Stevens, 14 Nov 1800; John Carrell, bm.

Ashly, William & Nancy Stevens, 7 Jan 1822; Jonathan Britt, bm.

Atkins, Isaac & Ann Penny, 31 Jan 1789.

Atkins, John & Irene Johnson, 19 Sept 1805; Henry Johnson, bm.

Atkins, Josiah & Frances Penny, 28 Dec 1799; E. Sanders, Hardy Penny, bm.

Atkinson, Amos & Julia Price, 9 Mar 1822; Elam Lockart, bm.

Atkinson, Ashly & Nancy Watson, 3 Dec 1847, Elijah Atkinson, bm.

Atkinson, Blake & Penellope Smith, 28 Jul 1824; James Hollomon, bm.

Atkinson, Cary & Willy Hinton, 26 Apr 1818; Wm. Oneal, bm.

Atkinson, Dick & Jane Langston, 30 Jun 1866; J. B. Alford, bm.

Atkinson, Elias & Sarah _____ [torn], 6 Oct 1795; Benjamin Hill, bm.

Atkinson, Harris & Caroline Baily, 1 Mar 1852; m 2 Mar 1852 by A. W. Richardson, J. P.

Atkinson, John & Fereby Stevens, 1 Jun 1790; William Stevens, bm.

Atkinson, John & Phereby Altmon, 14 Feb 1819; Etheldred Holt, bm.

Atkinson, John & Martha Watson, 27 Aug 1821; G. Grice, bm.

Atkinson, John & Betsy Lynch, 29 Nov 1832; James Raiford, bm.

Atkinson, John & Zilphia Aycock, 10 Sept 1862; Thos. D. Snead, bm; m 25 Sept 1862 by Jas. H. Sasser, M. G.

Atkinson, John Jr. & Patsy Roberts, 13 July 1820; Bright Jernigan, bm.

Atkinson, John T. & Ann W. Martin, 5 Mar 1867; H. Warrick, bm.

Atkinson, Madison (colored) & Pherebe Toler, 27 Aug 1866; Joseph Rhodes, bm; m 1 Sept 1866 by Bryant Williams, J. P.

Atkinson, Nathan & Nancy Moor, 29 May 1793; Henry Gray, bm.

Atkinson, Nathan & Nancy Moore, 9 Aug 1793; Robert Gulley, bm.

Atkinson, Nathen & Nancy Eason, 1 Mar 1815; Elam Smith, bm.

Atkinson, Oliver (colored) & Penny Whitley, 22 Jan 1867; W. P. Holt, bm; m 23 Jan 1867 by W. P. Holt, J. P.

Atkinson, Thomas & Patience Odom, 27 Feb 1798; John Atkinson, bm.

Atkinson, Thomas & Elizabeth Godwin, 26 Jan 1852; m 27 Jan 1852 by Jesse Parker, J. P.

Atkinson, Thomas H. & Martha A. R. Richardson, 11 Oct 1859; m 12 Oct 1859 at the house of Mrs. Richardson, by Semmon Shell.

Atkinson, Wilie & Appy Whitley, 23 Apr 1815; Etheldred Holt, bm.

Atkinson, William & Martha Godwin, 23 Feb 1846; William O'Neal, bm.

Atkinson, William & Elizabeth Harrison, ____; Josiah Houlder, bm.

Atkinson, Willis & Edith Allen, 4 Mar 1797; Robert Gulley, Jr., bm.

Austan, John & Sally Yongblood, 6 Apr 1803; Jonathan Auston, bm.

Austin, Alvin & Cyntha Coats, 14 Apr 1837; Samuel M. Utley, bm.

Austin, Elbert & Kiddy Barnes, 7 Oct 1846; James Roberts, bm.

Austin, Henry & Sophia Mitchener, 13 Dec 1858; m 14 Dec 1858 by J. F. Ellington.

Austin, M. L. & Amy Holt, 24 Nov 1857; J. J. Barney, bm; m 16 Nov 1857 at Joseph Holts, by A. J. Leach.

Auston, Alsey & Drusilla Tomlinson, 15 Apr 1820; William W. Bryan, bm.

Auston, Arrison & Betsy Roberts, 14 Jan 1829; Elisha Harrison, bm.

Auston, Asa & Lucretia Whitington, 27 Feb 1787; Richard Whittington, bm.

Auston, James & Patience Barns, 17 Nov 1849; Ransom Bridgers, bm.

Auston, John & Luvensy Johnson, 13 Jun 1826; Alsey Auston, bm.

Avera, Aventon & _____, 16 Nov 1800; Jesse Frost, bm.

Avera, Boling G. & Charity W. Brooks, 21 Dec 1822; Edwin Spivey, bm.

Avera, David & Rebeccah Tharp, 15 May 1805; Henry Avera, bm.

Avera, Hardy & Polly Rivers, 20 Oct 1810; Eliah Sanders, bm.

Avera, Hardy & Betsy Durham, 20 Feb 1833; Matthew Avera, bm.

Avera, Henry & Christian Durham, 23 Oct 1797; Aron Smith, bm.

Avera, Henry & Celia Tharp, 13 Oct 1802; David Avera, bm.

Avera, Jacob & Anne Faile, 14 Feb 1764; Wm. Bryan, John Smith Jr., bm.

Avera, John & Fanny Wilder, 18 Jan 1803; Young Bridgers, bm.

Avera, John Jr. & Ann Mariah Bell, 9 Aug 1843; James H. Durham, bm.

Avera, John C. & Sarah Penny, 24 Jan 1834; Needham Bryan, bm.

Avera, Jno. T. & Louisa Sanders, 18 Mar 1867; Thos S. Tharin, bm; m 19 Mar 1867 at John Sanders, by Jethro Thain, J. P.

Avera, Jonathan & Mary Draper, 10 May 1768, Alexander Avery, bm.

Avera, Kedar & Sally Johnson, 8 Oct 1807; John Turner Jr., bm.

Avera, Lewis & Lucrecy Avera, 9 Jul 1788; John Eason, bm.

Avera, Richard & Charllota Jones, 28 Nov 1822; William Coats, bm.

Avera, Samuel & Zilpha Ingram, 10 Feb 1779; John Smith, bm.

Avera, Samuel & Sarah Vinson, 30 Jan 1794; Henry Gray, bm.

Avera, Sander & Polly Oliver, 12 Nov 1797; William Jones, bm.

Avera, Thomas & Patience Avera, 24 Jan 1797; Etheldred Smith, bm.

Avera, Thomas & Judith Jones, 23 Dec 1804; Wm. Jones, Regdon Johnson, bm.

Avera, William & Sarah Pritchet, 9 Sept 1794; Robert Whittington, bm.

Avery, James & Nancy Love, 29 Sept 1830; Henry Duncan, bm.

Averyt, Alexander Jr. & Elizabeth Vinson, 31 Jan 1800.

Avra, Richard & Lucetta Jones, m 12 Feb 1853 by W. H. McCullers, J. P.

Aycoch, Albert & Joanny Bagley, 11 Oct 1848; James Faulk, bm.

Aycock, James & Martha Atkinson, 25 Feb 1861; m 28 Feb 1861 at John Atkinsons, by Jesse Parker, J. P.

Aycock, Simon Jr. & Mary Reval, 25 Jan 1843; William H. Aycock, bm.

Ayers, Thomas & Sarah Powell, m 16 Jan 1863 at Betsey Powells, by Ransom Lee, J. P.

Ayres, Counsel & Mary Carroll, 30 Apr 1866; Teagle Ballance, bm.

Bagget, Josiah & Edith Joiner, 26 Nov 1789; James Langdon, bm.

Bagley, Handy (colored) & Jane Bagley, 9 Jan 1867; Elbert Godwin, bm; m 10 Jan 1867 by B. R. Hinnant, J. P.

Bagley, Stephen & Martha J. Joyner, 22 May 1849; Minton M. Godwin, bm.

Bagly, Theophilus & Catherine Gisborn, 19 Oct 1815; Hilliard Starling, bm.

Bailey, Arnold & Betsy O'Niel, 27 Mar 1806; Benjamin O'Neil, bm.

Bailey, Arthur & Famy Parker, 27 May 1789; William Holleman, bm.

Bailey, Griffin & Rildy Hales, 27 Dec 1852; Stephen Hix, bm; m 30 Dec 1852.

Bailey, Hardy & Milchey Holliman, 30 Nov 1802; Harbard Gilman, bm.

Bailey, Hutson & Piety Oneal, 1 May 1834; Warren Bailey, bm.

Bailey, Isom & Elizabeth Parnold, 24 Feb 1789; Samuel Oneil, Arthur Bailey, bm.

Bailey, Jesse & Sarah Thom, 12 Jan 1796; E. Glasgow, bm.

Bailey, Jesse & Aby Tisdell, 15 Mar 1821; Burwell Johnson, bm.

Bailey, Levi & Beady Duck, 9 Oct 1801; Thomas Eatman, bm.

Bailey, Richard & Mildred Horn, 28 May 1792; John Hayles, bm.

Bailey, Ruffin & Cathern Woodard, 13 May 1851; m 15 May 1852 by Jas. Houlder, J. P.

Bailey, Thomas & Susan Davis, 22 Jan 1822; James Peaden, bm.

Bailey, Warren & Elizabeth Oneal, 29 Nov 1815; Arthur Bailey, bm.

Bailey, Warren Jr. & Polly Narron, 25 Sept 1838; Theophilus Dodd, bm.

Bailey, William & Martha Hillard, 26 Feb 1866; Jesse Hinnant, bm.

Baily, Evritt & Hailey Devaughan, 13 Aug 1802; Jesse Baily.

Baily, Gasten, & Mary Baily, 21 Feb 1850; Mabra Hinnant, bm.

Baily, Hilliard & Nicy Baily, 5 Mar 1828; Robert H. Helme, bm.

Baily, Osborn & Cresy Eatman, 23 Feb 1841; Simon Godwin, bm.

Bains, Henry & Bedie Jordan, 2 Jan 1808; Barry Wooten, bm.

Baker, B. A. & Kiziah M. Massingill, 29 Dec 1866; Gideon Keen, bm; m 2 Jan 1867 at Sarrah Massengales, by George Keen, J. P.

Baker, Clem & Polly Walston, 10 Mar 1824; James Baker, bm.

Baker, Elijah & Rosey Solomon, _____ ; Wm. Standley, bm.

Baker, Elijah & Sally Johnson, 16 Mar 1813; George Keen, bm.

Baker, Haywood, Bethania Ingram, 15 Nov 1849; George Keen, bm.

Baker, Jackson & Nancy R. Stanly, 4 Jan 1854; m 5 Jan 1854 by John C. Hood, J. P.

Baker, Jackson & Zelpha Jane Oliver, 1 May 1860; m 13 May 1860 by George Keen, J. P.

Baker, James & Polly Massingill, 25 Mar 1823; Noel West, bm.

Baker, James Jr. & Martha I. Baker, 18 May 1861; m 19 May 1861 by Right Ryals, J. P.

Baker, John & Ann Johnson, 4 Oct 1826; Clement Baker, bm.

Baker, John & Winiford Blaneford, 24 Jul 1844; John Stanley, bm.

Baker, Jonathan & Lewany Wallace, 17 Jan 1856; m 20 Jan 1856 by Right Ryals, J. P.

Baker, Needham G. & Polly Stanly, 5 Feb 1853; m 10 Feb 1853 by R. Masingill, J. P.

Baker, Starling & Lusenda Baker, 7 Jan 1853; m 11 Jan 1853 by R. Masingill, J. P.

Baker, William & Hannor Baker, 22 Jul 1795; John Blackman, bm.

Balance, Blackman & Martha Ward, 6 Apr 1837; Absalom Ward, bm.

Baldwin, Samuel & Elisabeth Reves, 13 Jan 1783.

Balkcom, Ichabud & Nancy Sasser, 12 May 1807; Jacob Stevens, bm.

Ball, William H. & Sally Powell, 3 Apr 1819; Chas. Stevens.

Ballae, Edmond & Caty Masburn, 6 Oct 1815; Theophilus Bagley, bm.

Ballance, John W. & Finettie Holland, 24 Feb 1860; m 16 Feb 1860 by Jas. Faulk, Jr.

Ballance, Martin & Lizzy Lucas, 23 Feb 1841; William D. Robertson, bm.

Ballance, Ruffin & Eliza Sasaser, 27 Apr 1852; m 2 Apr 1852 by S. Bagley, J. P.

Ballance, Teel & Zilpha Garner, 8 May 1824; John Rains, bm.

Ballard, James C. & Sarah Massey, 3 Sept 1866; N. G. Massey, bm.

Ballard, Peter & Sarah Williams, 19 Oct 1796; Wm. Hackney, bm.

Ballenger, George B. & Sarah R. Hinnant, m 26 Dec 1855 by Wm. H. Sellars, J. P.

Ballenger, Joseph D. & Laura L. Bridges, 6 Jul 1865; Jno. McC. Guy, bm.

Ballenger, William & Susanna Stephens, 3 May 1788; John Ballenger, bm.

Ballinger, Allen S. & Susanah Farmer, _____ 180-; Jno. Farmer, bm.

Banks, Adam & Susan Leache, 22 Jun 1829; Simon Smith, bm.

Banks, J. L. & Miss Pheribee H. Tomlinson, m at Mr. B. Tomlinson's, 30 Sept 1858 by T. M. Jones.

Barber, Absalem & Susan Johnston, 6 Sept 1817; Plyer Barber, bm.

Barber, Absalom & Polly Ann Massengill, 8 Dec 1858; m 9 Dec 1858 by George Keen, J. P.

Barber, Alvin & Tempa Eliza Jones, 30 Mar 1864; m 31 Mar 1864 at James A. Jones', by W. H. Lambert, J. P.

Barber, Ashly & Nancy Massengill, 14 Sept 1842; Theophilus Barber, bm.

Barber, Ashly & Wilsey Massingill, 25 Mar 1843.

Barber, Brittan & Susan Jones, 9 Feb 1841; Larkin Barber, bm.

Barber, Burwell & Lydia Jones, 27 Dec 1796; Thomas Barber, bm.

Barber, Charles L. & E. A. Beasley, 30 Apr 1860; m 2 May 1860 by A. Coats, J. P.

Barber, Doctor R. & Mary Johnson, 6 Oct 1866; Romulus Barber, bm; m 15 Oct 1866 at the residence of Isaler(?) Johnson, by W. F. Hall, M. G.

Barber, Drury & Edith Woodall, 13 Jan 1810; George Barber, bm.

Barber, Ezekiel & Mary Frances Johnson, 13 Feb 1867; L. H. Barber, bm; m 14 Feb 1867 at Lemuel Johnsons, by Rev. Parrot Creech.

Barber, George & Nancy Johnson, 5 Jan 1788; Reuben Barber, bm.

Barber, George & _____, 20 Jan 1807; Owen Barber, bm.

Barber, George & Carnan Barber, 3 Apr 1846; P. A. Barber, bm.

Barber, George Jr. & Cassandara Tomlinson, 1 Feb 1827; Thomas Lockart Jr., bm.

Barber, Gideon & Ritty Jones, 2 Feb 1835; Nathaniel Barber, bm.

Barber, Hardy & Ha----- ; 21 Apr 1831; Bailie Barber, bm.

Barber, Harry & Lusey Barber, 4 May 1816; Plyer Barber, bm.

Barber, Harry & Elizabeth Barber, 8 Jan 1834; Terry Barber, bm.

Barber, Harry & Smithey Byrd, 11 Aug 1860; m 14 Aug 1860 at John Byrds, by R. W. Stevens, J. P.

Barber, Haywood & Harriet E. Morgan, 22 Dec 1858; m 26 Dec 1858 by R. W. Stevens, J. P.

Barber, Irvin & Mary J. Jones, 18 Dec 1866; m 19 Dec 1866 at the R. of John R. Jones, by A. R. Duncan.

Barber, Isaac & Pollly Caudle, 14 Jan 1835; Reuben Barber, bm.

Barber, Jackson S. & Smithey A. Godwin, 19 Dec 1859; m 1 Jan 1860 at John L. Mangams(?), by R. W. Stevens, J. P.

Barber, James & Edith Averytt, 10 Apr 1827; Burwell Barber, bm.

Barber, James H. & Alcinda Barber, 16 Jan 1860; m 17 Jan 1860 at Elizabeth Barbers, by R. W. Stevens, J. P.

Barber, James K. & Charity Woodall, 10 Dec 1821; Reuben Barber, bm.

Barber, Jesse & Cassie Barber, 14 Mar 1862; m 16 Mar 1862 by N. B. Barber.

Barber, Jesse H. & Laney Massengale, 10 Aug 1835; John Barber, bm.

Barber, Jessie M. & Brazilla Barber, 7 Aug 1866; P. M. Barber, bm; m 7 Aug 1866 by B. A. Woodall, J. P.

Barber, John & Betsey Woodall, 19 Jan 1816; Terry Barber, bm.

Barber, John & Penny Woodall, 12 Nov 1830; Reuben Barber Jr., bm;

Barber, John R. & Eliza Ann Canada, 21 Feb 1866; John W. Hodges, bm.

Barber, Joseph A. & Caroline Hudson, 5 Jul 1866; W. C. Benson, bm.

Barber, Nathaniel B. & Lancy Dixon, m 26 Oct 1853 by D. H. Holland, J. P.

Barber, Owin & Elizabeth Gordan, 4 Oct 1791; George Barber, bm.

Barber, Parker & Mary Strickland, 22 Apr 1866; George Barber, bm.

Barber, Peola & Elizabeth Gurley, 26 Oct 1843; Hardy Barber, bm.

Barber, Plyer & Suquinna Duncan, 15 Oct 1842; Ruffin W. Tomlinson, bm.

Barber, Reuben & Edy Speight, 8 Apr 1783; Christopher Orr, bm.

Barber, Ruben & Elizabeth Barber, 14 Feb 1814; Etheldred Bell, bm.

Barber, Simeon & Casanda Barber, 6 Aug 1838; Needham Bryan, bm.

Barber, Simeon & Joseph Ann Adams, 19 Oct 1849; W. W. Morgan, bm.

Barber, Terry & Polly Woodall, 27 Feb 1821; Young Morgan, bm.

Barber, Terry & Anne Morgan, 15 Feb 1836; John Barber, bm.

Barber, Theophilus N. & Rosie F. Barber, 5 Apr 1862; m 6 Apr 1862 at Burwell Barbers's, by W. H. Lambert, J. P.

Barber, Thomas & Betsy Langdon, 5 Apr 1799; Burwell Barber, bm.

Barber, Thomas & Elizabeth Williams, 8 Jan 1834; Terry Barber, bm.

Barber, Thomas & Sarah Tomlinson, 6 Mar 1858; m 7 Mar 1858 by T. Garrard.

Barber, Thomas D. & Elizabeth A. Barber, 24 Jan 1867; R. M. Barber, bm; m 27 Jan 1867 at John Jones, Jr., by Rev. Robert Creech.

Barber, William & Pensey Lashley, 5 Aug 1853; m 7 Aug 1853 at Ransom Bridgers by Robert Massingill, J. P.

Barber, William G. & Sally Thomas, 3 May 1843; Robert W. Stevens, bm.

Barber, William G. & Piety Page, 18 Jul 1858; m 1 Aug 1858 at Samuel Byrds, by B. Godwin, J. P.

Barber, William R. & Catherine Barber, 21 May 1861; m 22 May 1861 at Ashley Barber's, by W. H. Lambert, J. P.

Barber, Younge & Rebeca Jordan, 9 Jan 1838; Daniel Gurley, bm.

Barfield, Cullen & Mary J. Westbrook, 17 Jul 1835; John Eason, bm.

Barefoot, Bythan & Jane Bryan, 24 Dec 1859; m 29 Dec 1859 at Nicholas Bryants, by John C. Hood, J. P.

Barefoot, Ezkiel & Mary Eldridge, 28 Apr 1866; Budd Johnston, bm.

Barefoot, George W. & Mary L. Hudson, 17 May 1864; m 24 Mar 1864 at Jane Tarts, by John A. Smith, J. P.

Barefoot, Joel & Esther A. Barefoot, 16 Feb 1856; m 20 Mar 1856 by John A. Smith, J. P.

Barefoot, John Q. & Elizabeth Lee, 25 Jan 1848; Wiley Barefoot, bm.

Barefoot, R. B. & Mary A. Lee, 25 Oct 1851; m 30 Oct 1851 by Joel Lee, J. P.

Barefoot, S. W. & Elizabeth Lee, 24 Nov 1857; James W. Allen, bm; m 26 Nov 1857 at James W. Lees, by R. Massingill, J. P.

Barfield, Bryant & Eleanor Adams, 31 Dec 1844; Right A. Adams, bm.

Barfoot, Miles & Meady Allen, 18 Apr 1817; John Barfoot, bm.

Barham, Eldredge & Maria Avera, 9 Apr 1833; Elisha Harrison, bm.

Barlow, Wilson & Barsheba Lee, 8 Mar 1816; Henry Lee, bm.

Barnes, Bennett & Celety Rentfrow, 17 Feb 1844; Mabury Rentfrow, bm.

Barnes, Elias & Edna Beel, 15 Dec 1837; William Ellis, bm.

Barnes, Henry & Cintha Davis, 3 May 1849; Pitts Kirby, bm.

Barnes, Henry & Jensey Woodard, 7 Nov 1855; m 22 Nov 1855 at B--- Woodards, by Robt. N. Gully, J. P.

Barnes, Jacob & Morning Hennant, 17 Feb 1827; Jacob Barnes, bm.

Barnes, Jacob Jr. & Penny Watson, 24 Mar 1849; Robert Roper, bm.

Barnes, John J. & Evaline Johnson, 29 Nov 1853; m 3 Dec 1853 by H. H. Finch, J. P.

Barnes, Needham & Catharine H. Avera, 28 Feb 1849; Isaac Munden, bm; m 20 Mar 1849 by Sims B. Sanders, J. P.

Barnes, Needham L. & Mary A. M. M. Youngblood, 9 Oct 1858; m 13 Oct 1858 at Ichabod Youngbloods, by R. N. Gully, J. P.

Barnes, Redick & Polly Prett, 30 Sept 1819; W. M. Penny, bm.

Barnes, Solomon & Nancy E. Spence, 26 Mar 1849; Joseph Barnes, bm; m 26 Mar 1849 by A. J. Leach, J. P.

Barnes, William & Mary Cox, 14 Mar 1840; Robert N. Gulley, bm.

Barnes, Wyrick & Polly Leach, 25 Feb 1800; Matthew Jones, bm.

Barnett, John A. & Mary E. Whitley, 19 Jan 1864; m 20 Jan 1864 by L. S. Burkhead.

Bartlet, Henry & Rebeckah Massengill, 27 Dec 1819; John Keen, bm.

Bass, John W. & Patience Ann Deans, 16 Mar 1859; m 17 Mar 1859 by Jesse Parker, J. P.

Bass, William A. & Chilly Ingram, 25 Aug 1835; W. H. Stevens, bm.

Bating, Matthew & Obedince Brown, 26 Feb 1844; Jess Parker, bm.

Battan, John & Elizabeth Adkerson, 12 Oct 1796; John Battan, bm.

Batten, Abraham & Ruth Starling, 8 Oct 1802; John Batten, bm.

Batten, Abraham & Willy H. Talton, 1 Feb 1859; m 3 Feb 1859 by Wilie Wellons, J. P.

Batten, Amos & Edith Watson, 28 Aug 1810; Jno. Gerald, bm.

Batten, Amos & Mary Corbin, 18 May 1812; Amos Batten, bm.

Batten, Charles & Elizabeth Bullock, 9 Nov 1816; Paton Vinson, bm.

Batten, Hardy & Pecy Starling, 9 June 1813; Abraham Batten, bm.

Batten, Henry & Zella Price, 10 Jan 1853; m 11 Jan 1853 by Ransom Kirby, J. P.

Batten, James & Sally Garner, 22 Jan 1824; Jonathan Sillivint, bm.

Batten, John & Betsy Garner, 7 Sept 1833; Samuel Batten, bm.

Batten, John & Martha Batten, 25 May 1858; m 27 May 1858 by Wilie Wellon, J. P.

Batten, John L. & Mary Ann Collier, 16 Sept 1859, m 18 Sept 1859 at Elwood Collier, by L. G. Boyette, J. P.

Batten, John W. & Cherry Snipes, 10 Oct 1866; Wm. H. Pearce, bm; m 11 Oct 1866 at David Snipes, by W. D. Holt, J. P.

Batten, Joseph & Amanda Pitmon, 1 Nov 1859; m 3 Nov 1859 at Elisha Pitmons, by P. Godwin, J. P.

Batten, Josiah & Martha Stansill, 1 Mar 1842; Ransom Sanders, bm.

Batten, Kinchen H. & Nancy Wallace, 2 Apr 1860; m 3 Apr 1860 at Spring Hill by McNab Earp, J. P.

Batten, Levi & Quilly Gerald, 7 Mar 1859; m 8 Mar 1859 by Wilie Wellons, J. P.

Batten, Levy & Louisa Wall, 29 Oct 1853; m 30 Oct 1853 by B. C. Richardson, J. P.

Batten, Matthew & Elizabeth Batten, 25 Jul 1835; John Batten, bm.

Batten, Pleasant & Betsey Gay, 16 Apr 1825; Charles M. Wellons, bm.

Batten, Richard & Tempy Atkinson, 25 Jan 1858; Perry Godwin, bm; m 24 Jan 1858 at H. Godwin, by P. Godwin.

Batten, Samuel & Jemima Starling, 8 Oct 1802; John Batten, bm.

Batten, Samuel & Barbara Starling, 25 Jan 1816; John Batten, bm.

Batten, Starling & Celia Brown, 15 Nov 1825; Jonathan Sillivant, bm.

Batten, Wesley & Lucinda Brown, 13 Oct 1863; m 15 Oct 1863 at William Browns, by P. Godwin, J. P.

Batten, William W. & Louiza Batten, 1 Jan 1847; Pleasant Batten, bm.

Battin, John W. & Dolly Battin, 30 Jan 1847; James Battin, bm.

Battin, Robert & Martha Stancell, 24 Oct 1849; Jesse Creech, bm.

Batting, Ephram & Cyntha EAtmon, 4 Aug 1845; John Broadwell, bm.

Batton, Henderson & Joanah Pitman, 20 Feb 1860; m 21 Feb 1860 at Elisha Pitmons, by P. Godwin, J. P.

Baucom, Hurious & Betsy Lee, 29 Sept 1815; Bennet Baucom, bm.

Baucom, Isom & Alcy Penny, 11 Jun 1798; Samuel Smith, bm.

Bawcum, Ichabird & Delanie Jarroll, 23 May 1806; Isaac Jarrell, bm.

Bawcum, Seth & Sally Elliot, 17 Oct 1808; Ichabard Balkcum, bm.

Bawcum, Urias & Sally Turner, m 28 Sept 1853 by W. H. McCullers.

Bawkham, James & Sarah Rogers, 30 Jan 1780; Green Rogers, bm.

Bayker, Starling & Caroline Griffin, 24 Jan 1857; m 26 Jan 1857 by A. Mitchener, J. P.

Bayley, Jesse & Lynchia Blanketship, 2 Apr 1800; Micagah Bagly, bm.

Beal, John & Edny Ellis, 19 Jun 1826; John Ellis, bm.

Beaman, Davis & Silvy Godwin, 12 Nov 180; James Carrell, bm.

Beaman, Jacob & Winifred Langdon, 2 Mar 1800; James Carrell, bm.

Beaman, Nathan & Betsy Wright, 24 Jul 1810; Bartley Stevens, bm.

Beaman, Samuel & Sally Langdon, 31 Jul 1811; Thomas Barber, bm.

Beard, Counsell & Nancy Stevens, 22 Mar 1823; David Stevens, bm.

Beard, William & Mary Ann Rose, 2 Mar 1803; Joseph Hearne, bm.

Bearfoot, John & Betsey Smith, 26 Dec 1815; Miles Bearfoot, bm.

Beasley, Ashley & Redly Byrd, 22 Jan 1851.

Beasley, Ephraim O. & Edith Avery, 18 Dec 1845; James Homes, bm.

Beasley, Isaac & Phereby Roberts, 7 Jul 1829; W. H. Johnson, bm.

Beasley, Jesse & Fanny Moore, 30 Sept 1841; J. Q. Adams, bm.

Beasley, Kinderick & Eny Bryan, 6 Aug 1835; Herom Homes, bm.

Beasly, James & Polly Jennigan, 29 Dec 1843; Henry Moore, bm.

Beckwith, John B. & Ann G. Thomson, 22 Feb 1849; Wm. H. Morning, bm.

Beckwith, John B. & Julia M. Sanders, m 20 May 1856 by P. J. Carraway, M. G.

Bedingfield, John & Maryan Price, 2 Jan 1792; John Price, bm.

Beesly, Barnaby & Polly Williams, 24 Dec 1806; Henry Johnson, bm.

Bell, Anthony (colored) & Willy Holland, 20 Dec 1866; Tobby Lassiter, bm; m 20 Dec 1866 by Jethor Hain, J. P.

Bell, Benjamin & Rebeckah Johnson, 8 Feb 1815; D. Bell, bm.

Bell, David & _____ [torn], 28 Sept 1778; Zadok Stallings, bm.

Bell, David & Sarah Hardy, 2 Dec 1848; William Thornton, bm.

Bell, David & Phebe Thorp, 29 Sept 1812; Etheldred Bell, bm.

Bell, Hardy & Patsy Pool, 9 Jul 1818; Baldy Sanders, bm.

Bell, Henry & Helen Mariah Clark, 18 Feb 1837; Benjamin Walston, bm.

Bell, Thomas & Sally Powell, 15 May 1824; Nicholas Lee, bm.

Bell, Willie A. & Agusta Jane Droughon, 18 Dec 1858; m 22 Dec 1858 by George Keen, J. P.

Bellington, Ezekiel & Elizabeth Penny, 8 Nov 1784; Edward Penny, bm.

Benifield, John & Lucy M. Hinton, 13 Nov 1833; Wm. P. Johnson, bm.

Bennet, William & Sally Stevens, 16 Aug 1828; Bold Robin Hood, bm.

Bennett, Isham & Sally Blanchet, 8 Aug 1799; Philemon Bennett, bm.

Bennett, William H. & Elizabeth Bulls, 3 Aug 1841; Wm. H. Morning, bm.

Benson, Alfred & Sarah Stanly, 19 Dec 1866; Lewis Stanly, bm; m 19 Dec 1866 at Jesse Standlys, by George Keen, J. P.

Benson, Ashley & Elizabeth Johnson, 7 Aug 1857; George Keen, bm; m 9 Aug 1857 by George Keen, J. P.

Benson, Charles & Elizabeth Capps, 28 Sept 1812; William Capps, bm.

Benson, Charles H. & Mary J. Jones, 16 Feb 1867; W. C. Benson, bm; m 28 Feb 1867 at Thos. Jones by P. Creech, M. G.

Benson, James R. & Susan H. Godwin, 15 Feb 1866; William C. Benson, bm.

Benson, John W. & Sarah Barber, 13 Sept 1860; W. C. Benson, bm; m 16 Sept 1860 by B. A. Woodall, bm.

Benson, W. C. & Sarah A. Dixon, 14 June 1866; E. D. Snead, bm.

Benson, William & Louisa Tyner, __ 1837; John Jackson, bm.

Best, Handy (colored) & Jemima Jernigan, 7 Aug 1866; Eli Morgan, bm; m 10 Aug 1866 by Bryant Williams, J. P.

Bishop, Moses & Lucy Rose, 1 Mar 1825; Counsel J. Beard, bm.

Bitten, William & Elizabeth Faulk, 13 Dec 1827; John Saser, bm.

Bingham, Charles J. & Casanda Longdon, 21 Oct 1846; John T. Sanders, bm.

Bird, Lemuel & Nancy Ennis, 15 Aug 1848; William W. Morgan, bm.

Bizzell, Everet A. & Bethany Barnes, 14 Nov 1853; m 17 Nov 1853 by E. L. Perkins, M. G.

Bizzell, Montraville & Fannie M. Ezzel, 19 Dec 1846; Joel Joyner Jr., bm.

Bizzelle, Montraville & Lucette Langston, 16 Aug 1861.

Blackburn, George & Mary Jones, 18 May 1790; Isaac Jones, bm.

Blackman, Arthur A. & Alder Jernigan, 8 Feb 1853; m 10 Feb 1853 by Powel Blackman, J. P.

Blackman, Ashly & Judith Beasley, 20 May 1847; Harry Blackmon, bm.

Blackman, B. C. & _____, 23 Aug 1847; Powell Blackman, bm.

Blackman, Barzilla Jr. & Sarah Rauser, 1 Jan 1824; Starling W. Temple, bm.

Blackman, Cullen & Evelina V. Boon, 29 Sept 1831; William H. Watson, bm.

Blackman, Edmond & Mournen Masingill, 4 Jan 1808; William Blackman, bm.

Blackman, Harrey & Polly Avery, 26 Dec 1844; George Keen, Bm.

Blackman, Jeremiah & Winifred George, 4 Mar 1823; Barzilla Blackman, bm.

Blackman, Jeremiah & Unity Jane Barnhill, 23 May 1864; m 5 June 1864 by John Harper, J. P.

Blackman, Jesse R. & Elizabeth E. Massingill, 29 May 1852; m 30 May 1852 by Needham Brigrow, J. P.

Blackman, John & Rachal Killingsworth, 4 Jan 1792; Ichabod Blackman, bm.

Blackman, John & Cadty Lee, 18 Jan 1821, Brazilla Blackman, bm.

Blackman, Joseph & Polly Standley, 4 Jan 1802; Etheldred Massingill, bm.

Blackman, Josiah & Betsey Jenergan, 10 Jan 1849; George Rose, bm.

Blackman, Josiah L. & Meady Smith, 23 Apr 1858; m 27 Apr 1858 by A. B. Peacock.

Blackman, Julius A. & Pettie J. Peedin, 1 Nov 1865; m __ Nov 1865 at James Peedens, by Perry Godwin, J. P.

Blackman, Kedar & Absabeth Wood, 26 Sept 1826; Loverd Eldredge, bm.

Blackman, Richard & Susan Temple, 7 Jan 1835; Robert Massingill, bm.

Blackman, Stephen & Gracy Proctor, 18 Dec 1801; Henry Massingill, bm.

Blackman, William & Nancy Jernigan, 19 Dec 1795; Ichabod Blackman, bm.

Blackman, William & Sally Webb, 25 May 1853; m 26 May 1853 by R. Wm. Stevens, J. P.

Blackman, William H. & Rutha Batten, 6 Mar 1857; m 7 Mar 1857 at Starling Battens, by W. F. Gerald, J. P.

Blackman, William P. & Elizabeth Price, 12 Dec 1851; m 17 Dec 1851 by M. Avera, J. P.

Blackmon, John & Thena Strickland, 22 May 1855; m 3 June 1855 by J. B. Jackson.

Blackmon, Sir WIlliam & Elizabeth Brunt, 4 Dec 1851; m 11 Dec 1851 by Powel Blackmon, J. P.

Blackwell, Hezekiah (colored) & Louisa Whitley, 1 Jan 1867; Iredell Godwin, bm; m 2 Jan 1857 by W. A. Smith, J. P.

Blackwell, Josiah & Anzy Mitchell, 13 Oct 1820; Jesse Grice, bm.

Blackwell, Thomas & Eveline Hathcock, 14 Dec 1841; Isaac L. George, bm.

Blenson, Thomas & Susannah Ferrell, 1 Mar 1809; Theo. Pool, bm.

Blinson, William & Lucy Stevens, 29 Aug 1836; Henry Penny, bm.

Blow, Merritt (colored) & Rachael O'neal, 1 May 1866; Wright Blow, bm.

Blurton, Henry & Edith Averet, 5 Jan 1785; Zadock Stallings, bm.

Bodery, Isaac & Edeth Hamilton, 26 Feb 1833; John Atkinson, bm.

Bodie, William & Tranquella Sanders, 2 Jan 1818; J. E. Bodie, bm.

Booey, George W. & Annatha Johnson, 1 Nov 1845; William A. Johnson, bm.

Boon, Demsey W. & Allice K. Boon, 18 May 1855; m 3 Jun 1855 by J. F. Ellington.

Boon, Dempsy & Lotty Stevens, 26 Jan 1818; Harris Clark, bm.

Boon, John W. & Alice Kelly, 14 Aug 1841; R. T. Sanders, bm.

Boon, Joseph & Lydey Powel, 12 Jan 1779; Joseph Sims, bm.

Boon, Joseph & Hesther Strickland, 28 May 1794; William Musselwhite, bm.

Boon, Willie L. & Bathaba Richardson, 27 July 1846; David H. Holland, bm.

Booth, Levi & Polly Eavens, 12 May 1845; Wm. James, bm.

Bowles, Thomas G. & Sarah Jane Smith, 14 Jul 1855; m 15 Jul 1855 by S. Bagley, J. P.

Boyet, Moses & Polly Stevens, 28 Feb 1810; Benjamin Stevens, bm.

Boyett, George & Cuzzy Walston, 25 Dec 1827; Isaac Boyett, bm.

Boyette, Stephen E. & Elizabeth Broughton, m 30 Aug 1859 at John R. Walls, by Wm. B. Wall, J. P.

Boykin, David W. & Agnes Snead, m 18 Jun 1861 at Smithfield, by John R. Brooks.

Boykin, Edwin & Jane C. Jones, 5 Nov 1838.

Boykin, Harris & Mary Kent, 22 Apr 1844; J. S. Boykin, bm.

Boykin, Hillory & Milly Narron, 10 May 1861; m 6 July 1861 at Jonathan Boykins, by A. H. Atkinson, J. P.

Boykin, John Stanley & Glatha H. Kent, 26 Nov 1845; Mabry Hinnant, bm.

Boykin, Lunsford H. & Harriet Renfrow, 15 Oct 1857; R. Raper, bm.

Boykin, S. & Milbry Boykin, 25 Apr 1866; J. G. Brewer, bm.

Boykin, Stephen & Milbry Kent, 19 Jan 1839; Nelson Kent, bm.

Boykin, Stephen & Sally Griswe, 30 Aug 1843; Jesse Boykin, bm.

Boykin, Isham (colored) & Maria Richardson, 20 Dec 1866; Isaac Ried, bm; m 27 Dec 1866 by M. K. Grantham, J. P.

Boylan, Peter (colored) & Isabella Smith, 13 Oct 1866; Adam J. Heath, bm; m 13 Oct 1866 by Adam J. Heath, J. P.

Boyt, Jehu & Caty Wilder, 30 Sept 1807; John Killingsworth, bm.

Boytt, Isaac & Betsy Watson, 27 Sept 1837; Jesse Hinnant, bm.

Boytt, Joseph & Larkey Bryant, 9 Dec 1853; m 11 Dec 1853 by Stanly Kirby, J. P.

Braddy, James & Martha Roberts, 30 Aug 1791; Barnaby Bulls, bm.

Braddy, James & Catharine Farrow, 24 July 1838; Mathew Avera, bm.

Braddy, Robert & Dizy Strickland, 27 Dec 1824; Levi Strickland, bm.

Braddy, William J. & Matilda Barber, 26 Oct 1853; m 1 Nov 1853 by Sims B. Sanders, J. P.

Braddy, William M. & _____, 9 Jan 1841; Cullen Strickland, bm.

Brady, Blake & Lucy Carter, 14 Oct 1801; Robert Culley, Jr., bm.

Brady, John & Mary Tiner, 19 Feb 1804; Joseph Boon, bm.

Brady, Levy L. & Harriet Davis, 17 Mar 1853; m 20 Mar 1853 by Elder Dixon Phillips.

Brady, Lewis & Elisabeth Giles, 13 Feb 1770; John Brady, bm.

Brady, Nathan & Cynthea Roberts, 8 Feb 1820; James Roberts, bm.

Brady, William Jr. & Elizabeth Harrell, 13 May 1820; John Atkinson, Etheldred Holt, bm.

Brady, William R. & Elizabeth Davis, 31 Dec 1847; Green Hill, bm.

Branan, Allen & Penny Eason, 11 Sept 1845; Josial Gay, bm.

Brandis, Mark & Polly Godwin, 23 Sept 1817; William Bryan, bm.

Branen, Ranson & Nancy Jones, 24 Aug 1841; Gray W. Thomas, bm.

Brannan, Allen & Lotty Jones, 13 Nov 1828; William Brannan, bm.

Brannan, Caron & Milly Green, 29 Sept 1826; Wm. Hinton, bm.

Brannan, James & Rose Martin, 27 Jan 1783; William Green, bm.

Brannan, John W. & Lucinda Batten, 9 Dec 1848; Edwin Batten, bm.

Brannan, Kader & Zelpha Pearce, 30 Jun 1851; m 1 Jul 1851 by Jas. Houldor, J. P.

Brannan, Kedar & Martha Price, 11 Sept 1860; m 15 Sept 1860 at Jos. Deans, by Wm. B. Wall, J. P.

Brannan, Ransom & Harriet Parish, 2 Sept 1866; W. C. Nowell, bm; m 2 Sept 1866 by W. C. Nowell.

Brannan, William & Mary Green, 27 Nov 1793; John Watson, bm.

Brannan, William Jr. & Culy Price, 31 Jul 1822; Wiley Brannan, bm.

Brannen, Kedar & Elizabeth Wilder, 8 Oct 1802; Cullen Wilder, bm.

Brannon, Joseph & Harriet Wilder, 7 Mar 1834; Isham Wilder, bm.

Brannon, Leroy & Rebeckah Cole, 4 Oct 1791; William Brannon, bm.

Brannon, Thomas & Mary Wilder, 14 Sept 1816; Cador Brannon, bm.

Brantly, Edwin & Susannah Corbit, 25 May 1819; Samuel Lee Jr., bm.

Branwell, William & Nancy Humphries, 19 May 1798; Robert Gully Jr., bm.

Brassel, George & Cintha Garner, 28 Jan 1848; Jacob Brassel, bm; m ___ by Wilie Holt.

Braswell, George & Kizziah Massey, 4 May 1861; m 12 May 1861 at Charles Massey's, by William Brown.

Braswell, Jacob & Sally Spencer, 23 Dec 1841; Arthur Woodard, bm.

Braswell, Lewis & Sally Bridgers, 29 Dec 1815; Joseph Edwards Jr., bm.

Brexton, Willie & Patience Pearce, 9 Sept 1846; James H. Hinnant, bm.

Bridgers, Braswell & Jane Jenkins, 3 May 1825; Tom D. Bridgers, bm.

Bridgers, David H. & Nancy Pamenter, 10 Oct 1849; Lewis Williams, bm.

Bridgers, Thomas & Fanny Wilder, 17 May 1826; B. Bridgers, bm.

Bridgers, William & Elizabeth Smith, 21 Dec 1785;

Bridgers, Young & Clarry Norris, 7 Jul 1789, Nahon Norris, bm.

Bridges, Benjamin & Bearshaba Giles, 19 Jun 1794; Hardy Bryan, bm.

Bridges, Braswell & Elizabeth Stallings, 1 Oct 1814; John Stevens, bm.

Bridges, Ransome & Adaline Barber, 23 Oct 1849; Wm. H. Buchanan, bm; m 23 Oct 1849 by Linn B. Sanders, J. P.

Bridges, William & Jane Smith, 16 Apr 1788.

Brint, Richard & Nancy Ingram, 16 Jan 1827; Richard C. Terry, bm.

Britt, David & Sarah Stevens, 22 Feb 1867; m 30 Apr 1865 at Boon Hill by H. H. Hinnant, J. P.

Britt, Gaston & Elizabeth House, 4 Mar 1859; m 20 Mar 1859 by John Dupree.

Britt, Gaston W. & Elizabeth Morgan, 26 Aug 1866; Joseph Crocker, bm; m 26 Aug 1866 by James Hay, J. P.

Britt, Hardy & Lotty Penny, 21 Jan 1823; Nathaniel Johnson, bm.

Britt, Jessy Jr. & Nancy Norris, 21 Apr 1792; Isaac Kindall, bm.

Britt, Jonathan & Vicy Brown, 20 Jul 1807; Willis Nelms, bm.

Britt, Marion D. & Elizabeth H. Horne, 12 Dec 1853; m 14 Dec 1853 by J. F. Ellington.

Britt, Reddin & Rachel Frost, 24 Jan 1813; Bennet Dodd, bm.

Britt, William & Mary Price, 10 Dec 1866; Stephen Faircloth, bm; m 13 Dec 1866 at Pency Crocker's, by B. Williams, J. P.

Broadsheet, William & Betsy Turley, 31 Aug 1796; David Evans, bm.

Broadwell, John & Any Gulley, 25 Nov 1811; Noah Nichols, bm.

Broadwell, John & _____ [torn]; N. G. Gulley, bm.

Brogden, John & Rebecca Thorton, 1 Sept 1820; William Passons, bm.

Brooks, Benjamin S. & Nancy Beel, 13 Dec 1820; Jno. W. Brooks, bm.

Brooks, John R. & Julia A. Hastings, m 23 Jun 1863 by L. S. Burkhead.

Broughton, Benjamin & Mary Bagwell, 25 Feb 1834; Stephen Broughton, bm.

Broughton, Calvin & Mary E. Lassiter, m 24 May 1858 at Reddick Lassiters, by J. F. Ellington.

Broughton, J. W. & Rebecca A. Johnson, 28 Jan 1867; S. R. Horne, bm; m 2 Feb 1867 by J. F. Ellington, M. G.

Broughton, John & Patsy Boyett, 8 Feb 1825; Thomas Rice, bm.

Broughton, Joseph & Nancy Stansill, 23 Mar 1796; Frederick Holleman, bm.

Broughton, Stephen & Milly Stallings, 19 Mar 1833; Jesse Broughton, bm.

Brown, Aden & Seney Pitman, 8 Nov 1845; Stephen Brown, bm.

Brown, Barden & Honor H. Johnson, 28 Mar 1859; m 31 Mar 1859 by Ray Phillips, J. P.

Brown, Burkehead & Marsaline Eason, 12 Feb 1863; m 26 Feb 1863 by McNab Earp, J. P.

Brown, Burkett & Mary Jones, 23 May 1866; N. L. Brown, bm.

Brown, David & Clary Windbourn, 31 May 1822; Alsey High, bm.

Brown, Edward & Elizabeth Morgan, 24 Jan 1866; Theophilus Whitfield, bm.

Brown, Elisha & Ann Bullock, 9 Oct 1783; Nicholas Thompson, bm.

Brown, J. A. & Islie J. Winborne, 10 Apr 1862; m 11 Apr 1862 at Earpsboro, by J. R. Brown, J. P.

Brown, Jesse & Elizabeth Stearling, 15 Mar 1848; Thomas Brown, bm.

Brown, John & Bedy Garner, 25 Dec 1835; James Garner, bm.

Brown, John A. & Sarah Lockhart, 19 Jan 1820; Simon T. Sanders, bm.

Brown, Joseph & Phereby Smith, 4 June 1793; Abner Sauls, bm.

Brown, Joseph & Polly Snipes, 29 May 1799; Robert Gulley, bm.

Brown, Josiah & Polly Horn, 24 Dec 1834; John Batten, bm.

Brown, Larkin & Nancy Battin, 2 Dec 1857; James M. Corbit, bm; m 3 Dec 1857 at Pleasant Pattens, by Wilie Wellons, J. P.

Brown, Lee & Anna Parker, 28 Feb 1825; Nicholas Rose, bm.

Brown, Little Berry & Betsy Simpkins, 2 Feb 1820; Joseph Brown, bm.

Brown, Needham & Edith Roberts, 28 Apr 1849; Austen Hatcher, bm.

Brown, Samuel & Sally Wilson, 10 Jul 1802; Henry Hobby, bm.

Brown, Samuel & Sally Wilson, 30 Jul 1802; Hary Bryan, bm.

Brown, Stephen & Lany Strickland, 17 Aug 1814; John Avera, bm.

Brown, Stephen & Louisa Pearce, 28 Sept 1831; Edwin Jones, bm.

Brown, Stephen & Willie Starling, 17 Feb 1841; Charles Hatcher, bm.

Brown, Thomas & Sarah Hatcher, 23 Dec 1822; Benjamin Hatcher, bm.

Brown, William & Nancy Warren, 10 Jun 1820; R. Warren, bm.

Brown, William & Betsey Bolton, 13 Sept 1826; John Brown, bm.

Brounin, Josiah & Willey Jones, 16 Nov 1845; James Hinnant, bm.

Bruce, James & John Clarrissa Blackman, 13 May 1862; m 14 May 1862 at Powel Blackman's, by J. C. Cason, J. P.

Bryan, Arthur & Mary McCullers, 10 Dec 1773; Needham Bryan, bm.

Bryan, Asa & Anne Lee, 18 Aug 1778; James Lee, bm.

Bryan Asa Jr. & Susanna Lee, 15 Mar 1809; Henry Lee, bm.

Bryan, Benjamin & Polly Stevens, 14 Jun 1800; Samuel Smith, bm.

Bryan, Buthan & Julia C. Smith, 11 Jun 1821; David Thompson, bm.

Bryan, David H. & Winnifred McCullers, 7 Oct 1816; Ray Helme, bm.

Bryan, David H. & Elizabeth Smith, 8 Jul 1826; David Thomson, bm.

Bryan, Edward & Earbia Bryan, 23 Dec 1824; Simon Bryan, bm.

Bryan, Elbert & Mary Ann Stallings, 25 Jan 1843; Elijah Lancaster, bm.

Bryan, Frederick & Elizabeth WOodard, 28 Nov 1809; West Woodard, bm.

Bryan, Frederick & Sally Gully, 30 Mar 1814; James Bryan, bm.

Bryan, Harry & Edith Eason 8 Mar 1810; William Sasser, Needham W. Bryan, bm.

Bryan, Harry & Spicey McLamb, 25 Mar 1858; m 8 Apr 1858 by John C. Hood, J. P.

Bryan, Henry & Penny Utley, 7 May 1798; James Penny, bm.

Bryan, James & Nancy Green, 23 Feb 1808; Sion Green, bm.

Bryan, Joel & Delilah Eatman, 23 Jan 1811; Robert Lewis, bm.

Bryan, John Arthur & Eliza Smith, 25 Nov 1801; Willis Watson, bm.

Bryan, Laury & Sally Hinton, 7 Dec 1801; Willis Watson, bm.

Bryan, Lewis & Sarah Hinton, 26 Oct 1769; Samuel Smith, Jr., bm.

Bryan, Lucius H. & Elizabeth Ellis, 11 May 1855; m 13 May 1855 by J. B. Jackson.

Bryan, Nathan & Nancy McDonnell, 12 Mar 1817; William Fail, bm.

Bryan, Needham & Sally Jones, 23 May 1818; James Jones, bm.

Bryan, Robert & Sarah Woodard, 23 Dec 1826; Larkin Hollimon, bm.

Bryan, Samuel A. & Julia Lockart, 10 Mar 1828; Edwin Spivey, bm.

Bryan, Simon & Lotty Grayn, 9 Jun 1819; William Fail, bm.

Bryan, W. W. & Patsy McCullars, 7 Nov 1810; Needham W. Bryan, bm.

Bryan, William & Amelia Vinson, 21 Aug 1793; John Eason, Hugh H. Whitaker, bm.

Bryan, William & Rainy Strickland, 19 Jan 1838; J. Hudson Bailey, bm.

Bryan, William & Elizabeth Dunn, 16 Mar 1861; m 18 Mar 1861 at E. O. Beasley, by R. Masingill, J. P.

Bryan, William H. & Sarah A. E. Vincent, 1 Nov 1859; m 16 Nov 1859 at Bentonsville Church, by Lemmon Shell, minister.

Bryant, John H. & Lucy E. Wall, 29 Sept 1846; David Adams, bm.

Bryant, Lewis & Celia Holleman, 18 Nov 1767.

Buler, Charles M. & Ann Webb, 24 Jun 1844; Redden Webb, bm.

Bulls, Barnaby & Harriet Eason, 11 Mary 1819; Willie N. White, bm.

Bulls, William & Rebeckah Capse, 25 Oct 1785; Jethro Bulls, bm.

Bun, Fredrick & Zilpah Altman, 26 Nov 1799; Nathan Altman, bm.

Bunch, James H. & Caroline Williams, 17 Dec 1841; Sam D. Horten, bm.

Bundy, George D. & Mary T. Austin, 29 Mar 1853; m 10 __ 1853 by H. H. Finch, J. P.

Bunn, Benset & Nancy O'nail, 24 May 1823; John Maner, bm.

Bunn, James & Beedy O'neal, 17 Nov 1821; Wm. Oneal, Jr., bm.

Bunn, Tobias & Johnny Lee, 25 Feb 1811; John Avera, bm.

Bunting, William--see Butting, William.

Burcket, Lemuel & Susan Shepherd, 22 Jul 1836; Robert W. Snead, bm.

Burk, Goldy & Sally Haithcock, 9 Feb 1837; William B. Allen, bm.

Burnett, Barna & Sally Powell, 25 May 1813; David Freeman, bm.

Burnett, Sandy & Julia Crawford, 29 Dec 1849; Stephen Dawson, bm.

Burnum, Joel Jr. & Edny Ellis, 29 Aug 1809; Gearmon Ellis, bm.

Busbee, Alfred & Betsy Ellington, 19 May 1828; Lewis M. Jinkins, bm.

Busbee, Kinchen, & Nancy Russell, 17 Nov 1823; Ranson Busbee, bm.

Busby, Alsey & Polly Sauls, 15 Nov 1812; Willie Jones of Wake Co., bm.

Busby, Daniel & Sally Hardy, 24 Dec 1806; Benjamin Carrell, bm.

Busby, Jonathan & Christian Smith, 14 Jun 1805; Abner Smith, bm.

Bush, John & Susannah Bryan, 15 Mar 1779; Bryan Whitfield, bm.

Butcher, John & Patience Peeden, 17 Feb 1814; John Peeden, bm.

Butler, Samuel & Milly Rose, 27 Mar 1832; Needham Richardson, bm.

Butting or Bunting, William & Martha High, 3 Sept 1833; Mark B. Richardson, bm.

Butts, Wilson & Zilpha Pugh, 21 Sept 1820; Jno. Farmer, bm.

Bynum, Drewry & Patience Howell, 30 May 1795; Wm. Darham, bm.

Byrd, Alexander & Mary F. Capps, 26 Jul 1860; m 29 Jul 1860 at L. S. Byrds, by R. M. Stevens, bm.

Byrd, Bright & Gracy Godwin, 20 Mar 181-; Benjamin Stevens, bm.

Byrd, Bruton & Sucky Richardson, 20 May 1810; John Chambe, bm.

Byrd, Curtis & Parizada Parrish, 7 Sept 1859; m 11 Sept 1859 at David Parrish's, by F. F. Ellis, J. P.

Byrd, George & Susan Byrd, 13 Mar 1812; Benjamin Stevens, bm.

Byrd, George & Penny Ritter, 6 Mar 1819; Benjamin Martin, bm.

Byrd, John & Nancy Jones, 29 Sept 1829; Thomas Jones, bm.

Byrd, Leroy & Rildey Barber, 23 Dec 1859; m 28 Dec 1859 by R. W. Stevens, J. P.

Byrd, Lemuel D. & Martha J. Draughorn, m 11 Apr 1861 at Richard Byrds, by Eld. James Turnage.

Byrd, Lewis & Lusetto Jones, 20 Jan 1846; James Jones, bm.

Byrd, Needham T. & Narcissa West, 20 Nov 1863; m __ Nov 1863 at Thomas Byrds, by R. W. Stevens, J. P.

Byrd, Richard & Jerusha Deloach, 13 Oct 1806; John Byrd, bm.

Byrd, Richard Jr. & Betsy Haislip, 16 Dec 1805; John Byrd, bm.

Byrd, Richard D. & Elenor Magee, 14 Sept 1858; m 16 Sept 1858 at Richard Byrd, by B. Godwin, J. P.

Byrd, Robert J. & Helen Wellons, m at her mother's residence, 10 Mar 1858 by J. H. Keneday.

Byrd, Sutton & Margret Johnson, 23 Oct 1845; Isaac Johnson, bm.

Byrd, Thomas & Rebecca Sanders, 7 Nov 1838; John Cordell, bm.

Byrd, William & Nancy Johnson, 10 May 1821; Robert Stevens, bm.

Cadell, Banks & Nancy Johnson, 6 Dec 1828; Right Byrd, bm.

Canaday, Joshua & Amy Ann Coats, 13 Dec 1860; m 21 Mar 1860 by George Keen, J. P.

Canaday, William H. & Elizabeth J. Barber, m 15 Apr 1858 at Apslaur Barbers, by B. Godwin, J. P.

Canady, Cannon & Patsey Johnson, 20 Jan 1835; James Carrell, bm.

Canady, William & Tabithey Bratcher, 27 Jun 1793; Robert Whittington, bm.

Cannon, Samuel & Winny Jones, 13 Feb 1827; Benj. Hatcher, bm.

Capps, Allen & Elizabeth Parnold, 7 Sept 1825; Dixon Davis, bm.

Capps, Allen & Sally Strickland, 9 Dec 1846; John G. Gully, bm.

Capps, Allen & Charlotte Davis, 18 May 1859; m 19 May 1859 by Wm. S. Brown, J. P.

Capps, Elijah A. & Rebecca Thomson, 7 Jan 1850; Elijah H. Phillips, bm.

Capps, Haywood & Julia Moore, m 12 Sept 1860 at Benjamin Moores by Right Ryal, J. P.

Capps, Henry & Chilly Thompson, 21 Dec 1818; Henry Guy, bm.

Capps, Jeremiah & Polly Edwards, 11 Apr 1815; Wm. Bulls, Jr., bm.

Capps, Jeremiah & Zilpha Massey, 17 Jan 1816; Isaiah Massey, bm.

Capps, Jeremiah & Deliah Baker, 16 Oct 1823; Nicholas Rose, bm.

Capps, John T. & Hawkins Talton, m 20 Aug 1862 at Lewis Taltons, by W. P. Raiford, J. P.

Capps, Joseph J. & Elizabeth Barber, 14 Jan 1867; D. A. Coats, bm; m 17 Jan 1867 at Gastin Barbers, by Isaac Wheeler, M. G.

Capps, Lewis & Sally Hall, 19 Dec 1843; William Capps, bm.

Capps, Littleton & Zilpha Price, 12 May 1827; Bright Jernigan, bm.

Capps, M. W. & Easter Price, 14 Jan 1861; m 9 Feb 1861 at the residence of B. Price by B. Lowe, J. P.

Capps, Matthew & Sally Parnold, 17 May 1825; Dixon Davis, bm.

Capps, Needham & Martha Davis, 24 Feb 1807; William Capps, bm.

Capps, Ruffin & Nancy Norriss, 27 Apr 1861; m 28 Apr 1861 by William F. Hall, elder.

Capps, William & Catharain Creech, 20 Jan 1847; Willie Holt, bm.

Capps, William Jr. & Polly Deans, 18 Mar 1822; William Capps, Sr., bm.

Capps, William H. & Emily Jane Rains, 3 Jan 1843; Elijah Capps, bm.

Capse, William & Zilpah Bulls, 16 Jan 1788; Daniel Duz, bm.

Cardell, Thomas & Lucetta Adams, 7 Feb 1866; L. T. Carroll, bm.

Carlile, Edward & Susan Hall, 11 Nov 1816; Kinchen Wheelley, bm.

Carpenter, Reuben & Caty Wilder, 12 Mar 1810; Hillary Wilder, bm.

Carr, Benajah B. & Mary Ryals, 13 Jul 1865; Julius A. Lee, bm.

Carr, James & Cynthia Britt, 8 Aug 1809; Samuel Willoby, bm.

Carrel, Benjamin & Nancy Ferrell, 16 Dec 1806; Drury Johnson, bm.

Carrel, Troy & Mary Stephens, 17 Sept 1850.

Carrel, William & Piety Fluellin, 18 Mar 1797; Abraham Perry, bm.

Carrell, Benjamin & Elizabeth Peedem, 17 Dec 1848; Hardy Pilkinton, bm.

Carrell, Britain & Betsey Austin, 1 Nov 1820; John Carrell, bm.

Carrell, Ceborn & Nancy Ellen, 15 Mar 1830; Carrell Johnson, bm.

Carrell, Dallas & Dillie Ann Parrish, 11 Aug 1851; m 14 Aug 1851 by C. Langdon, J. P.

Carrell, David & Polly Matthews, 29 Aug 1820; Britin Long, bm.

Carrell, Dennis & Elizabeth Johnson, 23 May 1795; John Carrell, bm.

Carrell, James & Rhoda Stevens, 30 Jan 1792; John Carrell, bm.

Carrell, John & Winefred Ferrell, 26 Feb 1839; Needham Bryan, bm.

Carrell, John R. & Lucy Artis, 19 Apr 1845; Isaac W. Stallings, bm.

Carrell, Mitchell & Sally Carrell, 3 Dec 1805; Benjamin Carrell, bm.

Carrell, Reuben & Margaret Matathews, 25 Apr 1826; David Carrel, bm.

Carrell, Ruffin & Betsey C. Eavens, 23 Apr 1846; Raiford Edwards, bm.

Carrell, Simeon & Sarah Hall, 18 Jul 1836; Richard H. White, bm.

Carrell, Thomas & Nowell Adams, 20 May 1797; Benjamin Segraves, bm.

Carrell, William & Sarah Stevens, 8 Feb 1790; John Carrell, James Carrell, bm.

Carrell, William & Sarah Penny, 29 Jul 1806; John Carrell, Edwin Smith, bm.

Carrell, William & Holly Gibbs, 12 Arp 1828; Ivy Richradson, bm.

Carrell, William & Polley Cordell, 19 Oct 1857; Dallas Correll, bm; m 21 Oct 1857 by A. Coats, J. P.

Carrell, William Jr. & Piety Hobby, 30 Nov 1851; Elisha Harrison, bm.

Carroll, Benjamin & Susan Dickens, 10 Sept 1840; Josiah Hollinson, bm.

Carroll, Hardy H. & Edith Johnson, 17 July 1857; W. H. Coats, bm; m 30 Jul 1857 by A. Coats, J. P.

Carroll, James & Betsy Wall, 8 Sept 1866; W. M. Murphrey, bm; m 17 Sept 1866 by W. C. Nowell.

Carroll, John & P. A. Jones, 1 Mar 1859; m 8 Mar 1859 by Moore Stephenson, bm.

Carroll, Joseph (colored) & Cazilla Tomlinson, 17 Sept 1866; J. Wesley Smith, bm; m 17 Sept 1866 by Wm. Hastins, J. P.

Carroll, Raiford (colored) & Courtney Sanders, 31 Dec 1866; Theophilus Whitfield, bm.

Carroll, Ransom & Lucinda Stevenson, 10 Aug 1849; Dallas Carroll, bm.

Carter, Charles & _____, _____ 1811.

Carter, Irvin & Mary Youngblood, 9 Aug 1790; Wm. Youngblood, bm.

Carter, James M. & Julia A. Roberts, 21 Jul 1857; J. H. Abell, bm.

Carter, John & Rilda Pearce, 21 Nov 1845; Stanley Kirby, bm.

Carter, Kindred & Luvey Eskridge, 1 Aug 1797; Peter Williams, bm.

Carter, Reuben & Penelopia Price, 26 Feb 1799; Hardy Parker, John Bailey, bm.

Carter, William & Rachill Frost, 25 Jul 1810; James Durham, bm.

Carter, William & Nancy Wellens, 12 Dec 1816; Neill Buie, bm.

Carter, William & Appy Oliver, 1 Jun 1818; David Thomson, bm.

Carter, Young & Lolly Tarver, 16 Dec 1829; Wm. Penny, bm.

Caudel, Camil & Sally Lee, _____ 180-; Harmon Caudle, bm.

Caudell, Cammel & Polly Harper, 2 Dec 1819; H. Guy, bm.

Caudle, Harman & Sally Massingill, 13 Nov 1810; Jonathan Caudle, bm.

Caudell, Harmon & Polly Warren, 13 Oct 1820; Isaac Wise, bm.

Caudle, John & Elizabeth Toler, 26 Dec 1804; Robrt Tolar, bm.

Celia, Henesbury & Wealthy Hodge, 24 May 1856; m 25 May 1856 at her own house by L. Richardson, J. P.

Chambers, James & Zilpah Jernigan, 25 Nov 1799; John Stevens, Jr., bm.

Chambers, Thomas & Mary Stanley, 22 Sept 1786; Dial Collins, bm.

Chamblee, Hiram & Patience Strickland, 16 Dec 1837; Fremon Chamblee, bm.

Chamblee, William & Martha Hardy, 23 Jul 1847; Stephen Johnson, bm.

Champane, Elijah & Olive Byrd, 11 Jul 1827; John Byrd, bm.

Champion, Isaac & Nancy Taylor, 3 Jun 1801; Henry CHampion, John Lee, bm.

Cheves, Thomas & Grace Brady, 1 Mar 1771; William Rand, Jr., bm.

Childers, Joshua Meilton & Jane Sellers, 28 Mar 1865; Elisha Moore, bm; m __ Apr 1865 by P. Godwin, J. P.

Chiles, Mathew & Nancey Tarlor, 13 Nov 1795; Saml Avera, bm.

Chrismon, Robert D. & Mary A. Hinnant, 25 Nov 1856; m 7 Dec 1856 by B. G. Richardson, J. P.

Christerfer, Christer & Sally Boon, 3 Nov 1824; Jno. L. Haywood, bm.

Christnall, L. & Martha Millenaner, m 21 Jan 1862 at Joseph Jones's, by McNab Earp, J. P.

Churchill, William & Cally Reesce (Pearce?), 24 Jan 1848; Charles Howell, bm.

Clark, Eli & Edeth Powell, 24 Mar 1810; Jno. Stevens, Jr., bm.

Clark, Francis & Ruth Powell, 7 Dec 1808; Jacob Powell, bm.

Clark, Harris & Lydia Gower, 14 Nov 1789; James Carrell, bm.

Clark, John & Rutha Powell, 10 Mar 1857; m 26 Apr 1857 by B. A. Wellons, J. P.

Clark, Stephen & Peggy Evans, 28 May 1833; Henry Lee, bm.

Clark, Stephen & Susan Barefoot, m 16 Feb 1860 at Joel Hudson's, by Jas. H. Adams, J. P.

Clemons, Samuel & Grizy Ann Daniel, 29 Dec 1854; m 31 Dec 1854 by J. W. Moody, J. P.

Clenny, William & Phereby Lee, 25 Nov 1807; Saml Lee, Jr., bm.

Clifton, Aeril P. & Ridley Jones, 1 Aug 1844; Jo Clifton, bm.

Clifton, Azel & Sarry Pool, 8 Dec 1796; Britain Suggs, bm.

Clifton, Henry A. & Elizabeth Kean, 12 Jan 1839; Joel Clifton, Sr., bm.

Clifton, James & Susanna Lewis, 19 Nov 1788; William Clifton, bm.

Clifton, James H. & Martha Cordal, 22 Feb 1859; m 24 Feb 1859 by R. W. Stevens, J. P.

25

Clifton, Joel & Sally Iveans, 23 Aug 1842; Henry A. Clifton, bm.

Clifton, Joel B. & Susan Lunceford, 24 Dec 1833; Joseph Clifton, bm.

Clifton, John & Polly Hinton, 31 Mar 1823; Hardy Avera, bm.

Clifton, John R. & Theterson Barber, 12 Apr 1827; Joel Clifton, bm.

Clifton, Joseph & Mason Parish, 28 Dec 1832; Lovet Spivey, bm.

Clifton, Rufus R. & Marzilla Byrd, m 17 Feb 1864 at Thurston Clifton's, by W. H. Lambert, J. P.

Clifton, Thomas G. & Joanna Lee, 20 Nov 1826; Col. Jno. Lee, bm.

Coates, P. P. & Susan Johnson, 3 Mar 1859; m 6 Mar 1859 by C. J. Bingham, J. P.

Coats, Amos & Polly Tellington, 1 Feb 1840; Wm. H. Coats, bm.

Clifton, Joel & Sally Iveans, 23 Aug 1842; Henry A. Clifton, bm.

Clifton, Joel B. & Susan Lunceford, 24 Dec 1833; Joseph Clifton, bm.

Clifton, John & Polly Hinton, 31 Mar 1823; Hardy Avera, bm.

Clifton, John R. & Theterson Barber, 12 Apr 1827; Joel Clifton, bm.

Clifton, Joseph & Mason Parish, 28 Dec 1832; Lovet Spivey, bm.

Clifton, Rufus R. & Marzilla Byrd, m 17 Feb 1864 by W. H. Lambert, J. P.

Clifton, Thomas G. & Joanna Lee, 20 Nov 1826; Col. Jno. Lee, bm.

Coates, P. P. & Lilay Stevenson, 18 Jan 1806; Benjamin Blunt of Georgia, bm.

Coats, William H. & Martha Penny, 20 Jul 1846; James Tomlinson, bm.

Cobb, James & Nancy Avera, 19 Dec 1837; Edwin Boykins, bm.

Coble, Willie & Martha Lee, 29 Nov 1825; Nicholas Rose, bm.

Cobles, Thomas & Sarah Hopkins, 2 Dec 1824; Benjamin A. Barham, bm.

Cockerell, Thomas & Patsy Garner, 10 Jan 1825; Simon Cockerell, bm.

Cockerl, Simon & Dicey Garner, 21 Mar 1803; Willis Garner, bm.

Cockrel, Jonathan & Willy Creach, 26 Apr 1836; Levy Yelventon, bm.

Cockrel, Ruffin & Willy Silivent, 1 Jan 1849; John Oliver Rains, bm.

Cockrell, John & Polly Folk, 4 Jan 1806; Sam'l Cockrell, bm.

Cockrell, Ruffin & Sylva Watson, 9 Dec 1836; Ervin Cockrell, bm.

Cockrell, Samuel & Polly Hatcher, 17 Jan 1797; Benjamin Hatcher, Jno. Vinson, bm.

Cockrell, Stephen & Anne Watson, 23 Dec 1807; Willis Garner, bm.

Cockrell, William & Theny Bagley, 1 Mar 1802; Willis Garner, bm.

Cogdell, John S. & Salley E. Stevens, 29 Mar 1836; Julius A. Stevens, bm.

Cole, James & Elizabeth Weaver, 9 Apr 1853; m ___ Apr 1853 by E. S. Jones, J. P.

Cole, John & Jane MacClain, 29 Mar 1831; Jonthan Fail, bm.

Cole, Josiah & Nancy Dunn, 28 Feb 1825; Nicholas Rose, bm.

Cole, Levi, of Orange Co., & Sarah Guess, of Johnston Co., 20 Dec 1866; J. T. Capps, bm; m 20 Dec 1866 at John M. Guess's, by W. P. Raiford, J. P.

Cole, Thomas & Elizabeth Fail, 28 Feb 1832; William Reaves, bm.

Cole, W. B. & Serena W. Langston, 5 May 1866; W. B. Flours, bm.

Cole, William H. & Sarah Thompson, 28 Dec 1855; m 30 Dec 1855 at the residence of Daniel Thompson, by Thos. D. Snead, J. P.

Cole, Willis & Mary Flowers, 29 Feb 1836; Alexander H. Thornton, bm.

Collens, John & Eliza Hamilton, 19 Feb 1866; E. H. Wilson, bm.

Collier, Elwood & Edith Littleton, 4 Nov 1861; m 5 Nov 1861 by Jethro Lewis, J. P.

Collins, Alexander S. & Agatha Whittington, 16 Feb 1823; William M. Whitinton, bm.

Collins, David & Nanny Peeden, 30 Sept 1800; Deal Collins, Robert Gulley, Jr., bm.

Collins, Mark & Elizabeth Dodd, 31 Jan 1846; Willie Dodd, bm.

Collins, Matthew & Penny Earp, 12 Aug 1803; Matthew Jones, Jr., bm.

Collins, Richard & Sarah Starling, m 26 May 1863 by W. D. Holt, J. P.

Collins, Samuel & Martha Nowel, 15 Sept 1778; James Holliman, bm.

Collins, Thomas & Charlotte Davis, 6 Apr 1791; Wm. Bull, Nathan Powell, bm.

Collins, Uriah D. & Aquilla Johnson, 8 Jan 1839; D. G. Collins, bm.

Collins, Urias, of Wake Co., & Salley Fish, 18 Jan 1791; John Fish, of Wake Co., bm.

Collins, Warren & Polly Sellers, 26 Mar 1822; Samuel Strickland, bm.

Collins, Zachariah & Welthy Beaman, 8 Oct 1802; Isaac Beaman, bm.

Colyer, John & Polly Pearce, 7 Feb 1828; David Thomson, bm.

Colyer, Jonathan & Martha Ann Sellers, 20 Nov 1866; Richard Sellers, bm; m 20 Nov 1866 by W. H. Wellons, J. P.

Conegy, Owen & Amy Oliver, 27 Oct 1845; Barna Creech, bm.

Cook, William & Lucy Massingale, 5 Sept 1811; James Stanly, bm.

Cooke, John & Betsy Parish, 16 Mar 1803; George Parrish, bm.

Cooper, Henry & Harriot Hinton, 20 Apr 1820; William Russell, bm.

Cooper, John & Morning Stancell, m 31 Jan 1862 at the residence of Jos. Edwards by S. W. Woody, J. P.

Coor, Blany & Appy Whitley, 30 Jun 1834; John C. Montague, bm.

Copeland, Charles Jr. & Barbary Jones, 10 Mar 1784; Charles Copeland, Sr., bm.

Copeland, Hezekiah & Patsy Boon, 8 Jan 1813; William Honeycut, bm.

Copeland, William & Ann Meeks, 17 Mar 1785; Samuel Smith, bm.

Copenter, Henry & Holly Hinnant, 15 Feb 1867; Jesse Hinnant, bm.; m 15 Feb 1867 by Jesse Hinnant, J. P.

Corbet, Augustus & Laurinda Gay, 29 May 1860; m 30 May 1860 at Mrs. Susan Hales(?), by Edwin S. Sanders.

Corbet, Joshua & Polly Blackman, 21 Dec 1816; John Owen, bm.

Corbet, Richard & Sarah Brantly, 25 May 1819; Samuel Lee, Jr., bm.

Corbin, William & Rebecca Wise, 3 Jan 1853; m 9 Jan 1853 by H. Johnson, J. P.

Corbit, James H. & Mary Adams, 13 Apr 1844; Robert Masingill, bm.

Corbit, James Merrit & Martha Crocker, 20 Apr 1849; Loderick A. Corbit, bm.

Corbit, John & Catharine Bawes, 7 oct 1846; Ransom Hinton, bm.

Corbit, Loderick A. & Chelly Wiggs, 7 Nov 1848; James Corbit, bm.

Cordell, Henry L. & Sarah Ann Avera, 6 Oct 1847; Edwin Boykin, bm.

Cotton, John & Charity Wright, 25 Jul 1769; Deonysius Wright, bm.

Covey, Thomas & Rhoda Wilson, 31 Dec 1799; John Wilson, bm.

Cox, John M. & Pattie Poole, 30 Apr 1864; m 4 May 1864 by J. F. Ellington.

Cox, Wilie W. & Mary Ann E. Pool, 29 May 1855; m 5 Jun 1855 by J. B. Jackson, J. P.

Cox, William (colored) & Caroline Mitchenen, 9 Nov 1866; Haywood ELlis, bm; m 12 Nov 1866 by J. F. Ellington, M. G.

Crabtree, Richard, of Orange Co., & Mary E. Griswold, of Johnston Co., 31 Oct 1866; W. H. Neal, bm; m 1 Nov 1866 by J. F. Ellington, M. G.

Cravey, Hugh & Kessey Norsworthy, 29 Apr 1797; Jno. Williams, bm.

Crawford, Daniel & Winnefred Thomson, 7 Mar 1826; Nicholas Thomson, bm.

Crawford, John H. & Patience A. A. Stevens, m 29 Jan 1852 by B. Jackson.

Crawford, William H. & Sarah Edwards, 26 Feb 1846; m by Willie Holt, J. P.

Crawley, John & Winifred Lane, 19 Feb 1800; Jonathan Turner, bm.

Creach, Ezekiel & Betsey Ingram, 4 Mar 1803; Joshua Creach, bm.

Creech, Alvin & Edney Bagley, 28 Dec 1846; Robert Edwards, bm.

Creech, Ashley & Penelope Bagley, 5 Dec 1854; m 7 Dec 1854 by James Faulk, J. P.

Creech, Benjamin & Sally Creech, 13 Feb 1808; Joshua Creech, bm.

Creech, Bennet & Lydia Wall, 11 Jan 1825; Joshua Creech, Jr., bm.

Creech, Cullen & Esther Hix, 18 May 1857; m 19 May 1857 by T. G. Boyett, Esq.

Creech, Edwin J. T. & Rebecca Thompson, 20 Nov 1806; Alex Thain, bm.

Creech, Eli & Sally Daughtry, 24 Sept 1839; Riddick Warren, bm.

Creech, Ezekiel & Polly Collins, 25 Dec 1841; Joshua Creech, bm.

Creech, Ezekiel & Nancy Fail, 28 Sept 1846; Sylvester Jones, Isakiah Creech, bm.

Creech, Ezekiel & Elenor Godwin, 23 Jun 1859; m 3 Jul 1859 at the residence of B. Godwin, by B. A. Woodall, J. P.

Creech, Haywood & Winiford Olion, 27 Jan 1849; Larkin Creech, bm.

Creech, Herrin & Luvenia Sellers, 1 Mar 1849; William Brown, bm.

Creech, James W. & Penelope Stephenson, m 25 Apr 1862 at Haywood Dixons, by R. W. Stevens, J. P.

Creech, Jarrott B. & Martha Spiers, 10 Jan 1867; James Creech, bm.

Creech, Jesse & Margarett Worley, 28 Nov 1798; William Worley, bm.

Creech, Jesse & Polly Wall, 9 Apr 1847; Stanford Creech, bm.

Creech, John & Betsey Gennett, 15 Nov 1825; Ezekiel Creech, bm.

Creech, John R. & Eveline Oliver, 5 Jan 1858; Hawood Creech, bm.; m 5 Jan 1858 at Hawood Creech's, by Wm. S. Brown, J. P.

Creech, Joshua & Nancy Edwards, 3 Aug 1838; John Massey, bm.

Creech, Joshua & Harriett Farmer, 28 May 1866; Wm. H. Creech, bm.

Creech, Josiah & Mary Fentrell, 10 Dec 1861; m 12 Dec 1861 at William Capps, by Wilie Wellons, J. P.

Creech, Kedar & Catherine Creech, 19 Nov 1839; Wm. J. Peedin, bm.

Creech, Larkin & Delany Gearald, 30 Apr 1849; Alvin Creech, bm.

Creech, Lewis & Polly Ingram, 30 Jan 1808; Joshua Creech, bm.

Creech, Lewis & Mrs. Alley Crawford, 19 Jun 1858; m 24 Jun 1858 at Jesse Crawfords, by Edwin Boykin, J. P.

Creech, Patrick & Cally Jones, 29 Nov 1859; m 1 Dec 1859 at Polly Jones's, by Wm. S. Brown.

Creech, Ransom & Elizabeth Atkinson, 29 Dec 1853; m 3 Jan 1854 by Jesse Parker, J. P.

Creech, Stanford & Martha Ellen Horn, 11 Apr 1848; Henry Hinnant, bm.

Creech, Stanford & Mary Broughton, 31 Mar 1862; m 2 Apr 1862 at John Broughtons, by Jas. H. Bryan, J. P.

Creech, Stephen E. & Elizabeth Creech, 17 Jul 1857; m 19 Jul 1857 by R. W. Stevens, J. P.

Creech, William & Nancy Spencer, 21 Jan 1850; Robert Edwards, bm.

Creech, William H. & Mary Raper, 30 Sept 1841; Kedar Creech, bm.

Creech, William J. & Polly Massingill, m 17 Nov 1853 by Jno. P. Cook, J. P.

Creech, Worley & Martha Hare, 19 Feb 1866; N. P. Parker, bm.

Crocker, Bardin & Hawkins Eason, 29 May 1852; m 30 May 1852 by H. Bradley, J. P.

Crocker, Harry & Emily Clark, 28 Jan 1843; James H. Durham, bm.

Crocker, Henderson & Nancy Anders, 25 Jul 1843; Josiah Gay, bm.

Crocker, Henderson & Viney Corbit, 11 Apr 1855; m 12 Apr 1855 by O. L. Dodd, J. P.

Crocker, James & Ruth Gay, 5 Dec 1822; Exum Futrell, bm.

Crocker, Joel & Spency Taylor, 24 Jul 1829; Samuel Crocker, bm.

Crocker, John & Celia Nahorn, 20 Oct 1834; Josiah Gay, bm.

Crocker, Samuel & Charity Crumpler, 25 Jul 1816; Solomon Futrell, bm.

Crocker, Samuel & Sally Adams, 3 Feb 1852; m 5 Feb 1853 by J. S. Gully, J. P.

Crocker, W. A. & Christion Boykin, 8 Jan 1861; m 9 Jan 1861 at R. Rapers, by A. B. Atkinson.

Cruise, Lewis & Sally Horn, 7 Jul 1820; Deal Collins, bm.

Crumpler, Asa & Nancy Oneal, 12 Nov 1808; William Crumpler, bm.

Crumpler, Edmund & Dellah Hodge, 17 Jan 1809; William Hinnant, Sr., bm.

Crumpler, Gary & Alsey Watson, 13 Apr 1846; Ransom Holloman, bm.

Crumpler, John & Olive Oneal, 14 Jan 1811; William Crumpler, bm.

Crumpler, Kenchen & Betsey Joiner, 18 Feb 1835; Thomas Davis, bm.

Cullom, Mortimer & Rachel Lockhart, 7 Sept 1848; Wm. Henry Cullom, bm.

Cullum, William H. & Esther Ann Avera, 4 Dec 1851; m 7 Dec 1851 by J. B. Jackson.

Daniel, John H. & Martha J. Rice, 3 Apr 1844; David Smith, bm.

Daniel, Joshua & Nancy Corbit, 27 Mar 1814; Lewis Sasser, bm.

Darden, James & Nancy Godwin, 22 Dec 1834; Willie Godwin, bm.

Daughdy, Matthew & Susan Creech, 24 Sept 1833; William Baker, bm.

Daughtery, Arthur & Nancy Tiner, 1 Feb 1816; Henry Doughtry, bm.

Daughtery, John & Patsy Strickland, 12 May 1848; George Daughty, bm.

Daughtery, Richard & Rebecca Creach, ___ 180-; Needham Warren, bm.

Daughtery, Robert & Sally Braddy, 30 Nov 1824; William Teal, bm.

Daughtry, Aden & Emily Strickland, 25 Apr 1862; m 1 May 1862 at John Smith's, by Jno. R. Brooks.

Daughtry, Benjamin & Apsy Turley, 26 Jan 1837; L. G. Futrell, bm.

Daughtry, Hardy & Elizabeth Rhodes, ____, Needham Warren, bm.

Daughtry, Jacob & Celia Edwards, 27 Mar 1827; William Brown, bm.

Daughtry, Solomon & Patsey Capps, 3 Jan 1842; Kedar Creech, bm.

Daughtry, Solomon & Esther Capps, 31 Jul 1843; John Massey, bm.

Daughtry, Thomas & Patsy Ragan, 3 Mar 1837; B. Bulls, bm.

Daughtry, William H., son of Solomon & Easter Daughtry, & Mary Gurley, dau. of Joseph & Elizabeth Gurley, m 29 Oct 1867 by Eld. W. M. S. Brower.

Davis, Aden & Elizabeth Perdue, 8 Dec 1851; m 11 Dec 1851 by Willie Holt, J. P.

Davis, Arthur & Elizabeth Patterson, 11 Sept 1788; John Harp, bm.

Davis, Dixon & Mourning Pope, 1 Jul 1818; Elteldred Holt, bm.

Davis, Dixon & Mary Poole, 26 Mar 1866; W. H. Cullom, bm.

Davis, Elisha & Polly Crofford, 28 Sept 1812; Daniel Ward, bm.

Davis, Elisha & Sarah Garner, 23 Mar 1859; m 24 Mar 1859 by B. R. Hinnant, J. P.

Davis, George W. & Patience Kirby, 16 Jan 1854; m 2 Jan 1854 by Stanly Kirby, J. P.

Davis, Henry & Elizabeth Edwards, 20 Apr 1798; Philip Raeford, bm.

Davis, Jacob & Rebecca Hollingsworth, 20 Oct 1843; Furney Langston, bm.

Davis, James & Patience Kirby, 25 May 1852; m 26 Jun 1852 by Stanly Kirby, J. P.

Davis, Jesse & Zilpa Boyett, 28 Feb 1820; Stevens Barnes, bm.

Davis, Jesse & Anny Crafford, 25 Oct 1836; David Parrish, bm.

Davis, John & Morning Pilkinton, 25 Feb 1802; Jeremiah Gurley, bm.

Davis, Jones & Sally Green, 30 Oct 1813; Jno. C. Guy, bm.

Davis, Joshua & Sylvia Ward, 4 Apr 1838; Henry M. Stevens, bm.

Davis, Joshua & Cherry Pitman, 10 Dec 1866; Alex Ward, bm.

Davis, Thomas & Nancy Sasser, 28 Nov 1823; Stephen Barnes, bm.

Davis, Thos. & Jane Roe, _____ ; H. Sasser, bm.

Davis, William & Sally Davis, 5 Mar 1815; Henry Capps, bm.

Dawson, Joseph & Nancy Lee, 16 Jan 1824; Samuel Lee, bm.

Dean, Calvin & Rebecca Edwards, 16 Jul 1836; Alsey Earp, bm.

Dean, Henry & Gincy Carrell, 9 Mar 1836; Simeon Carrell, bm.

Dean, James B. & Lisha A. Wilder, 6 Sept 1860; m 13 Sept 1860 at Isham Wilders, by S. W. Woody, J. P.

Dean, John & Jane Strickland, 1 Mar 1796; Joseph Langston, bm.

Deans, Mathew J. & Rilda Pace, 15 Dec 1860; m 22 Dec 1860 at John Paces, by P. Godwin, J. P.

Deans, Willie & Allana Broadstreet, 4 Jul 1836; Joseah Houlder, bm.

Deberry, Benja. & Crecy Hocut, 16 Jan 1834; Burwell Earp, bm.

Debnam, Edward & Nancy J. Bulls, 14 Aug 1834; W. R. Debnam, bm.

Debnam, James A. & Adeline Williams, 5 Mar 1840; Edward Debnam, bm.

Dees, Drury & Sally Stevens, 20 June 1795; John Pool, John Smith, Jr., bm.

Dees, Edmond & Betsey Braswell, 15 Nov 1803; David Braswell, bm.

Dees, Edmund & Mary Whitington, 16 Dec 1790; Phaddy Whitington, bm.

Dees, Hilliard & Sally Smith, 20 Mar 1800; Matthew Handy, bm.

Dees, Rigdon & Penelope Core, 3 Feb 1829; Bold Robin Hood, Jr., bm.

Delk, Jacob & Peggy Smith, 26 Jun 1794; Drury Masse, Abner Jordan, bm.

Deloach, Jesse & Polly Bridgers, 13 Jan 1800; David Braswell, bm.

Deloach, John & Esebel Hodgsdon, 24 Feb 1762; Saml Pearson, bm.

Deloach, Joseph & Leacy Johnson, 15 Apr 1795; William Spiur, bm.

Demont, John & Charity Bridgers, 11 Mar 1788; Drewry Bynum, John Fields, bm.

Denby, Henry & Delany Stevens, 19 Sept 1810; James Denby, bm.

Denning, Georg & Mary Woodard, 26 Jan 1847; Abram Dixon, bm.

Denning, Isaac & Mahala Mainer, m 26 Mar 1855 by Edwin Boykin, J. P.

Denning, Nathan & Susanna Morgan, 23 Aug 1847; Powell Blackmon, bm.

Denning, Robert & Polly Gart, 28 Mar 1848; Powell Blackman, bm.

Dennis, James & Caroline Helme, 24 Sept 1833; David Thomson, bm.

Dinkins, Henry & Mezaney Collier, _____ ; Godfrey Stansell, bm.

Divine, John & Jerusha Jernigan, 28 May 1794; Henry Stevens, bm.

Dixon, Abram & Louisa Adams, 26 Jan 1841; Crawford Futrell, bm.

Dixon, Abram & Sarah Barber, 15 Feb 1858; m 18 Feb 1858 at Gideon Woodalls, by B. Godwin, J. P.

Dixon, Guilford & Maria Ennis, 15 Aug 1866; J. F. Winter, bm; m 19 Aug 1866 at William Ennis, by B. Godwin, J. P.

Dixon, John & Tempe Matthis, 25 Dec 1838; Abram Dixon, bm.

Dixon, Lemuel & Lucy H. Johnson, 2 Jan 1849; R. W. Stevens, bm.

Dixon, Patrick & Lucy Woodall, 12 Feb 1863; m 2 Mar 1863 at Gideon Woodalls, by B. Godwin, J. P.

Dixon, Richard S. & Penelope Ryals, 8 Dec 1849; R. W. Stevens, bm.

Dodd, Demsy & Phereby Dodd, 14 Jan 1796; William Durham, bm.

Dodd, Isaac & Lugenia Turley, 4 May 1861; m 6 May 1861 by J. F. Ellington.

Dodd, John & Martha Johnson, 14 Dec 1788; William Youngblood, bm.

Dodd, John & Angeline Johnston, 4 Oct 1842; Willie Dodd, bm.

Dodd, Matthew & Emily Flowers, 7 Feb 1835; Bryan Harper, bm.

Dodd, Reuben & Tabitha Youngblood, 7 Oct 1815; John Parish, bm.

Dodd, Robert & Lydia Wood, 29 May 1778; John Wood, bm.

Dodd, Theofilus & Rebecca Oneal, 20 Feb 1832; Ransom Sanders, bm.

Dodd, William Jr. & Dedemiah Price, 27 Jul 1804; Thomas Price, bm.

Dodde, Bennet & Winifred Britt, 27 Dec 1805; Jonathan Britt, bm.

Doughlas, Rhodham & Patty Harrell, 20 Nov 1802; Francis Harrell, bm.

Dowdil, John & Betsey Durham, 7 May 1802; Young Bridgers, bm.

Dowdy, Benjamin & Alsy Eason, 26 Jan 1828; Andrew Bass, bm.

Dozier, Edmond & Sally Avera, 11 Jan 1826; Banister Harper, bm.

Draughorn, John & Pearcy Wood, 27 Aug 1828; Etheldred Futrell, bm.

Drawhorn, Richard & Nicy Pope, 27 May 180-; Jesse Adams, bm.

Driver, Gilburt & Edith Hall, 1 Mar 1820; John Driver, bm.

Driver, John & Clary Deans, 28 Aug 1822; John Windborn, bm.

Driver, John & Zelpha Pope, 8 Dec __ ; William Hobbs, bm.

Driver, Jonathan & Winefred Price, 22 Nov 1819; John Driver,bm.

Driver, Jonathan & Gincy Price, 17 Apr 1840; Thomas Price bm.

Driver, William & Tempe Todd, 9 Jan 1840; Thomas Price, bm.

Duglas, Thomas & Edith Thompsn, 29 Feb 1804; Samuel Lee, bm.

Duncan, A. R. & Bettie Turner, 12 Oct 1866; John L. Banks, bm.; m 16 Oct 1866 at Mr. Samuel Turner's.

Duncan, Alexander & Sabrian Duncan, 15 Jan 1838; George W. Duncan, bm.

Duncan, Everet & Patience Avery, 8 Dec 1826; George Duncan, bm.

Duncan, George & Louisa Durhame, 24 Oct 1848; Henry Duncan, bm.

Duncan, Henry & Keziah Averyt, 20 Mar 1792; William Durham, bm.

Dunkin, Henry & Emeline C. Boon, 30 Nov 1857; Willie S. Boon, bm.; m 30 Nov 1857 at C. Boon, by J. F. Ellington.

Dunn, Amos & Eliza Lee, 24 May 1859; m 2 Jun 1859 at Ambrose Lees, by R. Masengill, J. P.

Dunn, Barnaby & Margaret Massingill, 17 Dec 1819; John Keen, bm.

Dunn, Benjamin J. & Leacy C. Lasiter, 4 Feb 1859; m 6 Feb 1859 by George Keen, J. P.

Dunn, George & Sally Blackman, 26 Nov 1833; Cary Johnson, bm.

Dunn, George W. & Susan Lasetter, 24 Jan 1855; m 25 Jan 1855 by Robt. Massingill, J. P.

Dunn, James B. & Elizabeth Ford, 11 Mar 1853; m 13 Mar 1853 by M. Avera, J. P.

Dunn, Joel & Betsey Harrell, 25 Aug 1821; Francis Harrell, bm.

Dunn, John & Sarah Jump, 21 Apr 1859; m 28 Apr 1859 by John C. Hood, J. P.

Dunn, John R. & Mary A. Fail, 6 Aug 1858; m 12 Aug 1858 at John C. Hoods, by John C. Hood, J. P.

Dunn, Nathaniel & Polly Pool, 26 Mar 1813; Richard Johnson, bm.

Dunn, Robert & Elizabeth Cole, 22 Mar 1830; Nicholas Rose, bm.

Dunn, Sampson & Mizonine Langley, 22 Feb 1864; m 28 Feb 1864 at Lucinda Davis, by R. Masingill, J. P.

Dunn, Sir William & Ridly Stanley, 14 Aug 1858; m 15 Aug 1858 by George Keen, bm.

Dunn, Thomas & Susanna Harrell, 23 Feb 1824; Nicholas Rose, bm.

Dupree, John & Sally Pittes, 11 Jan 1820; William Welch, bm.

Dupree, Peter & Sally Johnson, 18 Apr 1806; Jonathan Johnson, bm.

Dupree, Peter C. & Martha W. Britt, 27 Sept 1859; m 16 Oct 1859 by John Harper, J. P.

Durham, Hardy & Betsy Penny, 1 Mar 1827; Bud Youngblood, bm.

Durham, Henry & Martha Shaw, 23 May 1844; Duncan McPherson, bm.

Durham, Huel & Sarah Mossingill, 31 Jan 1865; m 2 Feb 1865 at William Durhams, by George Keen, J. P.

Durham, James & Druzeilla Tomlinson, 20 Dec 1797; Henry Avera, bm.

Durham, James & Celah Avera, 22 Jun 1808; Harris Tomlinson, bm.

Durham, James & Martha Bridgers, 1 Jul 1844; David Thomson, bm.

Durham, Samuel & Betsy Stallings, 6 Nov 1835; J. H. Youngblood, bm.

Durham, Thomas & Zilpha Pearce, 26 Mar 1839; Jmes Durham, Jr., bm.

Durham, Thomas & Nancy Griswold, 27 Sept 1849; James Hinnant, bm; m 27 Sept 1849 by Tho. Bagley, Clk.

Durham, W. H. & Aurelia Turner, 18 Dec 1858; m 21 Dec 1858 at her father S. Turners, by T. Garrard, bm.

Durham, William & Ann Nichols, 11 May 1780; Britain Smith, bm.

Durham, William & Lurany Johnson, 27 Nov 1797; Joseph Deloach, bm.

Durham, William & Bedy Moore, 11 Nov 1833; William Johnson, bm.

Durham, William & Ammy Massingill, 4 Feb 1854; m 12 Feb 1854 by Right Ryals, Jr.

Earp, Alsey & Martha O'neal, 29 Jul 1836; Thomas Powers, bm.

Earp, Berry & Patsy Lee, 15 Jan 1822; Moses Jordan, bm.

Earp, Burrell & Nancy Trayway, 24 Feb 1846; Wyatt Earp, bm.

Earp, Hudson & Sally Gully, 13 Nov 1816; Jno. G. Gully, bm.

Earp, Izariah & Charity Wimberly, 6 Oct 1809; Charles A. Hood, bm.

Earp, James H. & Emly Johnson, m 27 Jan 1853 by C. Langdon, J. P.

Earp, John & Frances Eason, 21 Apr 1837; William Earp, bm.

Earp, John & Edney Godwin, 9 Dec 1847; Bryan Sanders, bm.

Earp, Moses (colored) & Janet Wall, 9 Jun 1866; McNab Earp, bm; m 9 Jun 1866 by McNab Earp, J. P.

Earp, Sherod & Edith Atkinson, 16 Apr 1799; Ichabod Blackman, bm.

Earp, William & Alsabeth O'Niel, 15 Feb 1792; James Shaw, Jr., bm.

Earp, William & Patherby Atkinson, 18 Aug 1837; Robert Bryan, bm.

Earp, Wyatt & Mariah Fountain, m 4 Nov 1852 by N. W. Richardson, J. P.

Eason, Adin & Sally Brannon, 12 Aug 1825; William Hayles, bm.

Eason, Alex & Joanna Batten, 30 Oct 1866; John Broadwell, bm; m 15 Nov 1866 by Wm. Hasting, J. P.

Eason, Benjamin & Polly Keal, 26 Dec 1801; Henry Horne, bm.

Eason, Benjamin & Bethaney Snipes, 15 Jul 1817; Jno. C. Guy, bm.

Eason, Benjamin T. & Maria Ullmer 5 Jan 1851; Allanson Thornton, bm.

Eason, Elisha & Edith Avera, 9 Jun 1804; Benjamin Eason, bm.

Eason, George & Jane Price, 29 Sept 1846; Avera Eason, bm.

Eason, Hardy & Mary Shaw, 8 Feb 1834; Buthan Bryan, bm.

Eason, Henry W. & Susan Williams, 15 Jul 1828; Samuel Mitchner, bm.

Eason, James & Lotty Moore, 19 Oct 1822; James Dosier, bm.

Eason, James & Haukins Barber, 18 Nov 1849; Benjamin Stewart, bm.

Eason, John & Oliver Avera, 23 Oct 1795; Hardy Bryan, bm.

Eason, John & Fameriah Eason, 14 Oct 1803; Benjamin Eason, bm.

Eason, John & Betsy Williams, 22 Jan 1827; Thomas Lockart, Jr., bm.

Eason, John S. & Elizabeth Brown, 15 Jan 1867; Alex Eason, bm; m 17 Jan 1867 by John Broadwell, J. P.

Eason, Joseph D. & Peninnah Hocut, 6 June 1866; Jesse S. Kirby, bm; m 17 Jan 1867 at John T. Hatchers, by John Broadwell, J. P.

Eason, Kearney & Cozzey Godwin, 25 May 1840; Lemel Jones, bm.

Eason, Moses & Anny Hayles, 12 Aug 1814; Jeremiah Parnold, bm.

Eason, Otheniel & Ann Norriss, 9 Dec 1767; John Norriss, bm.

Eason, Sanders & Willy Parnold, 18 Mar 1844; Solomon Parnold, bm.

Eason, Thos. & Harriet Gully, 17 May 1834; Edwin A. McCullers, bm.

Eason, William & Sally Broughton, 28 Mar 1826; Jesse Eason, bm.

Eason, William H. & Elizabeth Talton, 11 Dec 1854; m 15 Dec 1854 by Pharoah Richardson, J. P.

Eason, William & Betsy Broughton, 2 Jan 1819; Jonathan Stansill, bm.

Eatman, John & Zady Tisdell, 29 Sept 1812; Soloman Johnson, bm.

Eatman, Kimbrel & Nancy Bailey, 11 Oct 1837; Austin Hatcher, bm.

Eatman, Kimbrel & Nancy M. Batten, 3 Dec 1866; Wm. H. Batten, bm; m 4 Dec 1866 by John Broadwell, J. P.

Eatman, Labon & Temperance Hogg, 14 Aug 1838; Sampson Morgan, bm.

Eatman, Thomas & Celah Bailey, 1 Mar 1791; John I. Driver, John Thomas, bm.

Eatmon, Alsey & Elizabeth Richardson, 24 Apr 1826; Calvin Richardson, bm.

Eatmon, Kimbrel & Piety Price, 10 Apr 1840; Austin Hatcher, bm.

Eaven, Seth T. & Mary Johnston, 8 July 1845; J. Clifton, bm.

Eavens, Jessey & Margaret Powell, 8 Mar 1794; Nathaniel Giles, bm.

Edgerton, Joseph G. & Celie Elizabeth Snipes, 19 Feb 1867; Bridgers Snipes, bm; m 21 Feb 1867 at David Snipes, by W. D. Holt, J. P.

Edgerton, Thomas & Zilpha Pearce, 14 Nov 1843; Lazarus Pearson, bm.

Edgerton, Thomas & Sarah Wooten, 9 Oct 1845; Thomas G. Hinnant, bm.

Edwards, Benjamin & Sabry Tiner, 1 Oct 1793; Drury Musslewhite, bm.

Edwards, Benjamin & Exaline Worley, 13 Apr 1837; Needham Worley, bm.

Edwards, Benjamin Jr. & Evaline Overby, 6 Feb 1866; Wm. B. T. Edwards, bm.

Edwards, George & Axey Strickland, m 9 Aug 1853 by W. M. S. Brown.

Edwards, Henry & Zilpha Starling, 5 Oct 1849; Redding Jinkins, bm; m by Willie Holt.

Edwards, Henry G. & Elizabeth Ann Jernigan, 29 Jul 1840; John Edwards, bm.

Edwards, Henry G. & Nancy Overba, 5 Apr 1852; m 6 Apr 1852 by E. Atkinson, J. P.

Edwards, Jacob & Elizabeth Pilkenton, 12 Jun 1790; Gethrow Bools, bm.

Edwards, Jacob & Apsabeth Creech, 4 Jan 1827; Joshau Creech, Jr., bm.

Edwards, Jesse & Patty Peeden, 10 Aug 1798; Jeremiah Gurley, bm.

Edwards, Jesse & Pheraby Hall, 1 Sept 1813; Amos Peeden, bm.

Edwards, John & Sarah Oneal, 17 Nov 1787; Benjamin Oneal, bm.

Edwards, John & Carolin Edwards, 22 Apr 1846; William T. Ballenger, Bryan Sanders, bm.

Edwards, Joseph & Patty Collins, 12 May 1794; Joseph Ingram, bm.

Edwards, Joseph & Linsey Renfrow, 17 Apr 1863; m 30 Apr 1863 at Harres Renfrow, by J. Lewis, J. P.

Edwards, Joseph Jr. & Leucy Braswell, 19 May 1815; Elijah Thompson, bm.

Edwards, Joshua & Hawkins Talton, m 9 Jan 1862 by Jethro Lewis, J. P.

Edwards, Micajah & Polly Spencer, 22 Nov 1805; Stephen Edwards, bm.

Edwards, Micajah & Elizabeth Stucky, 13 Aug 1824; Jesse Whitley, bm.

Edwards, Needham & Polly Brassell, 6 Feb 1838; John Edwards, bm.

Edwards, Newsom & Mourning Davis, 12 Apr 1834; Isaac Sterling, bm.

Edwards, Robbin & Elizabeth Oliver, 22 Aug 1843; William Oliver, bm.

Edwards, Robert & Tempy Creech, 21 Jan 1845; Pelick Massey, bm.

Edwards, Robert & Apsabeth Daughterey, 20 Dec 1845; Benj. B. Bronson, bm.

Edwards, Sampson & Sally Braswell, 29 Sept 1812; Benjamin Edwards, bm.

Edwards, Sampson & Mary Edwards, 16 Aug 1836; William Peeden, bm.

Edwards, Stephen & Betsy Thompson, 20 Nov 1838; Sampson Edwards, bm.

Edwards, Thomas & Nancy Price, 8 Sept 1796; Thomas Price, bm.

Edwards, Thomas & Elizabeth Peedin, 16 Jul 1814; James Peedin, bm.

Edwards, Thomas & Sally Snipes, 25 Mar 1841; William Brown, bm.

Edwards, Thomas & Sally Jackson, 27 Oct 1838; Riddick Warren, bm.

Edwards, Vine & Patsy Peeden, 31 Aug 1840; Newsom Edwards, bm.

Edwards, William & Penny Parker, 25 Nov 1817; John Carter, bm.

Edwards, William & Disey Gerrald, 12 Oct 1838; Sampson Edwards, bm.

Edwards, William B. T. & Mary Overby, 15 Dec 1860; m 16 Dec 1860 at Joseph Overbys, by Wms. Brown.

Edwards, William E. & Amanda M. Jones, 8 May 1839; N. H. Blackwood, bm.

Edwards, Zacheriah & Zerilly Peeden, 9 Mar 1842; Wm. M. Creech, bm.

Eldridge, Lovard & Mary Williams, 24 Jun 1822; Willie N. White, bm.

Eldridge, Lovard & John Lacy Ellis, 29 Apr 1861; m 30 Apr 1861 by S. Wait.

Ellington, Jesse & Betsy Brannon, 5 Aug 1810; Samuel Willoby, bm.

Ellington, Joel & Betsy Hocut, 26 Nov 1816; Allen Richardson, bm.

Ellington, John F. & Christian Avera, 3 Jan 1831; Joseph Clifton, bm.

Ellington, John Farrar & Ader Carter, 17 Aug 1798; Kindred Carter, bm.

Ellington, W. P. & Martha Eatmon, 4 Jul 1862; m 6 July 1862 at Mrs. Emily Loncefords, by Jas. H. Bryan, J. P.

Ellington, Warsham, & Elizabeth A. Tucker, 2 Feb 1807; Penington Tucker, bm.

Ellis, Abel & Reney Dunn, 10 May 1845; Henry Guin, bm.

Ellis, Elijah & Patiance Collins, 20 July 1791; George Collins, bm.

Ellis, Ferdinand & Polly Ann Lunsford, 16 Oct 1844; John W. Ferrell, bm.

Ellis, Henry (colored) & Coria A. Banks, 7 Feb 1867; Jno. I. Ellis, bm; m 17 Feb 1867 by W. A. Ellis, J. P.

Ellis, Jackson, son of Betsey Ellis, & Helan Parish, dau. of Caswell & Nancy Ann Parish, 2 Dec 1867; m 5 Dec 1867 by G. G. Gulley, J. P.

Ellis, James & Patsy Powell, 7 Dec 1825; Isaac Hutchins, bm.

Ellis, James N. & Mary Blackman, 10 Aug 1852; m 12 Aug 1852 by Harry Johnson, J. P.

Ellis, James R. & Martha Pool, 27 Feb 1839; Saml. M. Turley, bm.

Ellis, John & Mary Ferrell, 9 Feb 1793; John Turner, bm.

Ellis, John & Leucy Ferrell, 26 Mar 1834; James R. Ellis, bm.

Ellis, John & Winny Blackman, 4 Sept 1848; Wm. Thornton, bm.

Ellis, Lofton & Penny Pool, 23 Mar 1842; Sam'l M. Turley, bm.

Ellis, William & Altna Parish, 15 Jan 1839; Samuel M. Turley, bm.

Ellis, William H. & Mary E. Hood, 21 Nov 1851; m 3 Dec 1851 by S. S. Horton, J. P.

Ennis, John A. & Winnifred Ennis, 26 May 1856; m 1 Jun 1856 at the residence of John Ennis, by R. W. Stevens, J. P.

Ennis, John A. & Abi Wheeler, 10 Oct 1859; m 13 Oct 1859 by Wm. F. Hall, elder.

Ennis, Needham & Elizabeth Grimes, 3 Feb 1834; Ramon Ennis, bm.

Ennis, Ramon & Sally Grimes, 23 Feb 1836; John W. Johnson, bm.

Ennis, Raymond & Emily Stephenson, 17 Dec 1866; J. H. Parrish, bm; m 19 Dec 1866 at Moore Stephensons, by Jno. R. Coates, J. P.

Etherdg, William J. & Lucy J. Sanders, 27 Feb 1844; W. R. Etheredge, bm.

Etheredge, Ryals & Jane Massengill, 22 Mar 1813; Martin Hall, bm.

Ethridge, Edward & Clarky Proctor, 1 Jan 1798; Jacob Woodall, bm.

Ethridge, William & Elizabeth Sanders, 22 Dec 1836; S. M. Utley, bm.

Evans, Ashley B. & Helon Wilkins, 31 Mar 1856; m 9 Apr 1856 by Edwin Boykin, J. P.

Evans, David & Zelpha Lee, 14 Jun 1817; William Wood, bm.

Evans, Etheldred & Nancy Collins, 5 Mar 1805; James Paden, bm.

Evans, Jeremiah & Celia Crawford, 1 Nov 1822; Alexander Sanders, bm.

Evans, John & Dilley Rains, 2 Mar 1801; David Evans, bm.

Evans, John R. & Caroline Rhodes, 4 Jan 1836; Ambrose Lee,bm.

Evans, Simpson & Elizabeth Hodge, m 20 Apr 1854 by R. Oneal, J. P.

Evens, Ephriam R. & Elizabeth Blackmon, m 26 Nov 1851 by R. Massingill, J. P.

Evens, Francis & Jenny Brewer, 13 Mar 1784; Ambrose Rains, bm.

Fail, Jonath. & Lucey Field, 26 Mar 1828; Francis Harrell, bm.

Fail, Needham & Pherebee Howell, 21 Mar 1860; m 22 Mar 1860 at Jethro Howels, by Jas. H. Sasser, M. G.

Fail, Osburn & Alice George, 21 Apr 1802; Francis Harrell, bm.

Fail, Thomas & Phereby Fail, 19 Apr 1792.

Fail, William & Elizabeth Bryan, 23 Jan 1804; Jeremiah Lee, bm.

Faircloth, Hardy & Martha Messer, 10 Jan 1867; J. M. Parrish, bm; m 10 Jan 1867 by Jno. R. Coates, J. P.

Faircloth, Stephen L. & Penny Gainas, 18 Feb 1867; W. B. Joyner, bm.; m 21 Feb 1867 at Simon Gaines, by B. Williams, J. P.

Farmer, Henry S., of Alabama, & Margaret Sneed, 17 Nov 1842; Allen S. Ballinger, bm.

Farmer, Jenkins & Susanna Hadley, 29 Aug 1798; William Farmer, bm.

Farmer, John & Elizabeth Ballinger, 22 Apr 1809; Allen S. Ballinger, bm.

Farmer, Joseph & Polly Nelms, 3 Aug 1819; Wm. Henry Guy, bm.

Farmer, Joseph & Mary Mitchner, 7 Aug 1821; Tho. Lockhart, Jr., bm.

Farmer, Joseph & Sarah Frost, 19 Jan 1825; David H. Bryan, bm.

Farmer, Turner & Peggy Boyland, 26 Feb 1867; Parrot Creech, bm; m 27 Feb 1867 at P. Creech's, by Rev. P. Creech.

Farrar, William & Sarah Tiner, 1 Mar 1804; James Tiner, bm.

Farror, William & Catharine Turley, 19 Mar 1816; Thomas Turley, bm.

Farrow, Joseph & Mariah Phillips, 10 Apr 1844; A. J. Lloyd, bm.

Faulk, Henry & Sarah Stearn, 11 May 1795; John Faulk, bm.

Faulk, Jones & Annie Kirby, 10 Mar 1866; Ray Phillips, bm.

Faulk, Nicklos & Rhoda Harman, 8 Apr 1802; Etheldred Futrel, bm.

Fearrell, James & Cherry Watson, 1 July 1848; Reddin Newsom, bm.

Feilick, James & Emily J. Hunter, 31 Jul 1822; Ray Helme, bm.

Fellows, John & Polley Germillon, 28 Dec 1807; Jno. Stevens, Jr., bm.

Fellows, John & Mary bell, 3 Jan 1820; David Bell, bm.

Ferrel, Isaac & Edith Pipkin, 25 Jul 1778; James Butler, bm.

Ferrel, James & Jincy Richardson, 28 Feb 1844; Calvin Richardson, bm.

Ferrell, Ephraim Jr. & Betsy Parish, 9 Dec 1800; John Ellis, bm.

Ferrell, Gabriel & Nelly Watson, 27 Dec 1852; m 2 Jan 1853 by Kinchen Crumpler, M. G.

Ferrell, Harrison & Nancy Tew, 19 Dec 1854; m 26 Dec 1854 by Eld. J. H. Keneday.

Ferrell, Jacob Jr. & Liddy Johnson, 20 Feb 1797; Plyer Barber, Jr., bm.

Ferrell, James J. & Adlade C. Ellington, 13 Dec 1852; m 15 Dec 1852 by W. H. McCullers, J. P.

Ferrell, Merrit & Winifred Turner, 22 Apr 1837; Gaston Parish, bm.

Ferrell, R. K. & Mary Ann Vinson, 4 Nov 1859; m 9 Nov 1859 by J. F. Ellington.

Ferrell, Thomas J. & Martha Ann O'neal, 15 Sept 1863; m 16 Sept 1863 by J. F. Ellington.

Ferrell, Willie & Edith Rentfroe, 27 Feb 1816; James Watson, bm.

Ferrell, Willis & Olive Branan, 18 Jul 1832; Isaac Stallings, bm.

Ferrill, John & Elizabeth Jones, 26 Oct 1816; Reuben Dodd, bm.

Fewtrel, Bud & Chason Boyett, 13 Jan 1848; Howel W. Yelventon, bm.

Fields, Needham & Zilpha Blackkmond, 16 Jan 1853; m __ Jan 1853 by J. Peacock, J. P.

Finch, Birty & Harrot Johnson, 9 Feb 1814; Wily Johnson, bm.

Fish, John & Pherebe Tomlinson, 13 Oct 1787; Edmund Tomlinson, bm.

Fish, William & Matilda Grimes, 23 Feb 1836; John W. Johnson, bm.

Flowers, Benjamin & Slomney Horn, 24 Feb 1807; Stephen Grice, bm.

Flowers, Henry & Elizabeth Marshall, 18 Jul 1797; John Coats, bm.

Flowers, Jacob & Penny Coats, 14 Nov 1843; Wm. H. Coats, bm.

Flowers, Jacob Jr. & Fereby Johnson, 8 Apr 1798; Henry Flowers, bm.

Flowers, John & Tempe Flowers, 31 Dec 1838; Stephenson Godwin, bm.

Flowers, Michael & Mary Keen, 27 May 1807; Stephen Grice, bm.

Flowers, Nathan & Nancy Brunt, 25 Mar 1839; Thomas Toler, bm.

Flowers, Needham & Elizabeth Broadrib, 28 Mar 1789; Wm. Blunt, bm.

Fluellin, Archibald & Nancy Parish, 7 Dec 1790; Ludom Smith, bm.

Fluellin, James & Clary Orton, 13 Nov 1813; Martin Overby, bm.

Folk, William & Sarah Futerell, 13 Oct 1803; Thomas Folk, bm.

Folsom, Thomas & Charity Norriss, 13 Aug 1795; James Norriss, bm.

Ford, Hardy & Caroline Kelly, 8 Jan 1861; m 9 Jan 1861 by J. F. Ellington.

Ford, John A. & Catharine Munden, 13 Feb 1852; m 15 Feb 1852 by M. Avera, J. P.

Fowler, Charles & Patsey Hollomon, 24 Feb 1824; Pattrick Fowler, bm.

Fowler, James & Elizabeth Crowden, m 23 May 1863 at Smithfield, by J. A. Stevens, J. P.

Fowler, Wesley & July Carrell, 22 Jan 1846; Ephraim A. Smith, bm.

Franklin, William & Sally Rivers, 31 Dec 1805; John Smith, Jr., bm.

Frazier, Curtis & Maledith Thornton, 27 Mar 1862; m 28 Mar 1862 at Elizabeth Thornton, by John A. Smith, J. P.

Freeman, Needham & Betty Rae, 26 Sept 1857; Wm. H. Cullem, bm; m 26 Sept 1857 by Wm. Potter, M. G.

Freemon, N. Y. & Rixy Horne, 22 Sept 1857; Joseph C. Freeman, bm; m 24 Sept 1857 by J. F. Ellington.

Frost, Cathezen & Penny Smith, 28 Nov 1809; Stephen Brown, bm.

Frost, John & Betsey Brown, 28 Mar 1803; Willis Nelms, bm.

Frost, Jonas & Polly McCullers, 5 Feb 1801; Samuel Smith, bm.

Fulgham, John & Zelpha Massey, m 16 Nov 1854 by William Rains, J. P.

Fulgum, Charles & _____, ____ 1808; Charles Wellons, bm.

Futeral, Solomon & Rachel Watson, 28 Aug 1809; Etheldred Futral, bm.

Futrail, Needham & Caty Sharp, 29 Nov 1808; Loverd Pearce, Lamul Pearce, bm.

Futrel, Nathanel & Nancy Deans, 4 Jul 1812; Josiah Hinnant, Jr., bm.

Futrell, Crawford & Mariah Davis, 10 Jan 1837; Jonas Davis, bm.

Futrell, Crawford & Caroline Peeden, 8 Aug 1856; m 14 Aug 1856 at Wm. J. Peeden's, by Wm. H. Sellers, J. P.

Futrell, Etheldred Jr. & Polly Gurley, 28 Sept 1819.

Futrell, Etheldred Jr. & Edney Gearold, 2 Jul 1821; Thos. Rice, bm.

Futrell, Exum & Rhodes Pooll, 10 Feb 1821; Nathaniel Futrel, bm.

Futrell, Jesse & Patience Joiner, 20 Mar 1833; Solomon Futrell, bm.

Futrell, Wilkerson & Polly Massey, 8 Oct 1817; Isaiah Massey, bm.

Gale, Solomon & Miriam Ferrell, 7 Apr 1787; John Turner, bm.

Gallaway, Richard & Sarah Porter, 18 Jan 1804; Josiah Baggell, bm.

Game, Josiah & Catty Crocker, 4 Sept 1827; James Crocker, bm.

Game, Josiah & Edney Ranes, 4 Nov 1823; Samuel Game, bm.

Game, Samuel & Apsabeth Edwards, 26 Jul 1852; m 28 Jul 1852 by Wm. Rains, J. P.

Game, Samuel S. & Zilpha Raines, 18 Jan 1821; Robt. Raiford, bm.

Ganas, Reuben & Elinor Lockabay, 4 Jul 1849; George Keen, bm.

Gardner, Daniel & Martha Earp, 16 Dec 1847; Henry H. Hobbs, bm.

Gardner, Eli & Dicy Yelvington, 26 Mar 1839; Thomas Bagley, bm.

Gardner, Larry & Emily Sasser, 30 Jun 1846; John Sasser, bm.

Garner, Asa & Nancy Price, 5 Sept 1836; James Stallings, bm.

Garner, Elisha & Sally Brown, 1 Oct 1799; Daniel Rogers, bm.

Garner, Gidion & Sindy Snipes, 19 Jul 1826; Drury Johnson, bm.

Garner, Henderson & Joanny Atkinson, 21 Feb 1848; Austin Hatcher, bm.

Garner, Joel & Martha Yelvington, 6 Feb 1841; Eli Garner, bm.

Garner, Mabry & Margaret Stansell, 28 Jan 1854; m 2 Feb 1854 by S. Bagley, J. P.

Garner, Moses & Mary Cockrell, 25 Aug 1800; John Brown, bm.

Garner, Moses & Anna Bailey, 13 May 1821; Levi Garner, bm.

Garner, Wilie & Polly Garner, 21 Apr 1865; Jesse Parker, bm.

Garner, William & Mary Hatcher, 29 Nov 1785; Rueben Wilkerson, bm.

Garner, William & Elizabeth Garner, & 10 Mar 1834; James Garner, bm.

Garner, William & Patsey Batten, 14 Nov 1843; James Garner, bm.

Garner, Willis & Sarah Cockrell, 12 Dec 1797; William Garner, bm.

Garrald, Enus & Bedie Starlin, 10 Apr 1816; Samuel Batten, bm.

Gatlin, James & Phereba Hobby, 1 Mar 1816; Thomas Barber, Jno. Sanders, Jr., bm.

Gay, William & Betsey Spencer, 15 Jan 1821.

Gay, William & Sarah H. Wall, 29 Nov 1859; m 6 Dec 1859 at H. L. Barnes, by R. N. Gully, J. P.

Gay, Willis & Crecy Faulk (no date, term of Gov. Swain); Wm. Bolten, bm.

Gearald, Willie & Patsey Gearald, 5 Jun 1824; Henry M. Stephens, bm.

George, David & Winnifred Lee, 24 Mar 1813.

George, Elias & Sarah Rains, 4 Jan 1779; Charles Wilkinson, bm.

George, Isaac & Sarah Fail, 28 Aug 1837; Aaron Lee, bm.

George, Jeremiah L. & Mary Hudtson, 20 Feb 1849; Sir William Blackman, bm.

Gerald, Wilie F. & Sarah Phillips, 22 Feb 1867; m 26 Feb 1867 at F. Phillip's house Boon Hill, by James Hay, J. P.

Gerhardt, John C. F. & Harriet C. Carer, m 3 Jul 1851 by C. P. Jones, M. G.

Gerheardt, Henry & Emily Jane Carter, 15 Mar 1842; m 17 Mar 1842 by D. McPherson, J. P.

Giles, Jacob & Selah Avera, 11 Feb 1788; David Hill, bm.

Giles, John & Betsy Johnson, 25 Jan 1808; Philip Johnson, bm.

Giles, John & Eliza Pittes, 28 Jan 1828; James K. Barber, bm.

Giles, Matthew & Sally Thornton, 13 Nov 1827; James K. Barber, bm.

Giles, Matthew & Elizabeth Robers, m 14 Apr 1853 by W. Bradley, J. P.

Giles, Nathaniel & Maryan Bridges, 10 Jun 1794; Hardy Bryan, bm.

Giles, Nathaniel & Anna Holmes, 24 Jan 1859; m 25 Jan 1859 at the Res. of John Holmes, by W. F. Hall, elder.

Giles, William & Lydia Wood, 17 Aug 1793; John Wood, bm.

Giles, William & Nancy Stansell, 12 Jan 1826; Bryant Adams, bm.

Gilman, Harbard & Winefred Garner, 18 Aug 1787; Benjamin Crumpler, bm.

Glover, Benjamin J. & Milley Atkinson, 27 Sept 1841; Perry Rentfrow, bm.

Godwin, Aaron & Lisba Bryan, 22 Aug 1789; William Bryan, bm.

Godwin, Aaron & Fereby Lee, 28 Nov 1826; Noel West, bm.

Godwin, Alexander & Mary Holloman, 25 Feb 1806; Stephen Grice, bm.

Godwin, Avera E. & Martha J. Easom, 23 Dec 1861; m 24 Dec 1861 at Hardy Easoms' by N. G. Gulley, J. P.

Godwin, Benjamin & Elizabeth Barber, 26 Nov 1842; Simon Turner, bm.

Godwin, Bennet & Martha Matthews, 8 Jan 1834; Terry Barber, bm.

Godwin, Edmund & Celah Nan Richardson, 3 Dec 1802; Willis Watson, bm.

Godwin, Eli & Sarah Atkinson, 1 Jan 1823; Stephen Barnes, bm.

Godwin, Elias & Nanncy Watkins, 30 May 1810; Allen Watkins, bm.

Godwin, Epram & Penelepy Thaughn, 26 Sept 1795; Thomas Cockrel, bm.

Godwin, George & Lethey Ann Smith, 26 Nov 1866; Josias Lee, bm; m 20 Dec 1866 at Henry Smiths, by John A. Smith, J. P.

Godwin, Griffin W. & Chery Rentfrow, 22 Nov 1844; Minton M. Godwin, bm.

Godwin, Henderson & _____, 12 Jun 1844; David H. Holland, bm.

Godwin, Jacob H. & Aurelia Barber, 26 Apr 1858; m 6 May 1858 at William G. Barbers, by B. Godwin, J. P.

Godwin, James & Sally Stevens, 9 Oct 1801; Jacob Beaman, bm.

Godwin, Jesse & Kitsey Jackson, 3 Feb 1859; m 20 Feb 1859 by R. Masingill, J. P.

Godwin, Jesse H. & Willey Wall, 3 Jan 1855; m 4 Jan 1855 by S. Bagley, J. P.

Godwin, John & Elizabeth Smith, 11 Nov 1849; Joel Lee, bm.

Godwin, Jordan & Elizabeth Feutral, 12 Dec 1857; Wilie Wellons, bm; m 17 Dec 1857 by Wilie Wellons, J. P.

Godwin, Newit R. & Sally Bowes, m 16 Sept 1851 by S. Bagley.

Godwin, Phelix (colored) & Aurelia Smith, 16 Jan 1867; Isaac Smith, bm; m 23 Jan 1867 by James Hay, J. P.

Godwin, Ransom & Clany Godwin, 25 May 1858; m 30 May 1858 by Jas. Faulk, J. P.

Godwin, Samuel & Polly Duck, 28 Feb 1797; Ephraim Godwin, bm.

Godwin, Silas & Elizabeth Stevens, 8 Sept 1804; James Carrell, bm.

Godwin, Theophilus & Esther Jones, 16 Oct 1860; m 24 Oct 1860 at Nehemiah Hicks, by A. H. Atkinson, J. P.

Godwin, Tobias & Creasy Richardson, 7 Jan 1811; Hardy Richardson, bm.

Godwin, Willie & Harriet Flowers, 18 Feb 1836; Elijah Godwin, bm.

Goodrich, George & Elizabeth Walston, 19 Apr 1808; Elijah Barker, bm.

Goodrich, James & Sally Crofard, 14 Jan 1811; John Wallace, bm.

Gorden, Rubin & Olive Richardson, 30 Nov 1790; Applewhite Richardson, bm.

Gorman, Thomas (colored) & Lany Sanders, 15 Dec 1866; Romeo McCullers, bm.

Gower, Abell & Clarky Holloman, 30 Nov 1858; m 1 Dec 1858 at Harrison Ferrells, by B. A. Wellons, J. P.

Gower, John K. & Elizabeth Hopkins, m 15 May 1855 at Gideon Gowers, by H. H. Finch, J. P.

Gower, Simeon H. & Eveline S. Barber, 4 Jul 1859; m 21 Jul 1859 at Thomas Barbers, by D. H. Holland, J. P.

Gower, William & Jane Overby, 26 Nov 1796.

Gower, William & Cyntha Smith, 26 Nov 1839; Jnona. Johnson, bm.

Gower, William & Harriett Holt, 18 Nov 1847; Baldy Sanders, bm; m ____ by Lime B. Sanders, J. P.

Gower, Zacheriah & Nancy Williams, 15 Sept 1803; William Gower, bm.

Gower, Zacheriah & Theny Massingill, 24 Jul 1809; William Roberts, bm.

Graham, Henderson & Easter A. Whitley, 5 Oct 1844; Redick Warren, bm.

Granger, H. F. & N. R. Williams, 4 Feb 1867; E. D. Snead, bm; m 6 Feb 1867 at Maj. N. Williams, by T. Page Ricaud, M. G.

Grant, Dennis & Mary J. Taylor, 8 Feb 1860; m 9 Feb 1860 by Ransom Lee, J. P.

Grantham, Barna & Sidney Stevens, 16 Nov 1839: Thos. Toler, bm.

Grantham, Fedrick & Sarah Ann Thornton, 31 Jan 1849; John H. Daniel, bm.

Grantham, M. K. & Caroline Bridgers, m 28 Mar 1861 at Smithfield, by J. R. Brooks.

Grantham, Whitly & Polly Rose, 12 May 1837; Thos. Toler, bm.

Gray, Alexander & Ann Lightfoot, 10 Feb 1783; Joseph Boon, bm.

Green, Bryan & Susey Smith, 27 Nov 1798; Sion Green, bm.

Green, Bryan & Milley Welch, 24 Feb 1801; Samuel Wilder, Jr., bm.

Green, Dempsy & Sally Jeffers, 24 May 1820; Reding Green, bm.

Green, Demsey & Lewey Smith, 20 Jan 1800; William Bryan, bm.

Green, Erwin & Nancy Green, 28 May 1823; John Cooper, bm.

Green, Furnifold & Mary Murphrey, 20 Oct 1831; Lewis W. Jinkins, bm.

Green, Harry S. & Mary H. Gurley, 25 May 1847; John H. Bryan, bm.

Green, James & Darcas Jones, 21 Feb 1820; Nathan Atkinson, bm.

Green, James & Sarah Porch, 23 Jun 1838; Solomon Lockart, bm.

Green, James & Seany Lee, 20 Feb 1867; Calvin Perry, bm; m 20 Feb 1867 by M. K. Grantham, J. P.

Green, Jesse & Polly Price, 28 Jan 1825; Josiah Hollomon, bm.

Green, John & Welthy Moore, 28 Feb 1791; Alexdr. Avera, bm.

Green, Laborn & Rebey Green, 23 Feb 1819; Wiley Green, bm.

Green, Nathan & Hasseltine Talton, 25 Jan 1859; m 26 Jan 1859 by J. F. Ellington.

Green, Thomas & Unity Yelverton, 5 Sept 1782; Amos Atkinson, bm.

Green, William & Caroline Broadstreet, 27 Sept 1820; Jos. Holliman, bm.

Green, William & Kiddy E. Wise, ____ 1827; Aaron Wall, bm.

Green, William & Alley Elizabeth Jones, 10 Dec 1853; m 14 Dec 1853 by H. H. Finch, J. P.

Green, Willie & Penny O'neal, 24 Dec 1822; Jno. G. Gulley, bm.

Gregory, James & Ann Cooper, 12 Dec 1812; John Parish, bm.

Gregory, John & Rebecca Mariah Britt, 29 May 1838; Samuel Lee, bm.

Gregory, M. W. & Mary Ann Brasier, 10 Mar 1862; m 11 Mar 1862 at Benjamin Woodels, by J. W. Stevens, J. P.

Gregory, Uz & Sally May, 21 May 1796; Littleberry May, bm.

Greswell, Ruffin & Matilda Bailey, 18 Jun 1852; m 13 Jun 1852 by S. W. Woody, J. P.

Grice, Calvin & Joanna Evans, 6 Sept 1837; Gideon Allen, bm.

Grice, David & Cula Johnson, 11 Feb 1840; Wm. Johnson, bm.

Grice, James & Precella Moonahorn, 30 Dec 1812; Josiah Hinnant, bm.

Grice, Thomas T. & Eliza Jane Hinton, 16 Aug 1836; Furnifold Green, bm.

Griffen, Major & Elizabeth Gully, 2 May 1824; James S. Murchie, bm.

Griffin, Albis & Beddy Hoilt, 29 Aug 1828; Owein Barber, bm.

Griffin, David & Betsy Adams, 13 Jan 1808; David Braswell, bm.

Griffin, James B. & Eliza Jane Holt, 21 Feb 1866; J. B. Kennedy, bm.

Griffin, John R. & Hawkins Honeycutt, 28 Dec 1863; m 29 Dec 1863 by John R. Coats.

Griffin, Laban & Sally Flowers, 18 Dec 1824; Wm. W. Bryan, bm.

Griffis, John A. & Mary Wren, 11 May 1844; Zachariah Tinor, bm.

Griffis, Laben & Susanna Carrell, 16 Jan 1811; Benjamin Carrell, bm.

Grimes, Benjamin F. & Milly Ennis, 5 Mar 1867; Raymond Ennis, bm; m 7 Mar 1867 at Mary Ennis's, by Jno. R. Coates, J. P.

Grimes, William & Frances Adams, 11 Jun 1795; Howell Adams, bm.

Grizzle, Bannister & Sally Pugh, 6 Feb 1810; Jesse Bailey, bm.

Guess, H. P. & Aurelia H. Durham, 12 Jan 1867; W. P. Raiford, bm; m 16 Jan 1867 by Jno. R. Brooks.

Guin, Abraham & Catharine Crawford, 27 Nov 1802; Jno. Searcy, bm.

Guin, Barna B. & Elenor Evans, 21 Jan 1835; Silas Webb, bm.

Guin, William & Rhoda Baker, 11 Sept 1857; m 13 Sept 1867 by George Keen, J. P.

Guin, William & Polly Blackman, 30 Apr 1859; George Keen, bm.

Gulley, George & Zilpah Barnes, 1 Nov 1790; John Ellis, bm.

Gulley, George G. & Joanah W. Deans, 6 Dec 1861; m 8 Dec 1861 by J. F. Ellington.

Gulley, John & Ann Brown, 26 Dec 1779; John Watson, bm.

Gulley, Nathan & Temperance Thomas, 30 May 1780; Geo. Warren, Robt. Gulley, bm.

Gulley, Robert & Elizabeth Stallions, 23 Mar 1778; Felps Smith, bm.

Gulley, Robert Sr. & Sally Bridgers, 15 Jan 1798; Joseph Brown, bm.

Gully, Erastus H. & Elizabeth Hinnant, 29 May 1855; m 5 Jun 1855 at Josiah Hinnants, by Wm. T. Robertson, J. P.

Gully, George & Willy Wilder, 15 Oct 1825; Aaron Wall, bm.

Gully, Mead & Avie Atkinson, 31 May 1796; Amos Atkinson, bm.

Gully, Robert N. & Elizabeth Wall, 5 Oct 1827; Jno. S. Powell, bm.

Gully, Samuel S. & Jane Fralick, 9 Oct 1833; John L. Haywood, bm.

Gully, Walter W. & Louisa Wall, m 20 Nov 1853 by Pharoh Richardson, J. P.

Gully, William B. & Pherebe Kelly, 4 Oct 1849; A. G. Thornton, bm.

Gurley, Arthur & Polly Peeden, 24 Jul 1803; Etheldred Holt, bm.

Gurley, Daniel & Allana Jordan, 21 Aug 1837; Plyer Barber, bm.

Gurley, Daniel & Edith Philips, 10 Feb 1838; Henry Hamilton, bm.

Gurley, Frederick & Patience Tiner, 24 Feb 1801; Wm. Capps, bm.

Gurley, Henry & Polly Jones, 27 Oct 1835; John C. Montague, bm.

Gurley, John G. & Francis E. Nichols, m 21 Jul 1853 by Edwin Boykin, J. P.

Gurley, Jonathan & Reve Bulls, 28 Nov 1809; Meurell Gurley, bm.

Gurley, Joseph & Elizabeth Thomas, 27 Oct 1835; John C. Montague, bm.

Gurley, Maurice & Elizabeth Gurley, 26 Aug 1812; Robert Raiford, bm.

Gurley, Munroe & Harriet Lynch, 6 Jan 1840; Ezekiel Stevens, bm.

Gurley, Raford & Cherry Howell, 2 Apr 1846; William H. Toler, bm.

Gurley, Robert & Nancy Green, 25 Sept 1816; Jones Davis, bm.

Gurley, Willie & Lydia Gurley, 26 Feb 1833; Francis Bridgers, bm.

Guy, Henry Sr. & Olive Eason, 20 Feb 1817; Allen S. Ballinger, bm.

Guy, John C. & Patsy Gully, _____ 1818; Asa Midgett, bm.

Guy, William H. & Susan McCullers, 24 Sept 1833; David Thomas, bm.

Hackney, James S. & Mary J. Chirstmon, 24 Apr 1847; Bryan H. Hinnant, bm.

Hadley, Thomas & Milicent Richardson, 15 May 1824; Acquilla Hardy, bm.

Hagens, John & Polly Crafford, 27 Nov 1851; m 16 Dec 1851 by R. Massingill, J. P.

Hails, Henry & Zilpha Woodell, 29 Nov 1808; Chatmon Hails, bm.

Hails, William & Tabethy Cooper, 19 Feb 1810; Thomas Lockhart, Jr., bm.

Haislip, Jeremiah & Rachel Mitchell, 20 Sept 1805; Isaac Beaman, bm.

Hall, Fernifold & Zilpha Price, 11 May 1833; Etheldred Holt, bm.

Hall, Matthew & Sintha Carrell, 31 Mar 1842; Thomas Ligon, bm.

Hall, William & Sally Ryals, 23 Nov 1847; Robert W. Stevens, bm.

Hall, William F. & Eliza Ivey, 11 Feb 1858; m 16 Feb 1858 at Druzila Iveys, by B. Godwin, J. P.

Hall, William G. & Jane Lepard, 19 Aug 1843; Thos. H. Legan, bm.

Hall, Willoughby & Nancy Eatmon, 23 May 1837; Benajah Horn, bm.

Halliman, James & Elizabeth Bryan, 16 Apr 1772; Charles Jones, bm.

Hambleton, Henry & Secrecy Oliver, 4 May 1824; Reddick Warren, bm.

Hambleton, Henry & Edith Woodward, 4 Jan 1826; Thos. Edwards, Sr., bm.

Hambleton, Henry & Peity Edwards, 6 Sept 1842; Kedard Whitley, bm; m by Willie Holt, J. P.

Hamilton, Barnaba & Edith Ann Fail, 6 Sept 1837; G. Futrell, bm.

Hamilton, Barry B. & Nancy Ann Peeden, 1 Jan 1850; T. W. Whitley, bm.

Hamilton, John & Tranquilla Price, 31 Oct 1859; m 3 Nov 1859 at B. Price's, by Wms. Brown.

Hamontree, Stephen & Civil Lucas, 13 Apr 1839; Peter Hamontree, bm.

Hardee, Magear & Elizabeth Bell, 7 Aug 1846; Abram Dixon, bm.

Hardy, Bright & Mary Jane Johnson, 11 Mar 1854; m 19 Mar 1854 by R. W. Stevens, J. P.

Hare, John & Willy Oneal, 4 Oct 1842; Henry Hayles, bm.

Hare, Joseph & Lucinda Stansel, 23 Oct 1845; Jno. Hare, bm.

Hare, Ransom & Sarah A. C. Bagley, 21 May 1866; Worley Creech, bm; m 22 May 1866 at Theophilus Bagleys, by Ray Phillips, J. P.

Harp, Gaston & Sarah Ann E. Whitley, 30 Mar 1859; m 31 Mar 1859 by W. H. Masingill, J. P.

Harp, John & Lucretia Capse, 27 Sept 1787; William Capps, bm.

Harp, W. S. & Winifred Eason, 6 Nov 1866; Perry Godwin, bm; m 8 Nov 1866 by Perry Godwin, J. P.

Harper, Banister & Patsy Barber, 7 Nov 1818; William W. Jones, bm.

Harper, Bartley & Sally Cardell, 3 Aug 1838; John Cordell, bm.

Harper, Bryan & Nancy Jones, 18 Feb 1839; Elisha Harrison, bm.

Harper, Daniel & Mary Harper, 28 Nov 1820; Absalom Harper, bm.

Harper, Devro & Julia Barber, 1 May 1847; John R. Harper, bm.

Harper, George R. & F. E. Smith, 10 Dec 1866; Jno. W. Avera, bm; m 12 Dec 1866 by J. F. Ellington, M. G.

Harper, Jacob J. & Willey Jane Atkinson, 15 Jan 1861; m 17 Jan 1861 at Blake Atkessons, by N. G. Gully, J. P.

Harper, John & Anne Wiggs, 13 Mar 1801; Benjamin Rose, bm.

Harper, John & Winifred Flowers, 24 May 1819; Solomon Whitenton, bm.

Harper, John R. & Rhoda Langdon, 1 Nov 1848; Bartlet Harper, bm.

Harper, Martin & Nancy Bailey, 28 Feb 1820; Garry Grice, bm.

Harper, Westly & Creacy Ann Jones, 21 Nov 1842; Ashly Barber, bm.

Hartsfield, William & Mary Carter, m 5 Jun 1855 by Paul J. Carraway, M. G.

Harrel, Francis Jr. & Mary Leach, 25 Feb 1794; Joseph Langston, Jr., bm.

Harrell, Asa & Betsy Goodrich, 25 Mar 1811; Willis Cole, bm.

Harrell, Asa & Jeany Broadstreet, 13 May 1825; Adin Powell, bm.

Harrell, Francis & Southey Jonier, 23 Nov 1819; Thomas Allen, bm.

Harrell, Henry & Elizabeth Baker, 8 Jan 1796; John Roads, bm.

Harrell, Jacob & Polly Whitten, 1 Dec 1802; Francis Harrell, bm.

Harrell, John & Nancy Benson, 27 Feb 1827; John Phillips, bm.

Harrell, Samuel & Polly Farmer, 2 Apr 1798; William Farmer, bm.

Harrell, William & Anna Langhorn, 12 Aug 1825; Nicholas Rose, bm.

Harrell, William & Katy Bass, 24 May 1803; Francis Harrell, bm.

Harris, Churchwell & Mary M. Beasley, 9 Jun 1855; m 10 Jun 1955 by J. B. Jackson.

Harris, Matthew & Mildred Brown, 20 Mar 1788; John Killingsworth, bm.

Harrison, Elisha & Jane Bridgers, 17 Mar 1835; Allen S. Ballinger, bm.

Harrison, J. B. & Bettie Johnson, 11 Dec 1866; A. R. Duncan, bm; m 14 Dec 1866 at the residence of Alvin Johnson, by A. R. Duncan, J. P.

Harrison, Zachariah & Betsy Avera, 1 Oct 1832; Abram G. Borden, bm.

Harvill, Moses & Polly Sims, 25 May 1812; James Adams, bm.

Hastings, Howell & Edith Edwards, 28 Nov 1826; John H. Rose, bm.

Hastings, William & Lucy Anne McCullers, 19 Jan 1841; William H. McCullers, bm.

Hatcher, Allen & Rebecca Strickland, m 28 Jan 1863 at Samuel Stricklands, by Ransom Lee, J. P.

Hatcher, Benjamin & Anne Wilkerson, 28 Feb 1789; Benjamin Wilkerson, bm.

Hatcher, Benjamin & Polly Watkins, 24 Jun 1813; Sampson Rogers, bm.

Hatcher, Hiram & Nancy Brown, 26 Feb 1866; L. D. Bailey, bm.

Hatcher, James & Polly Garner, 5 Dec 1839; John Hatcher, bm.

Hatcher, John & Susannah Watkins, 25 Feb 1815; Robt. Gully, Jr., bm.

Hatcher, John T. & Ailsey Earp, 16 Sept 18401 Robert Hatcher, bm.

Hatcher, Lee & Lany Moore, 8 Feb 1842; James G. Rainer, bm.

Hatcher, Robert & Piety Bailey, 17 Oct 1837; John T. Hatcher, bm.

Hatcher, William & Christian Garner, 1 Mar 1796; Thmas Cockrell, bm.

Hatcher, William & Charity McClenney, 10 Jan 1804; Benjamin Hatcher, bm.

Hathcock, David & Abisha Clark, 30 Dec 1837; Henry Massingale, bm.

Hayes, Amos & Nancy Stansell, 24 Aug 1840; Quinney Watson, bm.

Hayes, John & Apsilla Pearce, 6 Feb 1795; Nichols Tomson, bm.

Hayes, Willis & Nancy Porter, 24 Jan 1826; Lazarus Matthews, bm.

Hayles, Gilbert & Luizer Stansel, 9 May 1846; Stephen H. Stansell, bm.

Hayles, Guilford & Amanda Godwin, 16 Apr 1842; L. Richardson, bm.

Hayles, Henry H. & Patsey Pearce, 24 Apr 1847; John C. Allen, bm.

Hayles, John & Cynthia Thomas, 14 Dec 1785.

Hayles, John & Elizabeth Spicer, 13 Aug 1795; Nathan Gulley, bm.

Hayles, John W. & Emma Oneal, 30 Dec 1865; m 31 Dec 1865 at Gilbert Hayles, by P. Godwin, J. P.

Hayles, William & Elizabeth Ferrell, 28 May 1859; m 6 Mar 1859 by Wm. B. Wall, Esq.

Hayles, William H. & Nancy Jordan, 1 Jun 1843; Elijah Todd, bm. [Notation on margin: "It is believed that these married people are the murderers of his first wife."]

Hays, Demsey & Fanney Barefoot, 25 Feb 1845; Thos. H. Thornton, bm.

Hearn, Jonathan & Emily Carter, 24 Dec 1825; Bythan Bryan, bm.

Hearn, Jonathan & Edny Dodd, 21 Dec 1833; Young Bridgers, bm.

Hearn, Napolean B. & Henrietta Jones, 9 Oct 1861; m 14 Oct 1861 at the residence of A. Jones, by J. W. Hodges, J. P.

Heath, Dick (colored) & Trecy Whitley, 19 Jan 1867; David Edward, bm.

Helme, Green (colored) & Olive Smith, 17 Sept 1866; Jarrot Whitfield, bm; m 27 Sept 1866 by Joseph Wheeler, M. G.

Helme, Robert H. & Nancy Guy, 6 Jan 1811; Wm. W. Hopkins, bm.

Helme, Robert H. & Pherebe McCullers, 11 Nov 1817; Braswell Bridgers, bm.

Helms, Mordecai & Sarah L. Ennis, 25 Apr 1860; m 26 Apr 1860 by J. F. Ellington.

Hennant, Williamson & Cally Hennant, 25 Apr 1833; Jesse Hinnant, bm.

Henton, Joseph H. & Tempy Ann Grice, 11 May 1825; Phillip Johnson, bm.

Henton, Willis & Polly Deloach, 2 Jul 1825; Edwin Spivy, bm.

Heritage, James & Elizabeth Johnson, 14 Mar 1843; Henry Johnson, bm.

Herren, Matchet & Betsy Braswell, 26 Aug 1793; Jarrot Thompson, Benjamin Strickland, bm.

Herring, Daniel & Civil Clark, 29 May 1860.

Herring, Joel & Edith Fulgham, 2 Nov 1802; Jno. Spivey, bm.

Herring, John & Dorcas Strickland, 28 May 1799; Joshua Creech, bm.

Heth, James & Precillar Horn, 15 Feb 1807; Stephen Grice, bm.

Hews, Reddick & Gilly Rivers, 5 Jan 1813; Abner Smith, bm.

Hicks, Bishop & Wily Bryan, 23 Jan 1839; Stephen Hicks, bm.

Hicks, Isaac & Mary E. Murphy, 10 Apr 1858; m 11 Apr 1858 at Matthews Murphys, by R. N. Gully, J. P.

Hicks, James & Penelope Boyett, 14 Jul 1824; Stephen Hicks, bm.

Hicks, Micajah & Susannah Overby, 29 Jun 1786; Joseph Edwards, bm.

Hicks, Nemiah & Willey Jane Manning, 23 Jan 1861; m 24 Jan 1861 by A. H. Atkinson, J. P.

Hicks, Stephen & Emely Horn, 22 Feb 1836; Benajah Horn, bm.

Higdon, Daniel & Mrs. Mary Calvit, ___ 1762; Joshua Houghton, John Higdon, bm.

Higgs, Matthew & Penny Turley, 14 May 1823; Clem N. Shaw, bm.

High, John B. & Elizabeth J. Atkinson, 27 Nov 1843; Benjamin J. Glover, bm.

High, William & Patsy Richardson, 16 Nov 1823; Calvin Richardson, bm.

Hill, Abner & Charlotte Adkinson, 1 Nov 1792; James Holder, bm.

Hill, Benjamin & Mary Wootten, 28 Nov 1787; John Green, bm.

Hill, George A. (colored) & Anne Beckwith, 17 Sept 1866, Wesley Whitfield, bm; m 17 Sept 1866 by W. B. Jones.

Hill, Green & Sally Lee, 21 Aug 1799; John Carrell, bm.

Hill, John & Elizabeth Eldredge, 14 Setp 1818; Laban Green, bm.

Hill, Joseph & Elizabeth Johnson, 2 Sept 1825; Peter Lee, bm.

Hill, Moses & Absilla Howell, 25 Apr 1854; m 4 May 1854 by T. W. Whitly, J. P.

Hill, Moses Lloyd & Tranquella Gully, 1 Apr 1819; Thos. Lockart, Jr., bm.

Hill, Richard & Susan Barbee, 28 Feb 1853; m 7 Mar 1853 by L.(?) Langdon, J. P.

Hill, Sion & Starage Lee, 21 Oct 1800; Green Hill, bm.

Hill, Sion & Sally Stevens, 17 Aug 1813; Gedeon Warner, bm.

Hill, Thomas & Elizabeth Garner, 5 Jan 1782; John Garner, Richard Bailey, bm.

Hill, William & Sarah E. Jones, 1 Sept 1853; m 8 Sept 1853 by W. H. McCullers, Jr., bm.

Hill, Zechariah & Virginia Whitley, 7 Jul 1855; m 10 Jul 1855 by B. Lane, J. P.

Hilliard, Benjamin & Louisa Hinnant, 5 Dec 1866; J. H. Whitley, bm; m 6 Dec 1866 by Wm. C. Nowell, M. G.

Hilliard, Ezekil & Jane Wilder, 20 Dec 1816; Griffin Hollimon, bm.

Hilliard, George & Ale Snipes, 24 Feb 1809; Matthew Jones, bm.

Hilliard, Henry & Prissilla Sims, 5 Apr 1791; Noel Renfrow, bm.

Hilliard, James & Zelphia Turley, 28 Sept 1819; Wm. Penney, bm.

Hilliard, James & Cloe Penny, 298 Sept 1817; Tom D. Bridgers, bm.

Hilliard, William & Nancy Hocut, 22 Oct 1840; Matthew Avera, bm.

Hinnant, B. R. & Trecenda Bagley, 14 Jun 1852; m 17 Jun 1852 by James Hinnant, J. P.

Hinnant, Berry & Elizabeth Earp, 28 Jan 1825; William Nowell, bm.

Hinnant, Gaston & Joanna Copeland, 6 Jan 1858; m 7 Jan 1858 by Jesse Parker, J. P.

Hinnant, George W. & Julia Fail, 24 Mar 1842; Theohpilus Bagley, bm.

Hinnant, Hardy & Jemima Parrish, 8 Jan 1853; m 11 Jan 1853 by Ransom Kirby, J. P.

Hinnant, Henry & Martha Edwards, 24 Nov 1846; Josiah Hinnant, bm.

Hinnant, Hillory & Mary J. Corbit, 3 Apr 1866; John I. Barnes, bm.

Hinnant, James & Cynthie Barnes, 1 Mar 1831; Jonathan Woodard, bm.

Hinnant, James & Rebecca Roper, 21 Dec 1846; Joseph Roper, bm.

Hinnant, James & Elizabeth Copeland, 23 Sept 1851; m 6 Nov 1851 by S. Bagley.

Hinnant, James D. & Mary A. Barnes, 7 Oct 1857; E. H. Gulley, bm; m 8 Oct 1857 by R. N. Gulley, J. P.

Hinnant, Jesse & Nancy Sillvant, 28 Nov 1825; Jesse Sillivent, bm.

Hinnant, Jesse & Elizabeth Hawkins Hayles, 9 Dec 1835; William Hayles, bm.

Hinnant, Jesse & Caroline Whitley, 9 Nov 1853; m 10 Nov 1853 by A. V. Richardson.

Hinnant, Jesse & Cherry Barnes, 23 Feb 1858; m 24 Feb 1858 by L. G. Boyett, J. P.

Hinnant, John & Mary Hocut, 4 Mar 1796; R. Gulley, Jr., bm.

Hinnant, John & Elizabeth Wall, m 20 Jan 1863 at Wm. B. Walls, by R. N. Gully, J. P.

Hinnant, John F. & Adline Suggs, 8 Oct 1866; Gaston Hinnant, bm; m 9 Oct 1866 by W. H. Wellons, J. P.

Hinnant, John H. & Sarah Jones, 23 Apr 1866; Theo. Hinnant, bm.

Hinnant, Josiah & Bethana Gully, 11 Feb 1815; Wm. Hinnant, Sr., bm.

Hinnant, Josiah Jr. & Calley Hinnant, 1 Nov 1827; Rubin Wilkinson, bm.

Hinnant, Josiah Jr. & Ailsey Fail, 12 Mar 1849; Elihu N. Jones, bm.

Hinnant, Larry & Winny Creech, 26 Feb 1839; Nelson Kent, bm.

Hinnant, Mabry & Susan Wiggs, 23 Feb 1841; Noel Barnes, bm.

Hinnant, Robert D. & Relcy Talton, 9 Jan 1839; Jethro Yelventon, bm.

Hinnant, Ruffin (colored) & Alcy Tisdale, 13 Aug 1866; Jesse Hinnant, bm; m 15 Aug 1866 by Jesse Hinnant, J. P.

Hinnant, Stephen & Harriet Bagley, 5 Oct 1842; James FAulk, bm.

Hinnant, Theophilus & Martha Watson, 17 Jul 1865; Wm. Q. Hinnant, bm.

Hinnant, William & Luvey Smith, 8 Feb 1804; Needham Davis, bm.

Hinnant, William & Sara E. Williamson, 31 Dec 1860; m 1 Jan 1861 at Rayford Williamsons, by W. Earp, J. P.

Hinnant, William & Mary Ann Raines, 11 Feb 1864; m 12 Feb 1864 at Little River Bridge, by Jesse Parker, J. P.

Hinton, George & Zilpah Johnson, 9 Dec 1793; Peter Williams, bm.

Hinton, Henry & Polly Sanders, 30 Apr 1807; Reuben Sanders, bm.

Hinton, Hughel & Pennina Hayles, 3 Mar 1866; Raiford Pearce, bm.

Hinton, Isaac & Matilda Hinton, 15 Aug 1823; Isaac Stallings, bm.

Hinton, James & Betsy Hinton, _____ ; David Sauls, bm.

Hinton, Jacob & Sally Stallings, 1 Jan 1792; Zadok Stallings, bm.

Hinton, Job & Lucy Bedingfield, 14 Dec ___; John Bedingfeld, Hardy Hinton, bm.

Hinton, John & Charlotte Carter, 21 Dec 1789; William Hinton, bm.

Hinton, John & Elizabeth Hinton, 1 Mar 1796; Mathew Sturdivant, bm.

Hinton, John & Sally Cooper, 29 Feb 1820; Joseph Hinton, bm.

Hinton, Joseph & Esther Hinton, 23 Dec 1807; Wm. Hinton, bm.

Hinton, Malachi & Eliza Anne Hood, 22 Aug 1851; m 24 Aug 1851 by S. P. Horton, J. P.

Hinton, Matthew & Betsy Jones, 27 Sept 1816; Wilson Busbee, bm.

Hinton, Ransom & Betsy Wilder, 19 Oct 1830; Ransom Sanders, bm.

Hinton, Ransom & Betsey Floid, 20 Jan 1845; Aven Floid, bm.

Hinton, William & Temperance Pope, 25 Nov 1793; John Petty Cobb, bm.

Hinton, William & Lydia Hinton, 24 Dec 1801; Larry Bryan, bm.

Hinton, Willie & Polly Wilder, 3 Aug 1831; Ransom Hinton, bm.

Hinton, Willis & Sally Stallings, 15 Jan 1798; Joseph Brown, bm.

Hinton, Willis & Polly Hart, 20 Sept 1811; John Kelly, Jr., bm.

Hinton, Wimberly & Edith Hinton, 26 Nov 1822; Hugh Lee, bm.

Hix, William & Sarah Stansell, 8 Jun 1857; m 9 Jun 1857 by L. G. Boyett, J. P.

Hoalder, Israel & Sally Nichols, 18 Jun 1836; Clem M. Baker, bm.

Hoalt, Samuel & Sally Johnson, 28 May 1805; Sam'l Lee, Jr., bm.

Hoalt, William & Dianna Wellons, 21 Jan 1811; Charles Wellons, bm.

Hobbs, Bolling Green & Edith Williams, 30 Nov 1804; John Williams, bm.

Hobbs, Bolling G. & Agatha H. Speed, 22 May 1813; Hardy Sanders, bm.

Hobbs, Henry H. & Mary A. Northam, 31 May 1858; m 1 Jun 1858 at Smithfield, by Wm. E. Pell, Elder, M. E. Church, South.

Hobby, Henry & Nancy Wilson, 7 Jan 1801; John Wilson, bm.

Hobby, John & Polly Temples, 11 Feb 1814; Littleton Johnson, bm.

Hobby, William Sandy (colored) & Maria Snead, 11 Aug 1866; John Clarke, bm; m 30 Aug 1866 by Seth Woodall, J. P.

Hocot, William Brown & Aley Oneil, 5 Apr 1795; Benjamin Hill, bm.

Hocut, Atless & Allen Carroll, m 9 Oct 1862 by Jethro Lewis, J. P.

Hocut, Bryan & Nancy Wilder, 14 Oct 1832; Geo. S. Gulley, bm.

Hocut, Ervin W. & Bettie Borham, 6 Mar 1866; Jno. W. Lee, bm; m 11 Jul 1860 by S. W. Moody, J. P.

Hocut, William A. & Joanna Williamson, 16 Jun 1857; m by Burwell Temple.

Hocut, William Brown & Creacy Oniel, 24 Feb 1806; John Hinnant, bm.

Hocut, Zechariah A. & Sarah L. Richardson, 25 Apr 1866; m 26 Apr 1866 at Wm. B. Hocut's, by Wm. Hinnant, J. P.

Hocutt, Benjamin & Nancy Holoman, 26 Sept 1809; James Woodard, bm.

Hocutt, Lemuel & Lucy Ligon, 9 Jan 1841; William Moody, bm.

Hodge, Curtis & Sally Hobbs, 3 Feb 1843; Curtis Hodge, bm.

Hodge, Jesse & Lucinda Wall, m 10 Feb 1858 by P. C. Richardson, J. P.

Hodge, Wesley & Louiza Thomas, 6 Mar 1834; Roy Helme, bm.

Hodge, Wilie (colored) & Fanny Lassiter, 7 Sept 1866; Toddy Lassiter, bm; m 8 Sept 1866 by E. D. Snead, J. P.

Hodges, Horatio B. & Sarrah Giles, 29 Dec 1852; m 5 Jan 1853 by R. W. Stevens, J. P.

Hodges, James & Cynthia Whittington, 24 Nov 1835; James G. Woodall, bm.

Hodges, James W. & Elizabeth Rainer, 25 Apr 1859; m 28 Apr 1859 by R. Masingill, J. P.

Hodges, John W. & Rebecca E. Sanders, 8 Mar 1852; m 11 Mar 1852 L. W. Martin, M. G.

Hodges, Joseph & Sarah Allen, 21 Apr 1791; Bryant Adams, bm.

Hogg, Richard & Eastly Eatmon, 25 Nov 1824; Russel Sillevent, bm.

Holder, Esam (colored) & Dilly Richardson, 19 Oct 1866; Wm. H. Oneal, bm.

Holder, James & Penelopia Hayles, 28 Feb 1792; Joseph Irwin, bm.

Holder, Jonathan & Patty Finch, 14 Aug 1795; Henry Finch, bm.

Holder, Josiah & Mildred Holliman, 29 Nov 1798; James Holder, bm.

Holiman, Jesse & Jenny Godwin, 11 Mar 1843; Wiley Godwin, bm.

Holland, Alfred & Caroline Avera, 5 Mar 1856; m 6 Mar 1856 by P. J. Carraway, M. G.

Holland, Benajah & Amanda Johnson, 17 Jun 1839; Ransom Johnson, bm.

Holland, Bryant & Polly Lee, 15 Jun 1853; m 16 Jun 1853 by H. Johnson, J. P.

Holland, Charles & Tempy Holland, 7 Jan 1847; Eason Holland, bm.

Holland, Curtis & Nancy Holland, 1 May 1823; William Jackson, bm.

Holland, David H. & Sarah Avera, 11 May 1843; Wm. H. Morning, bm.

Holland, Elisha & Betsy Holland, 26 Mar 1822; Enos Holland, George Mitchell, bm.

Holland, Exum H. & Sarah Sasser, 4 Feb 1858; Philip E. Sasser, bm; m 11 Feb 1858 by Jesse Parker, J. P.

Holland, Ezekiel & Julia A. Woodall, 16 Feb 1846; Wm. H. Morning, bm.

Holland, Green & Elizabeth Garner, 15 Feb 1830; Asa Garner, bm.

Holland, James & Mary Carter, 17 Jan 1847; Bryant Holland, bm; m by Wilie Holt.

Holland, Jennet & Elizabeth Low, 8 Apr 1837; Bryan D. May, bm.

Holland, John H. & Julia Woodard, 5 Mar 1867; Berry Aycock, bm.

Holland, Thomas & Maria Earp, 2 Dec 1845; Elbert Austen, bm.

Holland, Thomas & Kesiah Johnston, 23 Jul 1847; Stephen Johnson, bm.

Holland, William & Cynthia Garner, 1 Feb 1823; Simen Cockrell, bm.

Holland, William & Martha Kirby, 30 Dec 1847; Harris Rose, bm.

Holland, William Turner & Mary J. Stephenson, 19 Dec 1866; Elbridge Stephenson, bm; m 20 Dec 1866 at Guary Stephenson, by H. A. Clifton, J. P.

Holleman, Jesse & Betsy Holland, 28 Mar 1820; Charles Crawford, bm.

Holleman, Richard & Asptil Bryan, 8 Jan 1768; David Holliman, bm.

Holleman, Willie & Betsy Green, 28 May 1823; John Cooper, bm.

Holliman, Jesse & Polly Jones, 2 Jul 1796; Wm. Hackney, bm.

Holliman, Joseph & Nancy Nairn, 5 Nov 1791; John Holder, bm.

Holliman, Josiah & Dedey Narron, 25 Jun 1838; Edwin Boykin, bm.

Holliman, Lary & Dusey Narron, 30 Aug 1827; Allen Jones, bm.

Holliman, Seth & Unity Godwin, 15 Aug 1786; Frederic Holliman, bm.

Holliman, Tobias & Prudence Holder, 29 May 1793; Hardy Parker, bm.

Holliman, William & Polly Davis, 22 Jan 1840; John Harrell, bm.

Holloman, Asa & Winnifred Holloman, 21 Dec 1824; Gideon Price, bm.

Hollomon Bardain & Patsy Hollomon, 28 Jan 1824; Garry Hollomon, bm.

Hollomon, Berry & Patience Parker, 11 Mar 1820; Tom D. Bridgers, bm.

Hollomon Berry & Dusey Narron, 10 Mar 1826; Thomas Brown, bm.

Hollomon, Berry & Margaret Jones, 25 Jan 1862; m 26 Jan 1862 at Margaret Jones's, by Ray Phillips, J. P.

Hollomon, Garry & Rhoda Hollomon, 28 Aug 1822; John Hollomon, bm.

Hollomon, James & Keron Bedingfield, 25 Sept 1827; James Carrell, bm.

Hollomon, William & Caroline Stallings, 21 Nov 1848; Ransom Hollomon, bm.

Hollowel, Thomas T. & Sophia Holt, 5 Oct 1833; Jesse Holt, bm.

Hollowell, Silas & Nannie Hines, m 30 Jul 1863 at Mrs. Hines's, by W. D. Holt, J. P.

Hollowell, Thomas S. & Nancy M. Holt, 12 Jun 1858; m 17 Jun 1858 at Ransom Holt's, by Edwin Boykin, J. P.

Holly, John C. & Betsey H. Langhaun, 23 Feb 1848; Frances Langhhan, bm.

Holmes, Benjamin & Celah Peacock, 22 Feb 1808; John Stansell, bm.

Holmes, Benjamin & Lucinda Parker, 20 Feb 1860; m 23 Feb 1860 at Sarah Parkers, by John C. Hood, J. P.

Holmes, Hardy, of Wayne Co., & Elizabeth Oquinn, 24 Aug 1808; Sam'l Lee, Jr., bm.

Holmes, Hiram & Susan Caroline Thornton, 8 Apr 1841; Right Ryals, bm.

Holmes, James & Mary Ann Beasly, 25 Mar 1844; Hiram Homes, bm.

Holmes, James W. & Dartha Young, 5 Jun 1866; Isaac Wheeler, bm.

Holmes, John & Sally Giles, 9 Aug 1828; James Ivey, bm.

Holmes, John & Easther Woodall, 27 Feb 1843; Robert W. Stevens, bm.

Hols, Gillis & Patsy Stansel, 27 Oct 1848; John T. Hatcher, bm.

Holt, Calvin A. & Elizabeth Howell, 26 May 1866; W. D. Holt, bm.

Holt, Etheldred & Elizabeth Wellons, 15 Oct 1804; William Hinnant, bm.

Holt, Henry & Delia S. Jones, 20 Jan 1860; m 25 Jan 1860 by Lemmon Shell, M. G.

Holt, James & Arebella Clark, 10 Jun 1848; Richd. Green, bm.

Holt, James M. & Sarah Ann Lee, 26 Dec 1863; m 27 Dec 1863 by R. W. Stevens, J. P.

Holt, John & Mary Jordan, 18 Feb 1795; Thomas Price, bm.

Holt, John & Luquinay Barber, 12 May 1855; m 15 May 1855 at the house of Owen Barber, by R. W. Stevens, J. P.

Holt, John & Emily Woodard, 30 Jan 1849; Elijah Capps, bm.

Holt, Joseph & Charlotte Lee, 8 Mar 1866; S. A. Smith, bm.

Holt, Osborn & Patsy Hobby, 9 Jan 1828; John Holt, bm.

Holt, Richard & Jemima Mason, 10 Oct 1823; John Holt, bm.

Holt, William D. & Kissiah C. Capps, 24 Apr 1858; m 29 Apr 1858 at Wm. P. Raifords, by Edwin Boykin, J. P.

Honecut, John & Elizabeth Kemp, 30 Mar 1853; m 14 Apr 1853 by B. C. Richardson, J. P.

Honeycut, Alexander & Dilla Parrish, 17 Sept 1839; Johnson Parish, Jr., bm.

Honeycut, Britain & Candiss Courdell, 20 Aug 1813; William Honeycut, Jr., bm.

Honeycut, Edmund & Polly Johnson, 6 May 1820; David Parish, bm.

Honeycut, James & Bethany Parish, 7 Dec 1841; Jestis Parrish, bm.

Honeycut, William & Betty Honeycut, 28 May 1794; Moses Johnston, bm.

Honeycut, William & Abby Cordell, 12 Apr 1821; Jonathan White, bm.

Honeycutt, Sir William & Nancy Emiline Ennis, 6 Oct 1860; m 7 Oct 1860 by C. J. Bingham, J. P.

Hood, Bryan & Elizabeth Willoughby, 18 Aug 1810; Samuel Willoby, bm.

Hood, Bryan & Edith Johnson, 10 May 1834; James Hinnant, bm.

Hood, Caswell & Martha Cimbrel, 5 May 1848; Jas. H. Bryan, bm.

Hood, Charles & Sally Ellenton, 30 May 1810; Malachi Hinton, bm.

Hood, John B. & Missouri B. Lee, 11 Jan 1867; L. Eldridge, bm; m 22 Jan 1867 at Thos. Lee, by S. W. Blackman, J. P.

Hood, John C. & Charlotte Peacock, 28 Nov 1848; W. S. Ballinger, bm.

Hood, Joshua & Betsy Cole, 26 Feb 1830; Bold Robin Hood, bm.

Hood, L. W. & Rachel Stevens, 4 Sept 1860 at the residence of J. A. Stevens, by R. D. Lunceford, J. P.

Hood, M. F. & M. Hinton, 28 Jun 1858; m 29 Jun 1858 by B. C. Richardson, J. P.

Hood, Nathaniel & Susanah Gurley, 13 Nov 1782; Kedar Powell, bm.

Hood, Pearce & Beneter Taylor, 6 Jun 1801; Wm. Davis, bm.

Hood, Robert & Dicy Grantham, 28 Aug 1839; Thos. Toler, bm.

Hood, Robert B. & Mary M. Thornton, 26 Nov 1854; m 27 Nov 1854 by E. S. Jones, J. P.

Hood, W. R. & Sarah J. Hinnant, 16 Mar 1867; Wm. H. Hood, Jr., bm; m 17 Mar 1867 at the residence of the bride's mother, by M. G. Todd, M. G.

Hooke, Robert & Sarah Raiford, 10 Mar 1784; Needham Whitley, bm.

Hooks, Hardy & Patience Pearce, 27 Dec 1830; Henry M. Stevens, bm.

Hooks, Jacob & Celah Noles, 26 Aug 1806; Wm. Williams, bm.

Hooks, Robert -see Hooke, Robert.

Hopkins, A. J. & Elizabeth Wilder, 13 Sept 1860; m 16 Sept 1860 at Isham Wilders, by S. W. Woody, J. P.

Hopkins, William W. & Sally Boon, 16 Jun 1812; David Lunceford, bm.

Horn, Benjah & Betsy Tarver, 15 Dec 1827; Edwin Spivy, bm.

Horn, Hilliard & Hawkins Stancell, 21 Jul 1847; Staton Johnston, bm.

Horn, Jesse & Nanny Boyt, 1 Nov 1820; James Stricklin, bm.

Horn, Jessee & Nancy Johnson, 28 Nov 1831; Jessee Hinnant, bm.

Horn, Joel & Zilpha Richardson, 26 Sept 1822; Stephen Barnes, bm.

Horn, Silas & Winifred Johnson, 24 Sept 1834; Warren Johnston, bm.

Hosea, Henry & Fereby Learey, 27 Mar 1809; Everett Renfrow, bm.

Houghton, Joshua Jr. & _____, 19 Apr 1764; Thomas Houghton, Cornelius Keith, bm.

Houlder, Jonathan & Piety Hackney, 12 Oct 1810; Tobias Hollimon, bm.

Houlder, Josiah Jr. & ___ Hocut, 14 Jul 1827; Drewry Snipes, bm.

Houlder, Ruffin & Temperance A. Whiteley, 2 Nov 1837; James W. Wilder, bm.

Houlder, Zachariah & Nancy Corbet, 23 Aug 1845; Allen Nichols, bm.

House, Warren, of Wake Co., & Delilah Carroll, 28 Feb 1809; Benjamin Carroll, bm.

Howell, Barnabas & Sarah Raiford, 9 Dec 1839; Willie Howell, bm.

Howell, Burrell & Betsy Brady, 27 May 1824; Lewis Thomson, bm.

Howell, Burwell & Patsey Boyt, 27 Jul 1857; Levi Carmack, bm.

Howell, David & Polly Strickland, 21 Sept 1826; Riddick Warren, bm.

Howell, Dupree & Willey Gay, 12 Nov 1859; m 15 Nov 1859 by Jas. H. Sasser.

Howell, Edmund & Fereby Strickland, 20 Aug 1798; Uriah Strickland, William Worley, bm.

Howell, James & Elizabeth Johnson, 7 Aug 1866; John D. Howell, bm; m 7 Aug 1866 by W. D. Holt, J. P.

Howell, Jasper & Winifred Dinkins, 17 Apr 1819; Bold Robin Hood, bm.

Howell, Levy & Betsy Hocut, 24 Feb 1809; Willis Cole, bm.

Howell, Osborn & Nancy Strickland, 25 Sept 1810; Edmond Howell, bm.

Howell, Osburn & Lotty Strickland, 29 Dec 1812; Edmond Howell, bm.

Howell, Richard Mills & Eliza Solace, 21 Jul 1866; Wili Holowell, bm; m 24 Jul 1866 by W. D. Holt, J. P.

Hubbard, Westley & Nancy Atkinson, m 31 Dec 1856 by B. C. Richardson, J. P.

Hudson, Buc. F. & Betsy Eldridg, 27 Aug 1849; J. J. Hudson, bm.

Hudson, Jarmon J. & Eliza Blackman, 24 aug 1857; J. C. Hood, bm; m 27 Aug 1857 by John C. Hood, J. P.

Hudson, Joel, of Sampson Co., & Elizabeth E. Westbrook, 26 Feb 1866; W. P. Hudson, bm.

Hudson, Joel Green & Mrs. Aley Allen, 20 Oct 1842; John L. Bryan, bm.

Hughes, Brazel & Alisor Hamilton, m 7 Jan 1861 at the residence of John Hamilton, by B. Lane, J. P.

Hughes, William & Nancy Worley, 12 Jan 1859; m 13 Jan 1859 at the residence of H. Lanes, by B. Lane, J. P.

Hughs, Benjamin & Rachel Tiner, 19 Sept 1806; Jeremiah Gurley, bm.

Hughs, Benjamin & Nancy Oliver, 3 Aug 1839; Wm. J. Peeden, bm.

Hughs, John & Betsy Guley, 27 Feb 1805; Sampson Edwards, bm.

Huneycut, William H. & Polly Ann Pender, 25 Apr 1853; m 26 Apr 1853 by Willie Holt.

Hunter, Thomas O. & Martha Jones, 29 Nov 1828; John MacLeod, bm.

Hurn, Napoleon B. & Rebecca Ann Jones, 6 Dec 1854; m 7 Dec 1854 by H. H. Finch, J. P.

Hutson, John W. & Elizabeth E. Johnson, 24 Dec 1851; m 28 Dec 1851 by Harry Johnson, J. P.

Ingram, Ambrose & Sally Norriss, 16 Dec 1806; Barnaby Ingram, bm.

Ingram, Barney & Edith Altman, 24 Jan 1797; William Lee, bm.

Ingram, Henry & Jane Green, 15 Mar 1842; G. W. Duncan, bm.

Ingram, Isaac & Frances Collins, 6 Feb 1799; Wm. Ingram, bm.

Ingram, Isaac & Tabitha Blackman, 3 Jan 1822; Jeremiah Blackman, bm.

Ingram, Isac & Winefred Lee, 25 Mar 1786; James Lee, bm.

Ingram, John B. & Nancy Walston, 12 Sept 1855; m 18 Sept 1855 by R. Massingill, J. P.

Ingram, Joseph & Rebeccah Thomson, 23 Dec 1833; Needham G. Bryan, bm.

Ingram, Joseph Jr. & Eliza Boon, 27 Apr 1818; Wm. Hen. Guy, bm.

Ingram, Joseph A. & Julia C. Morgan, 7 Mar 1844; Bevely D. Ballinger, bm.

Ingram, Jos. A. & Mary B. Smith, 18 Mar 1867; m 3 Apr 1867 by T. Page Ricaud, M. G.

Ingram, Michael & Rebeccha Stevens, 7 Mar 1827; Riddick Warren, bm.

Ingram, Nathan & Catharine A. Adams, m 23 Aug 1866 by R. Massingill, J. P.

Ingram, Shaderech & Polly Deloach, 3 Oct 1803; Samuel Deloach, Jr., bm.

Ingram, Sir William & Fanny Dowdy, 20 May 1849; Needham Ingram, bm.

Ingram, William & Nancy Johnson, 20 Jan 1823; Nicholas Lee, bm.

Ingrim, Isaac Jr. & Betsy Lee, 8 Apr 1848; James H. Corbit, bm.

Irwin, Joseph & Ann Shaw, 1 Mar 1793; John Watson, bm.

Ives, Thomas & Susan Avera, 26 Oct 1842; Hiram W. Husted, bm.

Ivey, Lovell & Fanny Morgan, 28 Dec 1796; Absalom Woodall, bm.

Ivey, Vine A. & Nicy Woodall, 13 Dec 1848; Wm. W. Morgan, bm.

Ivy, Bourbon & Fanny Martin, 29 Dec 1857; Alfred Holland, bm.; m 31 Dec 1857 by R. Masingill, J. P.

Ivy, David Jr. & Rachell Jones, 9 Aug 1805; David Ivy, Sr., bm.

Ivy, Hartwill & Poartlock Parish, 11 Aug 1809; Reeves Ivey, bm.

Ivy, Payton & Viney Avera, 27 Nov 1804; David Ivy, Sr., bm.

Jackson, Edin & Buny Smith, 27 Sept 1836; Zachariah H. Pope, bm.

Jackson, Wilie & Clarkey Barefoot, 19 Feb 1859; m 20 Feb 1859 by R. Masingill, J. P.

Jackson, William & Priscilla Price, 26 Aug 1784; John Brady, bm.

Jackson, William & Nancy Holland, 26 Jul 1820; John Jackson, bm.

Jackson, Willie & Polly Pearce, 16 Jun 1824; Thomas Holland, bm.

Jarrell, Thomas & Amelia Hinnant, 17 Jan 1797; John Gerald, bm.

Jeffery, James & Willy Atkinson, 13 May 1847; Ruffin Jeffreys, R. D. Atkinson, bm.

Jefferys, Willie & Patsy Hollomon, 3 Sept 1825; Russell Sillivant, bm.

Jeffeys, Thomas B. & Cora Elvira Worley, 24 Jul 1863; m 11 Aug 1863 by J. A. Stevens, J. P.

Jenings, Hezekiah & Sarah Johnson, 28 Aug 1790; Richard Rivers, bm.

Jernagan, Bright & Elizabeth Watson, 2 May 1816; Thos. Rice, bm.

Jernegan, William H. & Susan Allen, 9 Jun 1857; m 18 June 1857 by B. Godwin, J. P.

Jernegan, William M. & Polly Ann Coats, 8 Apr 1856; m 13 Apr 1856 by B. Godwin, J. P.

Jernigan, Alexander & _____, 29 Nov 1803; Deal Collins, bm.

Jernigan, Allen & Mary Toler, 28 Dec 1806; Willis Tiner, bm.

Jernigan, Arthur & Winifred Crafford, 8 Dec 1779; John Rayford, bm.

Jernigan, Bright & Jerusha Lindsay, 28 Sept 1830; Baldy Sanders, bm.

Jernigan, Budd & Sally A. Adams, 1 Nov 1848; John C. Hood, bm.

Jernigan, Calvin & Eady Lee, 26 Dec 1849; Absalum Barber, Sr., bm.

Jernigan, George & Sally Bass, 23 Jan 1836; Wm. B. Allen, bm.

Jernigan, Handy B. & Pollie Grant, 9 Aug 1866; m 21 Aug 1866 by B. Massingill, J. P.

Jernigan, James B. & Alleycola Lee, 2 Apr 1859; m 3 Apr 1859 by R. Masingill, J. P.

Jernigan, Joseph & Colin Adams, 22 Feb 1830; Simon Bryan, bm.

Jernigan, Keder & Seny Bryan, 29 Feb 1848; Benjamin F. Hudson, bm.

Jernigan, Lewis Jr. & Frances Douglas, 13 Jan 1801; Ben. Phillips, bm.

Jeter, Henry M. & Elina V. Blackman, 2 Nov 1839; C. Christophers, bm.

Jinkins, Lewis W. & Betsy Rivers, 7 Sept 1831; Harry Avera, bm.

Johnson, Aaron & Patsy Oniel, 1 Mar 1796; Willie Watkins, bm.

Johnson, Alexander & Ally Cotton, 9 Oct 1824; Noel West, bm.

Johnson, Alferd & Lydia M. Reaves, 7 Aug 1846; John B. Johnson, bm.

Johnson, Alfred & Ceny Whittington, 27 Jun 1843; Frederick Holmes, bm.

Johnson, Allen & Peggy Whitington, 30 Sept 1791; John Stevenson, James Langdon, bm.

Johnson, Allen & Edith Barnes, 30 Aug 1814; Willie Johnson, bm.

Johnson, Allen Jr. & Penney Allen, 23 Dec 1833; Allen Johnson, Sr., bm.

Johnson, Alsey & Delia Johnston, 24 Feb 1835; Edward Price, bm.

Johnson, Alsey & Polly Lee, 5 Nov 1842; Elijah B. Johnson, bm.

Johnson, Alvan & Betsy Duncan, 28 Mar 1836; Ambrose Lee, bm.

Johnson, Amos & Disa Bedingfield, 27 Feb 1797; John Farrell, bm.

Johnson, Amos & Sally Johnson, 25 Mar 1817; John Leach, bm.

Johnson, Amos & Sally Tomlinson, 23 Aug 1819; Solomon Whitenton, bm.

Johnson, Arthur & Nancy Woodward, 21 Dec 1824; Jonathan Woodard, bm.

Johnson, Arthur Baile & Cloe Thomas, 25 Jan 1779; David Bailey, bm.

Johnson, Balaam & Mary Inman, 10 Jul 178-; Thomas Spight, bm.

Johnson, Berry & Nancy Cole, 25 May 1824; Allen Richardson, bm.

Johnson, Berty & Rhody Stansel, 8 Feb 1847; R. N. Gully, bm.

Johnson, Burty & Edith Wilkinson, 15 Mar 1828; Hardy Bailey, bm.

Johnson, Burwell & Susan Naron, 12 Jan 1822; Geo. Barber, bm.

Johnson, Carey & Polly West, 10 Jan 1835; Reuben Johnson, bm.

Johnson, David & Delitha Lassitor, 18 Jan 1803; Allen Johnson, bm.

Johnson, David & Pherbee Byrd, 27 Sept 1836; Jno. W. Johnson, bm.

Johnson, David P. & Catharine M. Tiner, 31 Dec 1860; m 1 Jan 1861 by B. A. Wellons, J. P.

Johnson, Delia & Susan W. Bailey, 13 Aug 1852; m 5 Sept 1852 by S. W. Woody, J. P.

Johnson, Drury & Anna Overby, 17 Mar 1825; Gideon Gower, bm.

Johnson, Drury Jr. & Margret Jane Griffis, 25 Feb 1851.

Johnson, Duncan & Cissaley Low, 5 Apr 1844; William Johnson, bm.

Johnson, Edmund & Wilsy Johnson, 7 May 1819; Benjamin Carrell, bm.

Johnson, Edmund & Elizabeth Lassiter, 24 Sept 1839; Alfred Lassiter, bm.

Johnson, Elijah P. & Sally Lee, 1 Mar 1842; James Johnson, bm.

Johnson, Elisha & Corternea V. T. Harper, 17 Aug 1861; m 18 Aug 1861 by W. H. Lambert, J. P.

Johnson, Frederick & Parrizady Parrish, 15 Feb 1825; David Parrish, bm.

Johnson, Garry & Elizabeth Bailey, 9 Jan 1845; Baldy G. Bailey, bm.

Johnson, Gaston & Marry Jane Carrol, 14 May 1853; m 19 May 1853 by A. J. Leach, J. P.

Johnson, George D. & Grizzie Stewart, 22 Oct 1861; m 24 Oct 1861 by Moore Stephenson, elder.

Johnson, Green & Polly Smith, 7 Oct 1841; Allen Nichols, bm.

Johnson, Hardy & Nancy Morris, 30 Dec 1826; Thomas Hicks, bm.

Johnson, Harris & Elizabeth J. Strickland, 17 Apr 1866; John Pool, bm.

Johnson, Harry & Susan Adams, 9 Oct 1835; Joel Lee, bm.

Johnson, Harry & Eliza Thornton, 23 Mar 1847; James B. Bryan, bm.

Johnson, Harry & Sarah Lee, 29 Jan 1848; George Stephenson, bm.

Johnson, Haywood & Nancy H. Johnson, m 8 Feb 1855 by R. W. Stevens, J. P.

Johnson, Haywood & Elizabeth Oneal, 27 Nov 1858; m 28 Nov 1858 by S. W. Moody, J. P.

Johnson, Henry & Lydia Johnson, 28 Dec 1841; A. W. Stevens, bm.

Johnson, Henry & Fanny Welch, 30 Mar 1842; Haywood Martin, bm.

Johnson, Henry & Harriet Beasly, m 16 Aug 1859 by C. J. Bingham, J. P.

Johnson, Henry C. & Dilitha Johnson, 30 May 1849; R. W. Stevens, bm.

Johnson, Henry M. & Nancy A. Beasly, 3 Mar 1859; m 10 Mar 1859 by John C. Hood, J. P.

Johnson, Henry M. & Edith Ann Allen, 2 Jun 1863; m 9 Jun 1863 by B. Godwin, J. P.

Johnson, Henry W. & Eliza Smith, 14 Mar 1838; William W. Johnson, bm.

Johnson, Heron & Leueney Dirden, 29 Mar 1836; John W. Johnson, bm.

Johnson, Isaac & Jinny Stevenson, 28 Jul 1832; David Parrish, bm.

Johnson, Isaac & Lucy Honeycut, 28 Feb 1837; John W. Johnson, bm.

Johnson, Isom & Polly Stephens, 17 Dec 1788; Martin Johnson, bm.

Johnson, Jacob & Nancy Coats, 20 Jul 1795; Noel Johnson, bm.

Johnson, Jacob & Elizabeth Pope, 24 Mar 1835; Hillary Wilder, bm.

Johnson, Jacob & Rachel Bird, 26 Dec 1840; Isaac Johnson, bm.

Johnson, James & Phereby Smith, 23 Sept 1828; Alexander Johnson, bm.

Johnson, James & Harriet Stevens, 28 Apr 1836; Allen Johnson, bm.

Johnson, James & Airy Parish, 30 Jan 1839; George Stephenson, bm.

Johnson, James H. & Fanny Morgan, 17 Mar 1853.

Johnson, Jarod & Leanna Cotton, 2 Jan 1826; Nathan T. Allen, bm.

Johnson, Jarret T. & Susan Johnson, 16 Nov 1842; Moses A. Johnson, bm.

Johnson, Jeremiah & Crecy Wildair, 24 Jul 1817; Redding Bryant, bm.

Johnson, Jesse & Elizabeth Lewis, 14 Dec 1778; Zadock Stallions, bm.

Johnson, Jesse J. & Telitha C. Ellis, 16 Nov 1857 John W. Hudson, bm; m 16 Nov 1857 by John C. Hood, J. P.

Johnson, Jesse V. & Martha Jane E. Faison, 17 Mar 1856; m 25 May 1856 by Right Ryals, J. P.

Johnson, John Q. & Nancy C. Peacock, 13 Nov 1863; m 17 Nov 1863 at Smithfield, by Jas. H. Adams, J. P.

Johnson, John W. & Mary Jean Reaves, 19 Jan 1842; R. Greene, bm.

Johnson, Jonathan & Lucy Pinney, 8 Feb 1803; Henry Johnson, bm.

Johnson, Joseph & Viney Redding, 9 Feb 1830; Isaac Penny, bm.

Johnson, Joseph & Lucinda Gay, 10 Dec 1859; m 11 Dec 1859 at Dupree Howels, by Wilie Wellons, J. P.

Johnson, Joshua & Edith Ingram, 2 May 1849; Willie T. Sanders, bm.

Johnson, Joshua Jr. & Anna Hobby, 8 Jan 1810; John Lee, bm.

Johnson, Josiah & Susan Phillips, 7 Nov 1835; Elias Barnes, bm.

Johnson, Littleton & Nancy Lee, 13 May 1821; William Johnson, bm.

Johnson, McCoy & Sarah Johnston, 9 Feb 1848; Henry C. Johnson, bm.

Johnson, Mark & Sally Evans, 26 Nov 1823; Noel West, bm.

Johnson, Malcomb & Polly Ann Atkinson, 1 Feb 1862; m 4 Feb 1862 at Blake Atkinson's, by N. G. Gulley, J. P.

Johnson, Merritt & Mary Holland, 20 Sept 1837; Alsey Johnson, bm.

Johnson, Moses & Ann Baggley, 14 Nov 1778; John Gerrald, bm.

Johnson, Mosses & Susannah Clark, 6 Dec 1784; Thomas Tomlinson, bm.

Johnson, Myrach & Susan Barefoot, 13 Dec 1840; Thomas Barefoot, bm.

Johnson, Nathan & Diana Rhodes, 25 Jun 1859; m 30 Jun 1859 at Edw. Rhodes, by Edwin L. Sanders.

Johnson, Phillip & Nancy Giles, 26 Feb 1792; William Giles, bm.

Johnson, Redden & Ellender Flowers, 31 Jan 1797; Joseph Deloach, bm.

Johnson, Redden & Metildeth Powell, 2 Jun 1804; Joel Clifton, bm.

Johnson, Richard & Martha Johnson, 10 Oct 1795; Abner Sauls, bm.

Johnson, Richard & Polly Stallings, 6 Jan 1810; Kedar Avera, bm.

Johnson, Richard & Fanny Johnson, 11 Nov 1823; Reuben Gower, bm.

Johnson, Rigdon & Emily Johnson, 22 Mar 1832; Edmund Johnson, bm.

Johnson, Right A. & Wineford Allen, 8 Apr 1851; m 11 Apr 1851 by Right Ryals, J. P.

Johnson, Right H. & Joice Surles, 18 Mar 1853; m 23 Mar 1853 by R. W. Stevens, J. P.

Johnson, Robert & Ann Garrald, 26 Mar 1785; William Johnson, bm.

Johnson, Rufus A. & Margaret Johnson, 27 Sept 1866; W. C. Benson, bm; m 30 Sept 1866 at Ara Johnson, by Abram Dixon, J. P.

Johnson, Ryas & Jane Carrell, 28 Oct 1794; Joel Johnson, bm.

Johnson, Samuel & Charlottee Johnson, 15 Jan 1803; Isaac Johnson, bm.

Johnson, Sandy & Elizabeth _____, 4 Jul 1846; Abram Dixon, bm.

Johnson, Starling & Araminta Gower, 7 Sept 1858; m 12 Sept 1858 at Gideon Gower's, by D. H. Holland, J. P.

Johnson, Stephen & Cally Low, 23 Sept 1851; m 24 Sept 1851 by S. Woody, J. P.

Johnson, Thomas & Ann Allen, 11 Oct 1822; Benjamin Bell, bm.

Johnson, Vine Allen & Mary Johnson, 1 Jul 1851; m 15 Jul 1851 by B. Blackman, J. P.

Johnson, W. C. & Sarah J. Tiner, 1 Jan 1867; B. A. Wellons, bm; m 3 Jan 1867 by B. A. Wellons, J. P.

Johnson, W. R. & M. A. E. Penny, 14 Apr 1860; m 19 Apr 1860 by A. Coats, J. P.

Johnson, Walter & Parazadia Johnson, 1 Jan 1867; Nathan Johnson, bm; m 3 Jan 1867 at the house of Fred. Johnson, by Jethro Hair, J. P.

Johnson, Wiley & Winefrin Carvele, 15 Aug 1792; Amous Johnson, bm.

Johnson, William & Clary Gale, 27 Feb 1796; Charles Copeland, bm.

Johnson, William & Burchet Lee, 23 Sept 1807; Samuel Johnson, bm.

Johnson, William & Celah Watson, 29 Jul 1810; Isom Watson, bm.

Johnson, William & Sally Horn, 27 Sept 1814; Solomon Johnson, bm.

Johnson, William & Patsy Johnson, 24 Jan 1823; Reuben Johnson, bm.

Johnson, William & Betsy Harrison 5 Dec 1826; Nathaniel Johnson, bm.

Johnson, William & Sally A. Q. Pope, 1 Nov 1848; Stephen Johnson, bm.

Johnson, William B. & Sarah Strickland, 12 Mar 1867; Eli Olive, bm; m 14 Mar 1867 by George Keen, J. P.

Johnson, William B. & Polly Gay, 4 Dec 1866; Jacob Wheeler, bm.

Johnson, Willie & Phereby Sauls, 28 Sept 1835; R. T. Sanders, bm.

Johnson, Willis & Penny Stanly, 5 Aug 1842; Starling Massingill, bm.

Johnston, Edmund & Susan Allen, 22 Feb 1848; Thos. Allen, bm.

Johnston, German G. & Elizabeth A. Reeves, 23 Feb 1841;

Johnston, James Bartly & Emily Coats, 23 Mar 1842; William H. Coats, bm.

Johnston, Jesse & Moaning Parker, 3 Apr 1802; Jesse Pearce, bm.

Johnston, Mos. & Elizabeth Marshall, 24 Dec 1795; William Peeples, bm.

Johnston, Reading & Celah Wall, 4 May 1810; L. A. Bryan, bm.

Johnston, Staton & Patience Barnes, 26 Oct 1846; Stanley Kirby, bm.

Johnston, William & Mary Richardson, 20 MAr 1847; John D. Howell, bm.

Joiner, Daniel & Alsy Ingram, 29 Apr 1809; Allen S. Ballinger, bm.

Joiner, Henry & Elizabeth Parker, 20 Oct 1851; m 28 Oct 1851 by Jas. H. Sasser.

Joiner, Jessie & _____ , 30 May 1784; John Whittley, bm.

Joiner, Joel Jr. & Isabella Strickland, 27 Dec 1841; N. B. Stevens, bm.

Joiner, John & Sarah Pearce, 25 Oct 1808; William Hinnant, Sr., bm.

Joiner, Reddin & Elizabeth Wilder, 26 Nov 1838; John Whitley, bm.

Joiner, Stephen & Betsy Pitman, 20 Dec 1825; Thomas Cockwell, bm.

Joiner, Thomas & Mary Henniard, 8 Mar 1786; Amos Atkerson, bm.

Joiner, Thomas & Sarah Bailey, 31 Mar 1797; Freadrick Homes, bm.

Jolly, Charles & Martha Wheallen, 17 Jul 1844; Richardson Oneal, bm.

Jones, Augustus & Harriet G. Lockart, 6 Apr 1843; Jas. H. Durham, bm.

Jones, Benjamin & Mary Clenny, 1 Apr 1793; Jesse Morgan, bm.

Jones, Benjamin & Nancy Capps, 24 May 1813; Edward Stevens, bm.

Jones, Bennet & Polly Holt, 21 Nov 1826; William Jones, bm.

Jones, Bryan & Cally Boyte, 9 Dec 1822; John Spencer, bm.

Jones, Bud & Susanna Taylor, 22 Mar 1827; Redden Taunt, bm.

Jones, Burwell & Judith Smith, 8 Aug 1794; Charles Copeland, bm.

Jones, Burwell & Elizabeth Clifton, 4 Apr 1835; William Jones, bm.

Jones, Doctor C. & Patsey Johnson, 31 Aug 1842; Larkin Barber, bm.

Jones, Charles & Mahala Watkins, 23 Aug 1860; m 24 Aug 1860 at Ensel Watkins, by Jesse Parker, J. P.

Jones, Elly & Patsy Fail, 2 Mar 1841; Needham Fail, bm.

Jones, Gaston & S. E. Johnson, 18 Jan 1859; m 19 Jan 1859 by J. F. Ellington.

Jones, George & Nancey Ellis, 22 Oct 1860; m 24 Oct 1860 by J. H. Ellington.

Jones, Harrison & Emily Welsh, 25 Jul 1832; Benjamin Jones, bm.

Jones, Haywood & Martha Parish, 11 Mar 1861; m 12 Mar 1861 at Mrs. Parish's, by W. H. Lambert, J. P.

Jones, Henderson & Patsey Parish, 26 Nov 1854; m 28 Nov 1854 by E. Langdon, J. P.

Jones, Henry & Sally Smith, 4 Sept 1806; Reuben Sanders, bm.

Jones, Isaac W. & Samantha Coble, 31 May 1847; Henry J. Bell, bm.

Jones, Isaac W. & Martha Brannan, 12 Apr 1862; m 13 Apr 1862 at Isaac W. Jones's house, by N. G. Gully, J. P.

Jones, James & Ulrica Stallings, 8 Mar 1832; Needham Bryan, bm.

Jones, James & Millie Ann Deans, 26 Dec 1866; C. M. Holleman, bm.

Jones, James Alvin & Emeline C. Barber, 1 Feb 1847; Nathaniel B. Barber, bm.

Jones, James A. T. & Sarah E. Barnes, 16 Feb 1867; H. H. Pate, bm; m 20 Feb 1867 at Solomon Barnes's, by B. B. Holder.

Jones, James H. & Elizabeth Smith, 3 Nov 1847; Wilie Jones, bm.

Jones, Jeremiah & Unity Byrd, 11 Oct 1853; m 25 Oct 1853 by H. H. Finch, J. P.

Jones, Jesse & Winifred Spights, 1 May 1775; Etheldread Jones, bm.

Jones, John & Sarah Matthews, 6 Aug 1798; John Carrell, bm.

Jones, John & Cassanda Lashley, 10 Feb 1848; Benjamin Jones, bm.

Jones, Josiah & Jane Wilder, 1 Feb 1843; Simon Jones, bm.

Jones, Lemuel & Calley Spencer, 11 Feb 1840; Curtis Holland, bm.

Jones, Leroy & Elizabeth Barber, 18 Feb 1861; m 19 Dec 1861 at Owen Barber's, by W. H. Lambert, J. P.

Jones, Lucian H. & Tranquilla Johnson, 28 Mar 1853; m 3 Apr 1853 by Linn B. Sanders, J. P.

Jones, Mathew & Betsey Turner, 26 MAr 1820; Cader Avera, bm.

Jones, Matthew & Sally Leach, 1 Oct 1793; James Ogburn, bm.

Jones, Mark (colored) & Ann Barber, 18 Oct 1866; Jos. C. Ellington, bm; m 28 Oct 1866 by S. H. Hood, J. P.

Jones, Nathaniel & Polly Barnes, 7 Jan 1806; John Leach, bm.

Jones, Philip & Mary Benson, 27 Sept 1837; Wm. Brown, bm.

Jones, Revell & Margaret Creech, 2 Nov 1839; Ray Jones, bm.

Jones, Samuel & Martha Lassiter, 3 Jan 1862; m 5 Jan 1862 at William Lassiers's, by Calvin Lassiter, J. P.

Jones, Samuel M. & Elizabeth Parish, 1 May 1849; Zachariah Jones, bm.

Jones, Thomas & Esther Norris, 13 Aug 1795; James Norris, bm.

Jones, Thomas & Patsey Johnson, 19 Jan 1842; John Cordell, bm.

Jones, Turner & Margaret Creech, 17 Mar 1855; m 3 Apr 1855 at Bennet Breech's, by S. Bagley, J. P.

Jones, William & Winefred Avera, 26 Jan 1793; Zadok Stallins, bm.

Jones, William & Amy Barber, 30 Jan 1800; Burwell Barber, bm.

Jones, William & Ruthy Penny, 6 Oct 1819; Cader Avera, bm.

Jones, William & Sally Simpkins, 13 Jan 1835; Calvin Simpkins, bm.

Jones, William H. & Maria Barber, 11 Jan 1860; m 12 Jan 1860 at G. Barber's, by J. W. Hodges, J. P.

Jones, William J. & Harriet A. Sanders, 2 Mar 1859; m 30 Mar 1859 by J. F. Ellington.

Jones, Willie, of Wake Co., & Penny H. Jones, 24 Dec 1809; Robert H. Helme, Ellick Sanders, bm.

Jones, Willie & Lotte Stephenson, 13 May 1811; Reuben Sanders, Hardy Jones, bm.

Jones, Willie & Alsy Hicks, 25 Feb 1823; Allen Jones, bm.

Jones, Willie & Della Harrison, 13 Apr 1843; James J. Farmer, bm.

Jonson, Osborn & Jency Ethridge, 26 Aug 1832; Thomas L. Ethridge, bm.

Jordan, Bryan & Julia Ann Lee, 1 Sept 1852; m 2 Sept 1852 by Revd. Ellen Mann.

Jordan, Dickson & Judith Manor, 26 Sept 1803; Marmaduke Strickland, bm.

Jordan, Henry & Mary Stevens, 30 May 1797; William B. Hocot, bm.

Jordan, Henry & Edith Houlder, 12 Dec 1823; Mark Nowel, bm.

Jordan, Nichols & Nancy Jordan, 4 Jul 1836; Plyer Barber, bm.

Jordan, Rubin & Olive Richardson, 30 Nov 1790; Applewhite Richardson, bm.

Jordan, William & Elizabeth Johnson, 1 Apr 1856; m 2 Apr 1856 by W. H. Massingill, J. P.

Jorden, John & Elizabeth Barber, 25 Jun 1851; m 26 Jun 1851 by N. G. Gulley, J. P.

Jordin, Green & Dilley Honecutt, 3 Mar 1842; Haywood Martin, bm.

Jourdan, Green & Middy Matthews, 5 Jan 1825; Sol. Whitinton, bm.

Joyce, William & Narcissa Williams, 28 Apr 1865; John J. Harper, bm.

Joyner, Turner & Winnford Duncan, 14 Dec 1849; E. A. Bryan, bm.

Kearn, John & Elizabeth Whitington, 25 Jul 1783; Thomas Kearn, Aaron Vinson, bm.

Keen, George & Catern Goodrach, 28 Jan 1793; Drewry Bynum, bm.

Keen, George & Sarah Laster, 6 Feb 1850; Nathan P. Allen, bm.

Keen, Gideon & Sally Ann Stanly, 3 Feb 1848; George Keen, bm.

Keen, Isaac & Judith Kerby, 25 Feb 1799; Jesse Kerby, bm.

Kelly, James & Elizabeth Bell, 3 July 1822; James Murphey, bm.

Kelly, John & Tabitha Simpkins, 13 Feb 1811; Cader Avera, bm.

Kelly, Preston & Nancy Boon, 29 Apr 1840; Wm. Pool, bm.

Kelly, Quinton & Nicy Jones, 6 Sept 1836; William Jones, bm.

Kelly, Quinton & Phereby M. Jones, 27 Dec 1841; Jno. Westly Boon, bm.

Kemp, Green & Nancy Hopkins, 29 Nov 1843; Wyatt Earp, bm.

Kenneday. Jesse & Darcas Pittes, 25 Dec 1821; George Byrd, bm.

Kennedy, Henry H. & Pensey Whittington, 24 Mar 1835; William B. Whitenton, bm.

Kennedy, William & Ether Smith, 12 Sept 1807; Alexander Penny, bm.

Kent, Robeson & Ceneth Pew, 3 May 1826; Jonathan Hinnant, bm.

Kerby, Dixon & Martha Peele, 28 Feb 1853; m 17 Mar 1853 by Stanly Kirby, J. P.

Kerby, Jesse & Morning Feboash, 15 Aug 1823; Henry Sasser, bm.

Kerby, Ransom & Celia Holland, m 1 Feb 1853 by Stanly Kirby, J. P.

Keuster, Ferdinand & Rixey Freeman, 5 May 1866; S. R. Horne, bm.

Killingsworth, Freeman Jr. & Polly Raiford, 20 Apr 1798; Philip Raiford, bm.

Killingsworth, John & Sarah Blackman 9 Nov 1793; Wm. Hobby, bm.

Killingsworth, John & Patty Guley, 2 Oct 1798; Shadrach Eason, bm.

Killingsworth, John T. & Lucreacy Hays, _____ 1788; Freeman Killingsworth, bm.

Kindall, Isaac & Mary Pritchet, 10 Jul 1790; John Norriss, Sr., bm.

King, Bennett & Ritter Jane Blalock, 19 Feb 1866; E. N. Wilson, bm.

King, Daniel & Mary Pearce, 22 May 1860; m 23 May 1860 by W. D. Holt.

King, Henry & Sarah Williams, 29 Apr 1790; Josiah Blackman, bm.

King, James & Edith Johnson, 22 Jan 1822; Edward Stevens, bm.

King, Starkey & Patsey Stanly, 30 Nov 1853; m 1 Dec 1853 by R. W. Stevens, J. P.

Kingry, William & Jane Lustere, 25 Dec 1819; John Avery, bm.

Kirby, Erasmus & Zilpha Peele, 30 Aug 1841; Stanly Kirby, bm.

Kirby, J. S. & Margaret Eason 3 Jan 1859; m 4 Jan 1859 by P. Godwin, J. P.

Knox, Needham L. & Patsy Pilkinton, m 26 Oct 1858 at Winny Pilkintons, by Perry Godwin, J. P.

Lamb, Calvin & Nancy Raper, 20 Dec 1842; Isaac Boyett, bm.

Lamb, Isaac & Piety Peelle, 15 Feb 1849; Stephen Peelle, bm.

Lambert, William H. & Milla Ann Watkins, m 22 Oct 1851 by James Wilson, elder.

Lane, Harry & Narcissy Guy, 6 Jan 1820; Jno. Sanders, Jr., bm.

Lane, J. B. & Nancy L. Gulley, 16 Mar 1867; W. G. Gulley, bm; m 20 Mar 1867 by J. F. Ellington.

Lane, William & Margarett R. Whitley, 2 Sept 1857, m 3 Sept 1857 by B. B. Alford, J. P.

Langden, James & Pattey Stevens, 13 Sept 1778; Richard Whitington, bm.

Langdon, Briton & Winifred Jordan, 5 Aug 1836; Benjamin Martin, bm.

Langdon, Carrell & Nancy Byrd, 16 May 1839; Haywood Martin, bm.

Langdon, J. M. & Sarah Byrd, 18 Dec 1866; L. B. Langdon, bm; m 20 Dec 1866 at Peggy Byrd's, by Abram Dixon, J. P.

Langdon, Lemuel B. & Margaret Lassiter, 4 May 1861; m 7 Mar 1861 at Alfred Lassiter's, by George Keen, J. P.

Langdon, M. D. & Darcas Stephenson, 25 Feb 1867; James A. Smith, bm; m 28 Feb 1867 at Benjamin Stephenson, by James A. Smith, J. P.

Langdon, Merret & Margaret I. Stephenson, 30 Dec 1856; m 31 Dec 1856 at Benjamin Stephenson, by C. Langdon, J. P.

Langdon, Zechariah & Elizabeth Johnson, 4 Feb 1849; Carrel Langdon, bm.

Langier, John & Peggy Musslewhite, 27 Apr 1802; Jno. A. Smith, bm.

Langlay, William H. & Emely Jane Capps, 30 Sept 1852; m 5 Oct 1852 by E. Atkinson, J. P.

Langley, Arthur & Elizabeth Thompson, m 17 Apr 1864 by W. A. Smith, J. P.

Langley, David & Nancy Legon, 20 May 1829; Willie N. Pridgin, bm.

Langley, Loverd & Charlotte Toler, 9 Nov 1838; John Jackson, bm.

Langley, Martin & Thaney Davis, 25 Jan 1837; Henry H. Davis, bm.

Langley, Miles & Ann Clarke, 21 Sept 1782; James Lockhart, Jr., bm.

Langley, Miles & Sarah Garner, 25 May 1807; Elisha Garner, bm.

Langley, Ozwell & Olive Swearinggame, 26 Mar 1811; Philip Raiford, bm.

Langley, William & Sally Langley, 16 Mar 1838; Miles Langley, bm.

Langly, Arthur & Polly Collins, 17 Jan 1849; Nicholas Thawne, bm.

Langly, Nathan L. & Winny Pope, m 6 May 1858 at Joshua Johnson, by B. Godwin, J. P.

Langly, William & Julia Ann Parnell, 29 Apr 1865; W. W. Joyner, bm.

Langston, Elias & Jane Lewis, 24 May 1836; Joel Flowers, bm.

Langston, John & Mary Randol, 25 Feb 1794; Joseph Langston, bm.

Langston, Joseph & Sukey Baker, 20 Nov 1802; Francis Harrell, bm.

Langston, Joseph & Bashaba Jordan, 17 Oct 1804; James Rose, bm.

Langston, Westbrook & Patience Ann Britt, 28 Feb 1844; Joel Joyner, Jr., bm.

Lankford, James & Winifred Brady, 24 May 1791; Wm. Brady, bm.

Lanner, Larry B. & Catharine Batten, 15 Feb 1866; W. C. Renfro, bm.

Lashley, Daniel & Nancy Holt, 20 Jul 1815; Henry Smith, of Wake Co., bm.

Lashly, John & Sophia Turner, 2 Jan 1850; H. J. Bell, bm.

Lassiter, Calvin & Elenor Woodall, 17 May 1860; m 20 May 1860 by Jno. H. Keneday.

Lassiter, Campbell & Susan Lee, 7 Aug 1835; Stephenson Godwin, bm.

Lassiter, Elijah & Polly Tomlinson, 28 Mar 1826; Thos. Barber, bm.

Lassiter, Elijah & Beedy Carrell, 9 Jan 1827; James Lassiter, bm.

Lassiter, George & Elizabeth Johnson, 29 Feb 1804; Jacob Flowers, bm.

Lassiter, James & Lucy Lockart, 27 Nov 1827; Wm. Lassiter, bm.

Lassiter, James O. & Eleanor Johnson, 10 Jan 1860; m 15 Jan 1860 at the house of A. Johnson, by R. W. Stevens, J. P.

Lassiter, Jason & Thena H. Cotton, 11 Apr 1825.

Lassiter, Joseph A. & Martha Woodall, 14 Nov 1860; m 18 Nov 1860 by Jno. H. Keneday.

Lassiter, Shadrach & Lucy Johnson, 10 Sept 1825; James Lassiter, bm.

Lassiter, Shadrach B. & Martha Hardy, 26 Oct 1849; William Lassiter, bm.

Lassiter, William & Luvey Stevenson, 6 Jan 1813; Solomon Whitinton, bm.

Lassiter, William H. & Louisa Johnson, 28 May 1866; L. B. Langdon, bm.

Lassiter, Sir William & Tabitha Byrd, 20 Apr 1853; m 27 Apr 1853 by C. Langdon, J. P.

Lassitter, Alfred & Dianna Jones, 28 Jan 1840; William Lassiter, bm.

Laton, John Allen & Susan Eldredge, 12 Jan 1852; m 15 Jan 1852 by Powel Blackman, J. P.

Lawhon, Francis & Zilpha Weaver, 28 Aug 1849; Powel Blackman, bm.

Lawhorn, Young J. & Mary A. Lee, 9 May 1866; Wm. S. Eldridge, bm.

Leach, Jacks A. & Martha Whitly, 19 Sept 1837; Wm. A. Walton, bm.

Leach, James T. & Elizabeth W. Sanders, 19 Jul 1833; Matthew McCullers, bm.

Lee, A. J. H. & Elizabeth Allen, 7 Oct 1863; m 8 Oct 1863 at Wm. H. Allens, by Jas. H. Adams, J. P.

Lee, Alexander I. & Susannah Lee, 28 Apr 1842; David B. Adams, bm.

Lee, Alfred & Sally West, 2 Jan 1828; Kedar Lee, bm.

Lee, Alfred & Elizabeth Walston, 20 Apr 1843; James H. lee, bm.

Lee, Atha & Cynthia Powell, 27 Aug 1822; Noel West, bm.

Lee, Bailey A. & Tempy E. Barber, 3 Oct 1848; Ransom Lee, bm.

Lee, Blackman & Mary Blackman, 28 Feb 1837; Ivy Lee, bm.

Lee, Bryant & Elizabeth Faulk, 3 Feb 1784; Elisha Woodard, bm.

Lee, David & Anna Lee, 5 May 1821; Cader Lee, bm.

Lee, Edward & Nancy Fail, 25 Feb 1806; Jeremiah Lee, bm.

Lee, Edward & Martha A. Lee, 24 Sept 1866; Young J. Lee, bm; m 25 Sept 1866 at Littleton Lees, by Joel Lee, J. P.

Lee, Elijah & Peggy Young, 28 Mar 1826; Peter Lee, bm.

Lee, Elisha & Betsy Cupps, 2 Mar 1827; Needham Ingram, bm.

Lee, Erasmus & Lucinda Allen, 3 Apr 1859; m 12 Apr 1859 by B. A. Woodall, J. P.

Lee, Franklin & Sarah Allen, 26 Feb 1867; J. A. Lee, bm; m 4 Mar 1867 at S. W. Blaman, by S. W. Blackman, J. P.

Lee, Gideon & Mary Ann Hood, 25 Mar 1861; m 9 Apr 1861 at John C. Hoods, Sr., by Jas. H. Adams, J. P.

Lee, Handy (colored) & Madalena Eason, 27 Nov 1866; J. C. Eason, bm; m 1 Dec 1866 by J. C. Eason, J. P.

Lee, Handy H. & Betsy Ann Evans, 21 Sept 1838.

Lee, Harry & Nancy Wood, 31 Oct 1858; m 4 Nov 1858 at Whitfield Wood, by R. Massingill, J. P.

Lee, Henry & Delia Holt, 21 Mar 1866; James Holt, bm.

Lee, Henry H. Jr. & Elizabeth Masingill, 24 Aug 1848; Robert Masingill, bm.

Lee, Hopkins & Tabethey Lee, 16 Mar 1792; Robert Lee, bm.

Lee, Hugh & Patsy Hollomon, 9 Feb 1824; Kindred C. Ellington, bm.

Lee, Ingram & Martha Braswell, 26 Dec 1804; Levi Braswell, bm.

Lee, Ingram & Susan Caudle, 22 Sept 1845; Barzilla Blackmon, bm.

Lee, Isaac & Polly Fail, 18 Mar 1827; Wm. Lee, bm.

Lee, James & Elizabeth Rains, 6 Jul 1785; Stephen Lee, bm.

Lee, James & Polly Durham, 27 Sept 1819; Cader Lee, bm.

Lee, James Jr. & Ann Ingram, 20 Sept 1785; William Ballenger, bm.

Lee, James Sr. & Ellinder Ingram, 24 Dec 1821; Samuel Lee, the younger, bm.

Lee, James E. & Dicey A. Guin, 16 Feb 1859; m 17 Feb 1859 by R. Masingill, J. P.

Lee, James H. & Lueaser Avera, 1 Mar 1845; George Keen, bm.

Lee, James H. & Sally Tyner, 24 Sept 1851; m 20 Oct 1851 by Needham Bryan, J. P.

Lee, James H. & Mary A. Price, m at Calvin Simpkins, 31 May 1863 by B. A. Wellons, J. P.

Lee, James W. & Chelly Holmes, 10 Sept 1866; Warren Holmes, bm; m 18 Sept 1866 by W. F. Hall, M. G.

Lee, Jeremiah & Elizabeth Avera, 18 Jan 1790; Robert Whitington, bm.

Lee, Jesse & Henrietta Tart, 29 Mar 1859; m 7 Apr 1859 by John A. Smith, J. P.

Lee, John & Mourning Altman, 25 Oct 1783; Dixon Fail, bm.

Lee, John & Gracy Clark, 11 May 1801; Henry Proctor, bm.

Lee, John & Polly Narsworthy, 3 Jun 1801; Henry Champion, bm.

Lee, John & Dorithy Smith, 11 May 1826; C. Musgrave, bm.

Lee, John & Bethana Jones, 7 Apr 1837; Peter Lee, bm.

Lee, John & Candies Clifton, 11 Jun 1844; Acriel P. Clifton, bm.

Lee, John & Ann E. Lassiter, 25 Jan 1850; Wm. G. Adams, bm.

Lee, John H. & Sally Standley, 25 Sept 1839; John Strickland, bm.

Lee, John H. & Elizabeth A. Gwin, 11 May 1859; m 12 May 1859 at Barnabas Gwins, by R. Masingill, J. P.

Lee, John J. & Cathrin Caroline Bryan, 13 Oct 1852; m 14 Oct 1852 by Robt. Masingill.

Lee, Joseph & Margaret E. Bryan, 15 Nov 1866; N. T. McLain, bm; m 18 Nov 1866 at Asha Bryants, by B. Godwin, J. P.

Lee, Joseph A. & Martha E. Lee, 4 Jun 1847; John Lee, bm.

Lee, Julius A. & Charlotte L. Peacock, 20 Feb 1866; T. T. Lee, bm.

Lee, Lemuel & Nancy Alford, 2 Apr 1823; John Lee, bm.

Lee, Linsfer & Sintha Hogg, 3 Apr 1845; Matthew Hall, bm.

Lee, Littleton & Elizabeth H. Crocker, 11 May 1844; Joseph A. Lee, bm.

Lee, Lovet & Winny Grant, 2 Sept 1858; m 5 Sept 1858 at Kinchin Grants, by R. Masingill, J. P.

Lee, Moses A. & Betsey Eldridge, 11 Dec 1854; m 14 Dec 1854 by John C. Hood, J. P.

Lee, Nathan & Winifred Sellers, 20 Jul 1796; Ichabod Blackman, bm.

Lee, Nichols & Polly Allen, 12 Feb 1827; Isaac Lee, bm.

Lee, Peter & Amy Caudle, 4 Sept 1821; Peter Lee, bm.

Lee, R. T. & Bettie P. Parish, 2 May 1866; W. J. Jones, bm.

Lee, Rains & R. L. Blackman, 28 Feb 1859; m 3 Mar 1859 by R. Masingill, J. P.

Lee, Rainy & Nancy Wood, 16 Sept 1819; Cader Lee, bm.

Lee, S. D. & Ursula Smith, 17 Oct 1866; Wm. R. Lee, bm; m 30 Oct 1866 by J. C. Eason, J. P.

Lee, Samuel & Ann Harrell, 26 Nov 1822; Francis Harrell, bm.

Lee, Samuel & Nancy George, 28 Nov 1820; Loverd Eldridge, bm.

Lee, Samuel & Patsy J. Britt, 16 Jan 1837; J. H. Youngblood, bm.

Lee, Samuel Jr. & Betsy Ingram, 20 Mar 1821.

Lee, Seth T. & Martha Woodall, 23 Nov 1863; m 24 Nov 1863 at Major Dixons, by R. W. Stevens, J. P.

Lee, Simon & Lovey Jernigan, 25 Apr 1828; Simon Bryan, bm.

Lee, Simon P. & Charlotte Evans, 2 Aug 1842; Elijah B. Johnson, bm.

Lee, Stephen & Keziah Lee, 4 Dec 1785; James Lee, bm.

Lee, Stephen & Edith Blackman, 13 Oct 1821; Jeremiah Blackwood, bm.

Lee, Thomas & Betsey Allen, 22 Jan 1822; William Ingram, bm.

Lee, Westbrook & Esther Smith, 28 Feb 1837; Joel Lee, bm.

Lee, William & Milly Naron, 3 Feb 1784; Richard Price, bm.

Lee, William & Pherebee Fail, 27 Nov 1827; Edwin Lee, bm.

Lee, Wright A. & Margaret Ryals, 29 Jun 1857; Sir Wm. Barefoot, bm; m 30 Jun 1857 by Thos. D. Sneed, J. P.

Lee, Young & Joanna Ingram, 3 Jul 1858; m 11 Jul 1858 by George Keen, J. P.

Lee, Young J. & Julia Ann Lee, 19 Aug 1857; A. J. Lee, bm; m 20 Aug 1857 by R. Masingill, J. P.

Lee, Young J. Jr. & Ann Eldridge, 4 Jan 1854; m 5 Jan 1854 by Robt. Massingill, J. P.

Lee, Zachariah & Sally Johnson, 6 Sept 1807; Samuel Johnson, bm.

Lee, Zacheriah & Mary Hobby, 14 Aug 1801; Peter Johnson, bm.

Leesby, John & Edith Edwards, 22 Aug 1836; Bryan Smith, bm.

Leigh, Loammo & Narcissa Legon, 1 Feb 1848; Jacob B. Fulgham, bm.

Lemay, Z. J. & Amelia A. Sanders, 12 Nov 1866; C. R. Tomlinson, bm.

Lewis, Bryant & Sally Wood, 23 Sept 1828; Jesse Whitley, bm.

Lewis, Henry & Ruth Bailey, 26 Mar 1789; David Lewis, bm.

Lewis, Hillsman & Sarah Johnson, 2 Sept 1857; m __ Sept 1857 by P. Godwin, J. P.

Lewis, James & Sarah Crawford, 15 Dec 1804; William Giles, bm.

Lewis, Jethro & Zelpha Rentfrow, 15 Aug 1843; Hinton M. Godwin, bm.

Lewis, William & Patty Wright, 24 Jul 1798; William Williams, bm.

Ligon, Thomas H. & Rilda Hocut, 22 Jan 1840; Benajah Horn, bm.

Liles, Brian & Willy Price, 27 Feb 1849; Richardson Oneal, bm.

Liles, Micajah & Nancy Woodard, 9 Aug 1793; Jno. Rosser, bm.

Lindsey, Henry & Mary Burket, 16 Jun 1866.

Lindsey, Louis & Martha Gully, 18 Sept 1847; Alvin Thornton, bm.

Little, Churchwell & Winefred Starling, 1 Nov 1866; Calvin Starling, bm.

Little, James H. & Sally Cole, 19 Sept 1866; R. Lane, bm.

Little, Lewellin & Mary Oliver, 31 Jan 1840; Wm. J. Peedin, bm.

Littleton, Charles & Epsaba Armstrong, 1 Mar 1796; Henry Stevens, bm.

Littleton, Joel & Piety Pitmon, 7 Aug 1827; Savage Littleton, bm.

Littleton, Savage & Emily Parker, 31 Jan 1828; R. H. Hleme, bm.

Lockart, A. E. & Eliza Borcum, 22 Sept 1852; m 24 Sept 1852 by J. B. Jackson.

Lockart, Elam & Nelley Hardy, 20 Nov 1827; Edwin Spivy, bm.

Lockart, Gaston & Rachel Stevens, 26 Apr 1825; Jno. B. Allen, bm.

Lockart, Solomon & Winiford Avera, 25 Apr 1844; M. Avera, bm.

Lockart, Thomas & Winney Thomas, 18 Apr 1801; Osborn Lockhart, bm.

Lockart, Thomas Jr. & Temperance Eason, 11 Dec 1817; H. Guy, bm.

Lockart, Thomas Jr. & Edith Tharp, 4 Dec 1838; Matthew Avera, bm.

Lockhart, Britain & Mary Vinson, 22 Feb 1791; Osborn Lockhart, bm.

Lockhart, Orsborn & Lucy Thomas, 18 Nov 1793, request for a license by Jas. Lockhart.

Long, George & Elizabeth Bullock, 9 Dec 1805; David Ivy, Sr., bm.

Long, W. S. & L. W. Sanders, m 11 May 1861 at White Oak, by P. H. Dalton.

Lothorp, Francis & Laney Braswill, 22 Mar 1803; Abraham Webb, bm.

Love, Ephraim & Zilpha Keen, 25 Feb 1822; Hardy Hinnant, bm.

Love, Hinson & Clarry Turley, 28 Sept 1836; Needham Bryan, bm.

Love, James & Nancy Carliles, 21 Jan 1791; Hardy Bryan, bm.

Love, John A. & Sarah Johnson, 26 Dec 1841; Samuel Johnson, bm.

Lovet, Curnelus & Sally Fail, 1 Feb 1805; Francis Harrell, bm.

Lovett, Barna & Cally Cellars, 17 Feb 1816; John B. Watson, bm.

Lucus, William & Betsy Ryals, 21 Oct 1847; Young A. Barber, bm.

Lumsden, George W. & Nancy Busbee, 18 Feb 1820; Herberd Robertson, bm.

Lumsden, George W. & Maria Fail, 2 Dec 1839; John MacLeod, bm.

Lunceford, David & Susan Allen, 6 Jun 1839; Allen S. Ballinger, bm.

Lunceford, David & Emily Hicks, 26 Sept 1843; Thos. Lockart, bm.

Lunceford, Robert D. & Cornelia A. Powell, 7 Jan 1857; m 8 Jan 1857 at Ashley G. Powells, by A. Mitchener, J. P.

Luvett, Barnaby & Edny Broadstreet, 17 Nov 1821; Wm. Hinton, bm.

Lyles, Drury & Winefred High, 23 Oct 1801; Seth Holliman, bm.

Lyles, Kinchen & Penny Strickland, 28 Feb 1798; Samuel Wilder, Jr., bm.

Lynch, Benjamin & Sally Bass, 23 Aug 1866; Festus Oliver, bm; m 26 Aug 1866 by Elisha Holland, M. G.

Lynch, Cornelius & Cynthea Pinks, 27 Feb 1799; Needham Whitley, bm.

Lynch, Nicholas & Nancy Davis, 25 Jun 1814; Chs. Stevens, bm.

Lynch, William & Polly Lupo, 19 Aug 1809; Wm. Jones, bm.

Lynch, William A. & Mary Hughes, m 11 Dec 1860 at Bengeman Hughs, by B. Lane, J. P.

McCalep, James & Lurana Durham, 29 Mar 1805; Willis Watson, bm.

McClam, Thomas & Jane Barefoot, 24 Feb 1838; Handy Barefoot, bm.

McClam, William & Nancy Tartt, 26 Jan 1839; Jesse Weaver, bm.

McClendon, Jesse & Ferebe McConico, 29 May 1793; Henry Gray, bm.

McCloud, Roderick & Cady Godwin, 24 May 1808; Sam'l Lee, Jr., bm.

McCullers, Edwin S. & Sophrona Warren, 28 May 1835; William C. McCullers, bm.

McCullers, George & Sally Dupree, 6 Jan 1823; Bythan Bryan, bm.

McCullers, Green (colored) & Rachael McCullers, 3 Nov 1866; Bennett Ellington, bm; m 10 Nov 1866 by S. H. Hood, J. P.

McCullers, John & Ann Sanders, 19 Sept 1771; Zadak Stallings, bm.

McCullers, Lewis & Margaret Wilson, 27 May 1823; B. Robin Hood, bm.

McCullers, Matthew & Sally Farmer, 6 Jan 1834; Thos. Eason, bm.

McCullers, Matthew & Sarah S. Warren, 9 May 1846; Willie T. Jones, bm.

McCullers, William (colored) & Candis Horne, 16 Nov 1866; Romeo Smith, Haywood Ellis, bm.

McCullers, William H. & Salina Hinton, 18 Sept 1843; W. T. Jones, bm.

McCullers, William H. Jr. & Mary E. Bell, 25 May 1843; Jno. D. Pate, bm.

McGee, Thomas & Patsey Bell, 4 Aug 1843; Robt. W. Stevens, bm.

McGlauhon, William & Margarett Dement, 28 Oct 1793; Ryon Wood, bm.

McGloughhorn, William & Caty Keen, 23 May 1814; Allen S. Ballinger, bm.

McHondikie, John & Penny Lee, 2 Dec 1795; Henry Stevens, bm.

McLam, Isham & Harriet Webb, 16 Sept 1862; m 17 Sept 1862 by R. W. Stevens, J. P.

McLam, Ishum & Phebe Tart, 11 Jan 1848; Wm. McLam, bm.

McLam, John & Elizabeth An Young, 29 Nov 1842; Joel G. Hutson, bm.

McLam, Robert & Betsy Jonergan, 13 Dec 1848; Wm. McLam, bm.

McLam, Thomas & Juda C. Beasley, 9 Jan 1864; m 20 Jan 1864 at Phebe Wilkins', by R. A. Adams, J. P.

McLean, John & Louinza Leach, 1 Feb 1839; Leroy Jones, bm.

McLenny, Samuel & Elizabeth Noles, 29 Nov 1810; Samuel Lee, Jr., bm.

McPherson, Duncan & Edith Broadstreet, 4 Oct 1840; Jordan Cowell, bm.

McPherson, Duncan & Mary Jane Gurly, 26 Dec 1846; Wm. H. Morning, bm.

Mace, Jonas & Elizabeth Newsom, 26 Oct 1805; Equilla Mace, bm.

Mahanes, Raiford R. & _____, 26 Nov 1844; Thomas Cole, bm.

Mainard, John & Polly Howard, 10 Feb 1828; Green Adams, bm.

Malaby, Samuel & Rebecca Tucker, 17 Sept 1834; William Grier, bm.

Man, Jonas & Mary Sims, 17 Nov 1794; William Braswell, bm.

Manden, John & Phereby Johnson, 2 May 1843; Hardy Barber, bm.

Maning, Meritt & Charity Baily, 19 Aug 1828; Wm. R. Privett, bm.

Manker, Lewis & Mary Lynch, 21 Jan 1852, m 22 Jan 1852 by E. Atkinson, J. P.

Manning, James & Pherebee Bailey, 29 Nov 1836; John Manning, bm.

Manning, Richard & Mary Porter, 25 Sept 1841; Wm. R. Lee, bm.

Manor, George & Sally Whitington, 22 Nov 1799; Richard Whitington, Isaac Johnson, bm.

Manor, James & Polly Johnson, 21 Oct 1802; Willie Johnson, Henry Johnson, bm.

Marsall, William & Naomy Norris, 3 May 1790; William Blunt, bm.

Martin, Haywood & Emily Dixon, 1 Dec 1841; Benjamin Godwin, bm.

Martin, Walter D. & Elizabeth H. Roper, m 18 Feb 1854 by J. B. Jackson.

Martin, William & Patsy Barber, 4 May 1811; Benjamin Martin, bm.

Martin, William & Martha Adams, 26 Mar 1852; m 1 Apr 1852 by R. W. Stevens, J. P.

Masingill, George Jr. & Polly Cotton, 12 Sept 1820.

Mason, John & Susan Price, 19 Sept 1846; Richardson Oneal, bm.

Mason, William & Celia Woodard, 9 May 1836; William Oneal, bm.

Massey, Charles C. & Mary W. Toler, 23 Feb 1859; m 24 Feb 1859 by T. H. Atkinson, J. P.

Massey, P. T. & Laura Snead, 31 Aug 1863; m 1 Sept 1863 at Thos E. Sneads, by L. S. Burkhead, M. G.

Massey, Wesley & Zilphea E. Phillips, 26 Oct 1835; Charles Massey, bm.

Massey, West & _____, 4 Nov 1846; James Hinnant, bm.

Massingale, Ethreld & Esther Blackman, 22 Dec 1794; John Blackman, bm.

Massingale, Sterling & Sally Reaves, 4 Jan 1837; Needham Masingill, bm.

Massingale, Warren & Lucy Massingale, 17 Dec 1825; Noel West, bm.

Massingil, George & Elizabeth Blackman, 6 ___ 1797; Etheldred Massingill, bm.

Massingill, A. G. & Sarah A. Temple, 11 Feb 1860; m 12 Feb 1860 by George Keen, J. P.

Massingill, Aaron & Wilsey Harper, 25 Mar 1846; R. W. Stevens, bm.

Massingill, Aaron W. & Ammy Harper, 4 Aug 1851; m 12 Aug 1851 by H. H. Finch, J. P.

Massingill, Aaron W. & Nancy Willey Harper, m 15 Mar 1855 by C. Langdon, J. P.

Massingill, George & William[sic] Everytt, 23 Feb 1810.

Massingill, George & Nancy Ann Jernigan, m 6 Mar 1856 at Cader Jernigan, by W. H. Massingill, J. P.

Massingill, Henry & Henry & Lucy Temple, 28 Dec 1801; Sterling Temple, bm.

Massingill, Henry & Rhoda Blackman, 27 Nov 1866; Ezekiel Creech, bm; m 29 Nov 1866 at Winnyford Ellice, by George Keen, J. P.

Massingill, Josiah & Amy Baker, 11 Feb 1858; m 18 Feb 1858 by George Keen, J. P.

Massingill, Needham G. & Sally Temple, 17 Dec 1846; George Keen, bm.

Massingill, Robert & Sally Sellers, 15 Aug 1798; Equillah Mace, bm.

Massingill, Robert & Sally Lee, 1 Jan 1829; Sterling W. Temple. bm.

Massingill, Robert & Martha Flowers, 7 Jan 1846; Bartlet Harper, bm.

Massingill, Robbert & _____, 25 Oct 1849; R. H. Temple, bm.

Massingilll, W. T. & Martha J. Blackman, 21 Feb 1860; m 23 Feb 1860 at R. H. Blackman, by George Keen, J. P.

Massingill, William B. & Mary Lassiter, m 16 Feb 1861 at Alfred Lassiters, by George Keen, J. P.

Massy, Charles & Zelpha Stallings, 29 Apr 1824; Collin Stallings, bm.

Massy, Cogdell & Polly Hollowell, 10 Oct 1823; William Spencer, bm.

Massy, John & Dicy Killingworth, 12 Oct 1810l Maurill Gurley, bm.

Massy, John & Louisa Creech, 10 Aug 1829; Wm. Massey, Jr., bm.

Mathews, Isaac & Sarah Martin, 24 Dec 1836; Haywood Martin, bm.

Mathews, Isreal & Peney Dixon, 6 Jan 1846; William R. Lee, bm.

Matthews, Jacob & Sarah Farmer, 3 May 1800; Jinkins Farmer, bm.

Matthews, John & Polly Williams, 19 Dec 1787; Thomas Matthews, bm.

Matthews, Joseph & Rhoda Carrell, 14 Jul 1832; Robert Whitmore, bm.

May, Little Berry & Patty Gregory, 14 Jun 1790; Thomas Price, Edward Price, bm.

Medlin, Alfred & Ady Smith, 10 Sept 1806; William Johnson, bm.

Medlin, Burgess & Susan Lynch, 24 Jun 1808; Johnson Busbee, bm.

Medlin, Drury & Sarah Johnson, 21 Feb 1793; Isaac Jones, bm.

Medlin, Haywood & Winefred Batten, m 16 Jan 1854 by B. Oneal, J. P.

Medlin, Hillsmon H. & Lucy M. Strickland, 17 Apr 1855; m 18 Apr 1855 by S. W. Woody, J. P.

Medlin, Johnson & Tempy Ferrell, 24 Dec 1826; James Jones, bm.

Mercer, Jacob & Zilpha Page, 23 Aug 1813; William Smith, bm.

Mercer, William & Nancy Dosey, 15 Aug 1811; William W. Hopkins, bm.

Messer, Aldridge & Elizabeth Kenedy, 11 Mar 1835; John Messer, bm.

Messer, Alexander & Peggy Stephenson, m 29 Dec 1851 by A. Corts, J. P.

Messer, Bryant & Jane Shaw, 27 Dec 1826; John Messer, bm.

Messer, Green Parker & Mary E. Stephenson, 14 May 1852; m 15 May 1852 by A. Coats, J. P.

Messer, John & Nancy Flu Ellen, 2 Jun 1848; John B. Allen, bm.

Messer, Thomas & Winefred Norsworthy, 15 Aug 1808; Thomas Barber, bm.

Messer, Thomas & Polly Sills, 9 Sept 1821; William Sanders, bm.

Messer, Whitley & Susan Johnston, 24 Jun 1843; John Messer, bm.

Messer, Whitley & Winefred Stephenson, m 12 Dec 1861 at Nancy Messers, by R. W. Stevens, J. P.

Messer, Whitly & Thena Johnson, 17 Oct 1827; John Messer, bm.

Messer, William & Polley Barber, 2 Apr 1787; Phir Barber, bm.

Messer, William & Nancy Woodall, 13 Jun 1821; John Messer, bm.

Messer, William W. & Louenza Parnold, 10 Apr 1866; Wm. H. Morning, bm.

Mials, Isaac & Olivia Ruffin, 13 Jun 1866; W. M. Murphy, bm.

Mickleroy, Avington & Sarah Dawson 7 Mar 1770; William Dawson, William Mickleroy, bm.

Midyett, Asa B. & Elizabeth Hinton, 9 Oct 1820; Allen S. Ballinger, bm.

Midyett, Micajah & Nicy Brooks, 12 Feb 1821; Horn Midyett, bm.

Millinder, Furney & Susan Brown, 18 Dec 1854; m 19 Dec 1854 by E. L. Jones, J. P.

Milliner, Furney & Ailsey Lynch, 13 Mar 1839; James Roberts, bm.

Milliner, Henry & Mary Futrell, 27 Feb 1841; J. H. Stevens, bm.

Minga, Edward & Martha Lewis, 27 Mar 1860.

Mitchel, Fredrick & Betsy Thomas, 4 May 1822; Needham Warren, bm.

Mitchel, George & Nancy Howell, 7 Jul 1852; m 8 Jul 1852 by William Rains, J. P.

Mitchel, Hinnant & Mary Parnel, 10 Jul 1852; m 11 Jul 1852 by Wm. Rains, J. P.

Mitchell, Dealia & Mary Howell, m 29 Sept 1857 by William Rains, J. P.

Mitchell, Henry & Polley Avera, 4 Sept 1792; Alexander Avera, bm.

Mitchell, John & Nancy Stucky, 3 Jan 1827; Isaac Boothe, bm.

Mitchell, William & Emily Edwards, 10 Jun 1846; Wilie Holt, bm; m by Willie Holt, J. P.

Mitchell, William & Elizabeth T. Hood, m 15 Dec 1852 by R. C. Richardson, J. P.

Mitchell, Willie & Polly Ann Pearce, 20 Jul 1852; m 22 Jul 1852 by William Rains, J. P.

Mitchener, Agrippa & Nancy Ann Atkinson, 6 May 1847; Henry H. Hobbs, bm.

Mitchener, Festus & Polly A. Wilder, 11 Sept 1845l; John Mitchener, bm.

Mitchner, Samuel & Frances Norris, 28 Jan 1799; John Bryan, Jr., bm.

Mitchner, Samuel & Patsey Lockhart, 8 Sept 1802; Jno. Stevens, Jr., bm.

Mobley, William & Lucy Allen, 1 Mar 1770; Edward Mobly, bm.

Monk, Willis & Celia Pool, 16 Jun 1788; Simon Watson, bm.

Montague, John C. & Eliza Dees, 14 Dec 1824; Wm. Hen. Guy, bm.

Moody, David & Patsy Edward, 29 Sept 1808; John Williams, bm.

Moody, William & Joanna Hocut, 6 Jul 1849; Lunford Bailey, bm.

Moanaham, John & Frances Tant, 28 Feb 1823; William Moonahan, bm.

Moor, James & Seney Rentfrow, 10 Jan 1850; G. W. Godwin, bm.

Moore, Benjamin & Lucy Adams, 24 Mar 1830; Bryan Allen, bm.

Moore, Benjamin & Polly Webb, 27 Aug 1816; Hardy Adams, bm.

Moore, Haywood & Darkas Green, m 6 Jan 1859 at H. L. Sanders by George Keen, J. P.

Moore, Henry & Celia Ann Beasley, 20 Oct 1843; Simeon Woodall, bm.

Moore, John & Sarah D. Cross, 15 Feb 1858; m 21 Feb 1858 at the residence of Sarah Ryals, by W. F. Hall, Elder.

Moore, Josefus & Ruthey Simpson, 11 Feb 1850; Thomas Price, bm.

Moore, Lewis & Elisabeth Sanders, 11 May 1779; John Moore, bm.

Moore, Lewis & Rachael Britt, 19 Feb 1805; Thomas Folsom, bm.

Moore, Nathaniel & Sally Raiper, 28 Jan 1852; m 26 Feb 1852 by Noel Barnes, J. P.

Moore, Randolph & Elisabeth Stansel, 10 Jun 1783; Amos Atkerson, bm.

Moore, Right & Elizabeth Pugh, 23 Mar 1824; Josiah Houlder, bm.

Moore, Stansell & Patsey Barnes, 3 Jan 1810; Elias Barnes, bm.

Moore, Walter R. & Amanda Barber, m 28 Jun 1864 at Mrs. Dorcas Windhams, by R. W. Stevens, J. P.

Morgan, Allen & Crecy Oliver, 29 Mar 1825; Kinchen Q. Adams, bm.

Morgan, Allen & Angeline Barber, 26 Oct 1844; Peter R. Temple, bm.

Morgan, Bryant & Sally Johnson, 19 Feb 1853; m 6 Mar 1853 by R. W. Stevens, J. P.

Morgan, Eli & Maria Sasser, 21 Jun 1845; Jacob A. Stevens, bm.

Morgan, James W. & Lucy Johnson, 1 Sept 1847; Zachariah Tiner, bm.

Morgan, Jesse & Esther Allen, 2 Jan 1795; James Woodall, bm.

Morgan, John & Patsey Blackman, 23 Oct 1845; Wm. Rilie Tart, bm.

Morgan, Kinchen & Polly Johnson, 16 Jan 1854; m 19 Jan 1854 by R. W. Stevens, J. P.

Morgan, Nathan A. & Penellope Barber, 6 Feb 1825; Young Morgan, bm.

Morgan, Needham & Sally Denn, 28 Apr 1851; m 1 May 1851 by Wm. Bugram, J. P.

Morgan, Needham & Martha Johnson, 14 Nov 1853; m 17 Nov 1853 by Needham Ingram, J. P.

Morgan, Needham & Elizabeth Werly, m 1 Oct 1860 by B. A. Wellons, J. P.

Morgan, S. R. & Martha A. Thornton, 31 Jan 1860 m by R. D. Lunceford, J. P.

Morgan, Simeon R. & Manizur Simpkins, 7 May 1856; m 8 May 1856 at the Smithfield Hotel, by P. J. Carraway, M. G.

Morgan, Thomas & Patsey Freeman, m 24 Aug 1859 by Lemmon Shell.

Morgan, William & Edith Johnson, 14 Nov 1818; William Johnson, bm.

Morgan, William & Rebecca Barefoot, 1 Jan 1852; m 4 Jan 1852 by Harry Johnson, J. P.

Morgan, William & Martha Ann Hicks, 12 Jan 1853; m 13 Jan 1853 by S. N. Moody, J. P.

Morgan, William G. & Martha Wood, 1 Nov 1859; m 3 Mar 1859 at Whitfield Woods, by John C. Hood, J. P.

Morgan, Young & Kiddy Oliver, 2 Mar 1822; Henry Lane, bm.

Morgan, Young & Zilpha Gurly, m 29 Mar 1856 at Smithfield, by J. G. Gulley, J. P.

Morning, William H. & Phebe T. Babcock, 1 Jun 1848; Edwin Boykin, bm.

Morris, John & Elizabeth Beal, 17 Jan 1825; John Beal, bm.

Morris, Riddick & Alley Grantham, 28 Mar 1837; Thos. Toler, bm.

Morris, Stephen & Martha Atkinson, 23 Oct 1845; John Holt, bm.

Morris, Stephen & Caroline Grantham, 1 Feb 1867; Thos. Cole, bm; m 2 Feb 1867 at Sidney Granthams, by Bryant Williams, J. P.

Mott, Benjamin & Ester Guven, 31 Aug 1784; Solomon Staton, bm.

Munden, John & Julia Y. Hines, m 31 Aug 1857 by B. A. Wellons, J. P.

Munden, W. H. & Harriet Johnson, m 14 Apr 1859 by B. A. Wellons, J. P.

Munden, William & Sally Vinson, 1 Feb 1826; John Sanders, bm.

Munford, James & Nancy Watson, 28 Feb 1859; m 17 Mar 1859 by Thos. Faulk, J. P.

Munds, Alexander & Elizur Barber, 24 Jan 1855; m 28 Jan 1855 by R. W. Stevens, J. P.

Munns, Samuel & Mary Huneycut, 7 Oct 1852; m 10 Oct 1852 by R. W. Stevens, J. P.

Murfry, John & Phereby Wall, 23 Aug 1831; Bennet Wall, bm.

Murphey, William M. & Lucretia Gay, 23 Nov 1859; m 24 Nov 1859 at Johnson B. Wall, by Wm. B. Wall, J. P.

Murphree, John & Polly Green, 23 Sept 1828; Bryan Whitley, bm.

Murphrey, Mathew M. & Sally Johnson, 1 Aug 1835; Furney Green, bm.

Murphrey, Woodruff & Amanda Eason, 26 Jan 1867; B. G. Carroll, bm; m 29 Jan 1867 at Avera Eason's, by Jesse Hinnant, J. P.

Murphy, W. G. & Sarah C. Hinton, 5 Feb 1859; m 20 Feb 1859 by R. N. Gully, J. P.

Murry, Duncan & _____, 2 Nov 1784; John Barefoot, bm.

Murry, James & Eliza Ryals, 7 Oct 1852; m 8 Oct 1852 by R. W. Stevens, J. P.

Musgrove, F. M. & Manerva A. Wall, 2 Apr 1862; m 20 Apr 1862 at Aaron Wall's residence, by Wright Blow, J. P.

Musslewhite, Drury & Annis Capse, 10 Dec 1782; Matthew Capse, bm.

Musslewhite, William & Margaret Stricklon, 11 Mar 1780; Edmond Griffin, bm.

Musslewhite, William & Patsy Overby, 4 Dec 1821; William Tule(?), bm.

Naaron, John & Nanny Watkins, 22 Mar 1827; Burwell Johnson, bm.

Nairn, Aquilla & ____ Bailey, 15 Nov 1782; William Holliman, bm.

Nall, Martin, of Wake Co., & Aley Carrell, 7 Sept 1823; Reuben Sanders, bm.

Naron, Aquilla & Eliza Talton, 29 Sept 1857; Riley Naron, bm; m 30 Sept 1857 by A. H. Atkinson, J. P.

Naron, Barden & Renda Talton, 24 Feb 1852; m 28 Feb 1852 by S. W. Woody, J. P.

Naron, Braswell & Tempy Prker, 1 Oct 1799; Joseph L. Broughton, bm.

Naron, John & Milly Price, 22 Nov 1819; Wm. Johnson, bm.

Naron, John & Patience Watkins, 4 Jul 1842; Josiah Holliman, bm.

Naron, Richmond & Delsey Baily, 14 Jan 1825; Calvin Lee, bm.

Naron, Wriley & Gilly Bailey, 29 Nov 1842; Samuel W. Woody, bm.

Narriz, Bryant H. & Suzan C. Jordan, 20 Apr 1849; R. W. Stevens, bm.

Narron, Aquilla & Elizabeth Bailey, 11 Oct 1822; Josiah Holliman, bm.

Narron, Aquilly & Polly Lee, m 26 Aug 1866 by J. W. Woody, J. P.

Narron, Larken & Martha Shellington, 6 Jul 1863; m 30 Jul 1863 by J. Lewis, J. P.

Neal, W. H. & Sarah M. Edwards, 26 Feb 1867; W. P. Raiford, bm; m 5 Mar 1867 at Mrs. Sarah Edwards's, by W. P. Raiford, J. P.

Nelms, William & Polly Tarver, 5 Oct 1825; Ryal W. Frost, bm.

Nelms, William & Polly Deloach, 24 May 1825; Ryal W. Frost, bm.

Nelson, Wilson & Sarah Wall, 6 Aug 1784; Jesse Wall, bm.

Nicholas, Moses & Nancy Car, 26 Feb 1806; Dempsey Car, bm.

Nichols, Benjamin & Ferreby Boyet, 28 Aug 1811; Henry Sasser, bm.

Nichols, David & Harriet Crocker, 13 Jan 1859; m 18 Jan 1859 at Mrs. Crockers, her mothers, by Edwin Boykin, J. P.

Nichols, Etheld. & Cenith Harrell, 9 Dec 1837; John Worley, bm.

Nichols, Josiah & Nancy Hocut, 11 Jan 1823; Gibson Martin, bm.

Nichols, William & Sarrah Ann Terry, m 18 Feb 1853 by Jno. P. Cook, bm.

Nichols, William W. & Sarah Ann Roberts, m 6 Apr 1863 at Smithfield, by Wm. H. Morning, J. P.

Nordan, William & Edith A. Adams, 8 Oct 1857; T. Ives, bm; m 8 Oct 1857 by J. H. Keneday, J. P.

Norris, Haywood & Sallie Ann Holmes, 1 Sept 1862; m 2 Sept 1862 at James Narn, by Wm. F. Hall, Elder.

Norris, Reuben & Elizabeth Britt, 14 Jan 1797; Thos. Folsom, bm.

Norris, William & Winefred Honeycut, 1 Jan 1849; R. W. Stevens, bm.

Norris, Winfrey & Amy Eliza Rainer, 22 Mar 1866; J. B. Holmes, bm.

Norriss, James & Jane Holmes, 5 Aug 1831; Plyer Barber, bm.

Norriss, Nahor & Sally Averyt, 22 Feb 1797; John Sanders, bm.

Norsworth, Samuel & Elizabeth Hawkins Hinton, 22 Jul 1802; Matthew Handy, bm.

Nowell, Mark & Vicy Jourdan, 13 Jun 1817; Henry Jourdan, bm.

Nowell, William & Martha Earp, 23 Oct 1819; John Howell, bm.

Nutt, Bennet & Leucy Smith, 11 Feb 1815; Benjamin Smith, bm.

Odam, William & Rebecca Hill, 28 Mar 1814; Isaac Williams, bm.

Odom, James & Betsy Hearne, 24 Sept 1798; Mason Hearne, bm.

Odom, John & Nancy Low, 4 Jul 1834; Jesse Hinnant, bm.

Odom, Levy & Zilpha Lamb, 13 Jun 1829; Jacob Odom, bm.

Ogbourn, Stephenson & Mary Ann Price, 27 Sept 1853; m 29 Sept 1853 by J. T. Leach, J. P.

Ogburn, James & Edith Youngblood, 5 May 1791; Thomas Youngblood, bm.

Oliver, Asa & Nancy Wise, 9 Jan 1812; William Oliver, bm.

Oliver, Ashly R. & Cathran A. Bosweth, 5 Aug 1847; Wilie Holt, bm.

Oliver, E. M. & Julia A. Adams, 24 Oct 1857; John U. Oliver, bm; m 27 Oct 1857 by George Keen, J. P.

Oliver, E. R. & Susan L. Tiner, 11 Jan 1859; m 13 Jan 1859 at James Tiners, by George Keen, J. P.

Oliver, Henry & Winey Ingram, 13 Nov 1799; William Powers, bm.

Oliver, Henry & Hulday Woodard, 24 Apr 1838; Jesse Holt, bm.

Oliver, James & Edith Johnson, 22 Jul 1825; Robert H. Helme, bm.

Oliver, James B. & Arcady Futrell, 14 Apr 1866; Alexander Thain, bm; m 15 Apr 1866 at Jesse Futerals, by Perry Godwin, J. P.

Oliver, John & Sarah Edwards, 22 Jan 1783; Elisha Thomas, bm.

Oliver, John & Evaline Watson, m 11 Jan 1856 by Wm. H. Sellers, J. P.

Oliver, Levy & Barsheba Raiford, 4 Jan 1820; William M. Carter, bm.

Oliver, Lewis & Polly Strickland, 24 Sept 1822; Stephen Oliver, bm.

Oliver, Lewis B. & Julia H. Tiner, 18 Oct 1858; m 31 Oct 1858 at Zachiea Rea, by George Keen, J. P.

Oliver, McKinnie & Lotty Raiford, 30 Aug 1821; Levi Oliver, bm.

Oliver, Robert & Moliana Wellons, 11 Feb 1840; McKinne Oliver, bm.

Oliver, Robert M. & Mary A. Melvina Starling, 13 Jan 1857; m 5 Feb 1857 by Wm. H. Sellers, J. P.

Oliver, Stephen & Polly Brasswell, 7 Oct 1795; John Oliver, bm.

Oliver, Thomas & Elizabeth Pool, 13 Aug 1790; Isac Stallings, bm.

Oliver, Thomas & Ancy Watson, 24 Aug 1829; Soloman Futrell, bm.

Oliver, W. Berry & Mary Pauline Peeden, 8 Apr 1856; m 10 Apr 1856 by Edwin Boykin, J. P.

Oliver, William & Winifred Teel, 28 Jan 1815; Asa Oliver, bm.

Oliver, William & Joannah Creach, 22 Mar 1834; Stephen Oliver, bm.

Oneal, Bryan & Pherebee Pool, 9 Dec 1826; Reuben Sanders, bm.

Oneal, Buck & Leasey Richardson, 22 Sept 1866; Perry Godwin, bm; m 27 Sept 1866 at Henderson Barnes, by Josiah Hinnant, J. P.

Oneal, Condarey & Leasy Bailey, 5 Oct 1826; Micajah Oneal, bm.

Oneal, Hopson & Lany Oneal, 1 Aug 1833; Benjamin Hocut, bm.

Oneal, James & Elizabeth Richardson, 25 Nov 1806; Allen Richardson, bm.

Oneal, Manly & Rebecca Hare, 22 Nov 1848; S. R. Stansell, bm.

Oneal, Micajah & Clarany Richardson, 21 Jan 1768; Thomas Tomlinson, Isom Oneal, bm.

Oneal, Samuel & Esther Price, 14 Oct 1806; Allen Richardson, bm.

Oneal, Stephen & Nancy Richardson, 11 Jan 1817; Benjamin Hocut, bm.

Oneal, William & Elizabeth Stevens, 29 Jan 1788; Frederick Holliman, bm.

Oneal, William Jr. & Harriet Richardson, 20 Jan 1827; Wm. Oneal, Sr., bm.

Oneal, William Jr. & Sally Hare, 9 Feb 1842; Nathan Oneal, bm.

Oneal, Willie & Polley Holmes, 24 Feb 1819; Joshua Musgrove, bm.

Oneil, Bridgers & Polly Hinton, 29 Aug 1798; Simon Price, bm.

Oneil, Isom & Ann Arrundell, 23 Apr 1779; Elisha Thomas, bm.

Oneil, Isom & Ann Pearce, 14 Oct 1800; Moses Oniel, John Pearce, bm.

Oneil, Isom Jr. & Savel Hill, 20 Nov 1808; Lodwick Oneal, bm.

Oneil, Kendrid & Culia Hayles, 21 Feb 1810; Moses Oneil, bm.

Oneil, Lodwick & Betsy Wilder, 5 Jan 1807; Thomas Oneal, bm.

Oneil, Samuel & Kiddy Hinton, 18 Feb 1802; Silas Oneil, bm.

Oneil, Samuel & Bedith Horton, 28 Feb 1804.

Oneil, Silas & Mary Grizzell, 25 Nov 1800; Harbard Gilman, bm.

Oneil, Thomas & Barsheby Richardson, 7 Oct 1795; Wm. Hackney, bm.

Oneil, Warren & Sally Richardson, 1 Oct 1799; James Gregory, bm.

Oneil, William & Pherebe Claney, 1 Dec 1784; Thomas Gray, bm.

Oneil, William & Elizabeth Hocut, 21 Nov 1789; William Richardson, bm.

Oniel, Samuel & Phereby Bailey, 27 Aug 1788; Wm. Oneal, bm.

Oniel, William & Rene Hinton, 1 Dec 1801; Bryant Richardson, bm.

Orr, Samuel & Mary Durham, _____ ; Matthew Durham, bm.

Overby, Edwin & Penny Barber, 2 Sept 1837; Wm. T. Roberts, bm.

Overby, Jesse & Betsy Errant, 11 Jan 1820; Joseph Edwards, bm.

Overby, Martin & Sarah Fluellen, 9 Aug 1811; William Roberts, bm.

Overby, Parker & Rachel Waddell, 1 Nov 1848; William A. Jones, bm.

Owen, Elijah & Teresa Stokes, 18 Dec 1835; Sterling Temple, bm.

Pace, Alsey & Zilpha Hall, 21 Sept 1820; James Carrell, bm.

Pace, Alsey & Cassanda Dean, 6 Mar 1837; Hiram Chamblee, bm.

Pace, Bartly & Zilphey Batten, 15 Jan 1850; Henry Starling, bm.

Pace, Larry & Cinthy Batten, 8 Apr 1856; m 9 Apr 1856 at James H. Bettens, by Ransom Kirby, J. P.

Pace, Stephen & Lucy Walker, 8 Mar 1799; Majer Walker, bm.

Page, Allen & Polly Lee, 27 Sept 1820; Plyer Barbee, bm.

Page, Britain & Nancy Garner, 9 Sept 1809; Thomas Page, bm.

Page, John & Mary Johnson, 29 Oct 1788; Thomas Page, bm.

Page, Sion & Eliza Burnett, 24 Jul 1827; Hardy Holmes, bm.

Page, Thomas & Candis Honeycut, 23 Mar 1826; William White, bm.

Page, Tobias & Polly Johnson, 19 Sept 1794; Isom Johnson, bm.

Pair, Nelson D., of Wake Co., & Emily Richardson, 27 Nov 1843; Edwd. Debnam, bm.

Parish, Alsey & Emily Hocott, 24 May 1852; m 25 Aug 1852 by A. W. Richardson, J. P.

Parish, Augustus & Edith Ellington, 30 Dec 1835; Lovet Spivy, bm.

Parish, David & Betsey Johnson, 25 Nov 1819; Joel Clifton, bm.

Parish, Gaston & Thebes Ferrell, _____ ; Lovet Spivy, bm.

Parish, Isham & Sarah Stevens, 23 Feb 1841; James Lassiter, bm.

Parish, James & Elizabeth Jones, 7 Dec 1827; William Jones, bm.

Parish, John & Betsy Ferrell, 28 Nov 1801; John Ellis, bm.

Parish, John F. & Delany Hocutt, 12 Jan 1861; m 13 Jan 1861 at E. D. Whitleys, by W. Earp, J. P.

Parish, Johnson & Patsy Stevens, 11 Mar 1815; Britin Langdon, bm.

Parish, Johnson & Harriet Parrish, 5 Aug 1842; Ransom Parish, bm.

Parish, Justis & Avy Fluellen, 20 May 1797; Jno. Jones, bm.

Parish, Nathan & Edith Parish, 12 Mar 1859; m 16 Mar 1859 by Moore Stephenson.

Parish, Peter & Edith Stevenson, 16 Nov 1819; Garard Stevenson, bm.

Parish, Ransom & Harriet Johnson, 4 Feb 1846; McCoy Johnson, bm.

Parish, William & Edith Langdon, 25 Jul 1821; David Parish, bm.

Parish, William & Temperance Stevens, 1 Dec 1840; Isam Parish, bm.

Parke, Pharaoh & Jane Young, 25 Nov 1851; m 9 Dec 1861 by N. L. Phillips, J. P.

Parker, Amos & Patience Jarrell, 18 Aug 1794; Matthew Parker, bm.

Parker, Benjamin & Betsy Rentfrow, 7 Jan 1837; Jesse Parker, bm.

Parker, Edward L. & Ellen C. Northam, 19 Dec 1863; m 23 Dec 1863 by L. S. Burkhead.

Parker, Elijah & Sally Barefoot, 23 Feb 1836; John C. Hood, bm.

Parker, Gabriel & Olive Moore, 29 Nov 1798; Joseph Richardson, bm.

Parker, Hardy & Phereby Bailey, 25 Feb 1789; Joseph Irwin, bm.

Parker, Jesse & Martha Rentfrow, 26 May 1852; m 15 Jun 1852 by James Hinnant.

Parker, Joel B. & Elizabeth E. Johnson, 29 Oct 1857; Joshua Johnson, bm; m 1 Nov 1857 by John C. Hood, J. P.

Parker, John H. & Elizabeth Massey, 1 May 1866; N. G. Massey, bm.

Parker, John W. & Alie Wood, 12 Jan 1861; m 17 Jan 1861 at Whitfield Woods, by J. C. Hood, J. P.

Parker, Leonard & Esther Ann Ingram, 3 Jan 1867; N. R. Parker, bm; m 6 Jan 1867 at Joseph B. Parkers, by Jas. H. Adams, J. P.

Parker, Matthew & Elizabeth Hinnant, 15 Oct 1829; Josiah Hinnant, Jr., bm.

Parker, Matthew & Vetura Wellons, 12 Jun 1849; Henry Bagly, bm.

Parker, Matthew Jr. & Mary Odom, 27 Aug 1793; Hardy Parker, bm.

Parker, Noah B. & Jane E. Tart, 24 Jan 1861; m 27 Jan 1861 at William Tarts, by John C. Hood, J. P.

Parker, Powell & Cyntha Parker, 7 Feb 1825; Wiley Jones, bm.

Parker, Stephen & Rachel Johnson, 1 Oct 1798; Matthew Parker, bm.

Parker, Stephen & Patsey Peebles, 11 Sept 1845; Jesse Parker, bm.

Parker, William F. & Mary L. H. Creech, 2 Feb 1867; R. W. Stevens, bm; m 6 Feb 1867 at Noah Creeches, by Abram Dixon, J. P.

Parnel, Alsey & Louenza Holt, m 17 Nov 1859 at Joseph Holts, by R. W. Stevens, J. P.

Parnel, Solomon & Viney Eason, 13 Apr 1821; Henry Parnel, bm.

Parnell, Archibell & Ann Caps, 15 Jan 1806; John Eason, bm.

Parnell, Curtis & Polly Ingram, 16 Mar 1835; Barnaba Hamilton, bm.

Parnell, Devreaux & Martha Parnell, 19 Jan 1867; Robt. Watson, bm; m 20 Jan 1867 by W. F. Gerald, J. P.

Parnell, Jeremiah & Nancy Strickland, 22 Jul 1824; Redick Warren, bm.

Parnell, John & Peggy Clemmons, 25 Mar 1794; Jethro Bulls, bm.

Parnold, Archibald & Penny Tedder, 4 Feb 1808; Henry Parnel, bm.

Parnold, Gideon & Elizabeth Brown, 26 Dec 1823; Jesse Sterling, bm.

Parnold, Henry & Nancy Starling, 27 Feb 1798; Arthur Bailey Johnson, bm.

Parnold, Henry & Edith Starling, 8 Apr 1824; Alvin L. Smith, bm.

Parnold, Irven & Anne Gerrald, 29 Oct 1835; Enos Gerald, bm.

Parnold, Jeremiah & Caty Stevens, 28 May 1816; Micajah Wilkinson, bm.

Parnold, Moses & Welthy Parnold, 26 Mar 1826; Young Morgan, bm.

Parnold, Solomon & Sarah Tomlin, 26 May 1801; Burwell Johnson, bm.

Parnold, William & Clarky Parnold, 10 May 1843; Ely Garner, bm.

Parrish, Augustus W. & Harriet Hocott, 6 Jun 1853; m 8 Jun 1853 by C. J. Bingham, J. P.

Parrish, Caswell & Elizabeth Jones, 18 Jul 1853; m 21 Jul 1853 by C. J. Bingham, J. P.

Parrish, David Davie & Nancy Ann Eliza Jones, 30 Jan 1849; David Parrish, bm.

Parrish, James & Louisa Stephenson 30 Mar 1860; m 8 Mar 1860 at Tempy Parrish, by Eld. Moore Stephenson.

Parrish, Justus & Martha H. Godwin, 28 Jan 1856; m 29 Jan 1856 by J. G. Gully, J. P.

Parrish, Mordecai J. & Harriet E. Peacock, 8 Jan 1853; m 13 Jan 1853 by James Wilson, elder.

Parrish, Paschal B. & Nancy E. Langdon, 12 Oct 1866; L. Eldridge, bm; m 14 Oct 1866 by James A. Smith, J. P.

Parrish, Richard & Culie Ann Johnson, 19 Aug 1861; m 21 Aug 1861 at William Lambert, by W. H. Lambert, J. P.

Parrish, Samuel & Delaney Garner, m 27 Jan 1864 at Jacob Parrish, by Jesse Parker, J. P.

Parrish, Troy & Mary Parrish, 8 Jan 1851.

Parrot, Bridgers & Morning Crocker, 13 Sept 1838; Mark Freeman, bm.

Parsons, Nathan & Elizabeth Munden, 19 Jan 1836; John C. Montague, bm.

Partin, William H. & Sarah Ogburn, 11 Apr 1842; Washington Partin, bm.

Passons, William & Cuzzy Brogden, 24 Aug 1818; Loverd Eldridge, bm.

Pate, Edmund & Peggy Johnson, 18 Jan 1814; John Williams, bm.

Pate, Thomas J. D. & Susan Ann Holland, m 17 Aug 1864 at Aron Basses residence, by William Rains,

Pate, Travis & Ann Tomlinson, 28 Nov 1791; John Williams, bm.

Patterson, Warren & Theaney Eason, 23 Mar 1805; Levy Reavis, bm.

Peacock, Bryan & Polly Rains, 19 Jan 1836; John H. Rains, bm.

Peacock, C. C. & Bethany Jones, 17 Apr 1866; George Collins, bm.

Peacock, Carter & Nancy Rains, 11 Feb 1836; William Rains, bm.

Peacock, David & Charlotte Bryan, 26 Feb 1789; John Bryan, bm.

Peacock, Irdell & Harriet Ballance, 29 Feb 1848; G. H. Holland, bm.

Peacock, Jacob & Sally Holmes, 25 Aug 1806; Fredrick Homes, bm.

Peacock, John & Winefred Allen, 26 Dec 1835; Vin H. Adams, bm.

Peacock, John B. & Elizabeth Johnson, 18 Jan 1867; W. B. Tart, bm; m 22 Jan 1867 at Allen Johnson, by B. Godwin, J. P.

Peacock, Uriah & Zepha Hayles, 5 Nov 1815; Jno. A. Smith, bm.

Peacock, William & Nancy Roberson, 18 Jul 1836; Bryan Peacock, bm.

Peacock, William R. & Elenor Evans, 7 Jan 1836; Jonathan Evans, bm.

Peacok, Zadock & Nancy Hinnant, 26 Mar 1844; Stanford Creech, bm.

Pearce, Alfred & Patience Hinnant, 25 Mar 1858; m 28 Mar 1858 at James Hinnants, by Jesse Parker, J. P.

Pearce, Asa & Betsey Davis, 20 Mar 1802; Isaac Jarrell, bm.

Pearce, Barden & Tilethy Howell, 28 Jul 1847; David Thompson, bm.

Pearce, Dixon & Polly Godwin, 7 Feb 1827; David Thompson, bm.

Pearce, Edwin E. & Mindy Snipes, 24 Fev 1824; Allen S. Ballinger, bm.

Pearce, Ephraim I. & Clarkey Godwin, 17 Jul 1865; Bryant R. Hinnant, bm.

Pearce, Everitte & Kezziah Whitehead, m 23 Nov 1858 at Boon Hill, by Willie Holt, J. P.

Pearce, Frank M. & Tabitha Burden, 11 May 1866; Jethro Howell, bm.

Pearce, Henry & Ann Eliza Parrish, 10 Feb 1852; m 12 Feb 1852 by John F. Ellington.

Pearce, Iredell & Bethaney Williamson, 25 Feb 1840; Thomas Durham, bm.

Pearce, John & Charity Watkins, 20 Oct 1823; Loverd Pearce, bm.

Pearce, John & Jane Whittington, 31 Jan 1828; Samuel Peebles, bm.

Pearce, John P. & Pereby Godwin, 26 Mar 1834; James A. Turnel, bm.

Pearce, Kedar & Rhoda Waddell, 27 Aug 1805; Philip Pearce, bm.

Pearce, Larken & Sally Pearce, 26 Feb 1836; George W. Griffin, bm.

Pearce, Leavey & Nancey Davis, 4 Jun 1795; James Davis, bm.

Pearce, Philip & Patience Oliver, 31 Jul 1778; Averet Pearce, bm.

Pearce, Richard & Clarky Pearce, 4 Apr 1827; Simon A. Pearce, bm.

Pearce, Samuel & Nancy Bulls, 29 Jul 1813; Jno. Stevens, J. P.

Pearce, Simon & Polly Rains, 22 Sept 1807; John Rains, bm.

Pearce, Simon & Phereby Taylor, 15 Apr 1811; Simon Pearce, bm.

Pearce, Simon & Chloe Ann Wiggs, 25 Jan 1867; J. T. Bridgers, bm; m 28 Jan 1867 at Joseph Woodans, by Eld. Wms. Brown.

Pearce, Simon Jr. & Polly Rains, 20 Oct 1807; John Gully, W. Watson, bm.

Pearce, William & Betsy Hatcher, 31 Oct 1800; Levi Pearce, Robt. Gully, Jr., bm.

Pearce, William & Rany Hinnant, 14 May 1849; McC. Talton, bm.

Pearce, William & Elizabeth Lane, 7 Aug 1861; m 8 Aug 1861 by W. D. Holt, J. P.

Pearse, Eli & Peggy Watkins, 23 May 1809; Philip Raiford, Freeman Killingsworth, bm.

Pearson, John & Penny Taylor, 26 Feb 1806; Simon Pearce, bm.

Pearson, Peter & Elizabeth Stevens, 24 Mar 1807; Simon Pearce, bm.

Pearson, Solomon & Mary Sasser, 23 Feb 1836; Benja. W. Raiford, bm.

Pearson, Solomon & Julie Ann Talton, m 30 Dec 1844 by Willie Holt, J. P.

Pearson, William & Josephin B. Vantassel, m 10 Feb 1851 by Willie Holt.

Peebles, Lemuel & Cherry Parker, 17 Nov 1818; John Lee, Jr., bm.

Peebles, Williams & Rebeckah Johnson, 17 Feb 1795; Moses Johnston, bm.

Peden, Amos & Ann Ritor Howell, 17 Nov 1793; Joseph Edwards, bm.

Peden, Larken & Mary Sasser, 16 Feb 1853; m 10 Mar 1853 by Wms. Brown.

Pedin, W. W. & Lucinda Starling, 6 Apr 1859; m 7 Apr 1859 by Wms. Brown, C. M.

Peeden, Alvin & Marcy Ann E. Edwards, 22 May 1845; Newit Peeden, bm.

Peeden, Amos & Polly Edwards, 11 Aug 1815; Micajah Edwards, bm.

Peeden, Amos J. & Elizabeth Creech, 7 Sept 1852; m 12 Sept 1852 by Jesse Parker, J. P.

Peeden, Edward & Drusilla Futrell, 29 Oct 1825; Handy Peedin, bm.

Peeden, Elisha & Caley Capps, 15 Jul 1815; Henry Peedin, bm.

Peeden, Handy & Keziah Johnson, 31 Jul 1824; Hardy Pilkenton, Major Griffin, bm.

Peeden, Handy Festno & Trecindo Rains, 29 Mar 1866; Stephen Sneed, bm.

Peeden, Isaiah & Tillitha Rose, 26 Jun 1852; m 1 Jun 1852 by Edwin Boykin, J. P.

Peeden, James & Celia Massy, 29 Oct 1825; Wilkerson Futrell, bm.

Peeden, James & Betsy Pilkinton, 24 Feb 1827; Clinch Pilkinton, bm.

Peeden, James & Sally Starling, 26 Sept 1837; Ezikiel Stevens, bm.

Peeden, James, son of James, & Linsey Crocker, 26 Dec 1843; Willie Peeden, bm.

Peeden, James & Lucretia Sellers, 16 May 1854; m 18 May 1854 by Ransom Kirby, J. P.

Peeden, James Jr. & Nancy Raiford, 26 May 1826; Needham Warren, bm.

Peeden, John & Edith Copps, 25 Aug 1814; Lemuel Pearce, bm.

Peeden, John & Axcy Spencer, 5 Feb 1842; Newit Peeden, bm; m by Willie Holt, J. P.

Peeden, Newit & Polly Spencer, 21 Sept 1804; Amos Peeden, bm.

Peeden, Newit & Sally Tiner, 8 Apr 1811; James Peeden, bm.

Peeden, William & Patsy Cooke, 11 Sept 1829; John Rains, bm.

Peeden, William James & Nancy Creech, 17 Mar 1830; Newit Peeden, bm.

Peele, John & Edy Price, 7 Mar 1845; Pery Renfrow, bm.

Peele, Matthew & Mary Jones, 18 May 1863; m 19 Mar 1863 at C. G. Hollands, by Jesse Parker, J. P.

Pender, James & Patty Edwards, 23 Dec 1795; Jesse Spencer, bm.

Pender, John Core & Theney Stevens, 2 Feb 1784; William Fellow, bm.

Pender, William & Anna Radford, 15 Aug 1852; m 16 Aug 1852 by Wm. Rains, J. P.

Pender, Willie & Polly Ann Davis, m 4 Jan 1863 at the residence of John Davis, by F. F. Ellis, J. P.

Penny, Alexander & Phereby Johnson, 28 Aug 1787; Caleb Penny, James Penny, bm.

Penny, Caleb & Polly Turner, 3 Nov 1823; Harry Penny, bm.

Penny, Caleb Sr. & Lizay Averyt, 23 Oct 1824; Henry Penny, bm.

Penny, Claud (colored) & Sarah Vinson, 12 Jan 1867; Ransom Hinnant, bm; m 17 Jan 1867 by M. R. Grantham, J. P.

Penny, Edward & Edith Bagget, 1 Sept 1784; William Ryals, bm.

Penny, Henry & Martha Smith, 13 Jul 1787; Henry W. Johnson, bm.

Penny, James & Mary Jane Wood, 11 Jun 1840; Caleb Penny, bm.

Penny, Jesse & Milley Broadstreet, 24 Apr 1792; Edward Stevens, bm.

Penny, Jesse & Sally Leeps, 12 Jan 1807; Philip Johnson, bm.

Penny, Leonedas H. & Elizabeth Byrd, 6 Dec 1856; m 18 Dec 1856 at Lemuel Byrds Snr, by C. Langdon, J. P.

Penny, Seth & Mary C. Byrd, 28 Dec 1858; m 13 Jan 1859 at the residence of R. Byrd, by R. W. Stevens, J. P.

Penny, William & Sally Penny, 9 Mar 1805; Philip Johnson, bm.

Peoples, Drury & Ann Coalts, 26 Mar 1785; John Eliot, bm.

Peoples, Matthew & Edith Evans, 21 Oct 1846; Isaac Munden, bm.

Peples, Archable & Sarah Renn, 16 Jun 1790; Jeremiah Powell, bm.

Perdue, L. W. & Annie E. Utley, m 20 Jan 1864 at Parsonage in Smithfield, by L. S. Burkhead.

Perkinson, William W. & Mariah Ballenger, 4 Sept 1852; m 5 Sept 1852 by J. S. Jackson.

Perry, Alsey & Edith Stallings, 28 Dec 1831; Thos. Rice, bm.

Perry, Calvin & Rebecca Davis, 12 Dec 1839l; Silas Webb, bm.

Perry, Harrod & Augusta C. Phillips, 4 Jun 1840; James R. Pearce, bm.

Perry, Stephen & Elizabeth Oneil, _____ ; CHarles Stevens, bm.

Perry, William & Betty Cooper, 25 Aug 1812; Jesse Wall, bm.

Pettes, Stephen & Edith Messer, 23 May 1813; Thomas Barber, bm.

Pettis, John & Betsey Garner, 8 Feb 1825; Matthew Barber, bm.

Philips, Barnaby & Sally Gully, 11 Sept 1821; Dixon Phillips, bm.

Philips, Dickson & Edith Oliver, 16 Apr 1814; Will. Phillips, bm.

Philips, Hamilton Guy & Eveline Pitmon, 28 Jul 1847; Turner Joyner, bm.

Philips, Henry & Sarah Lawhorn, 1 Dec 1778; William Dodd, bm.

Philips, William & Nancy Caudle, 29 Apr 1806; John Caudle, bm.

Phillips, Eligah H. & Winifred H. Capps, 14 Jan 1850; Elijah Capps, bm.

Phillips, Fort T. & Elizabeth Rains, 11 Jan 1847; Wm. Hastings, bm.

Phillips, Franklin & Zelphia Strickland, 10 Dec 1834; Jacob Yelventon, bm.

Phillips, George & Helon Kelly, m 12 Nov 1852 by Jesse Parker, J. P.

Phillips, Hamilton & Sarah Faulk, 9 Sept 1812; Dixon Phillips, bm.

Phillips, Henry & Emily Bond, 25 Oct 1833; Lewis H. Phillips, Allen Ballenger, bm.

Phillips, John Sr. & Mary THomson, 4 Oct 1824; Loverd Pearce, bm.

Phillips, John W. & Caroline Pitman, 20 Sept 1848; Bryan R. Hinnant, bm.

Phillips, Ray & Nancy Jones, m __ Jun 1856 by P. Godwin, J. P.

Phillips, W. D. & Martha Q. Gearald, 13 Oct 1858; m 19 Oct 1858 at C. F. Geralds, by Wilie Wellons, J. P.

Pickett, J. B. & Mary Eatmon, 1 Aug 1859; m 4 Aug 1859 at the dwelling of A. Eatmon, by Chs. W. Lee, J. P.

Pierce, Larkin & Mary Ann Corbett, 21 Dec 1846; Wm. H. Oneal, bm.

Pike, Jonathan Q. & Mary Ann E. Johnson, 6 Mar 1852; m 9 Mar 1852 by S. Bagley, J. P.

Pilkenton, Hardy & Sally Crockell, 29 Mar 1825; Handy Peeden, bm.

Pilkenton, Willie & Sally Fort, 28 Nov 1823; Allen Price, bm.

Pilkinton, Green B. & Elizabeth Tisdale, 4 Apr 1866; Moses Nichols, bm.

Pilkinton, John & Pheraby Caps, 13 Jan 1809; Barnaby Bulls, bm.

Pilkinton, John & Nancy Daughtry, 31 Dec 1860; m 1 Jan 1861 at Solomon Daughtrys, by Wms. Brown.

Pilkinton, Richard & Maryan Davis, 11 Oct 1791; Joshua Creech, bm.

Pilkinton, William & Sarah Edwards, 28 Mar 1791; Richard Pilkinton, bm.

Pitman, Calvin & Ranzey Gay, 23 Sept 1859; m 25 Sept 1859 by Jesse Parker, J. P.

Pitman, Elijah & Orpah Pugh, 19 Oct 1819; Micajah Wilkinson, bm.

Pitman, Jesse & Polly Killingsworth, 26 Feb 1813; Jno. Sanders, Jr., David Hollimon, bm.

Pitman, Joel & Winnefred Wilder, 4 Jun 1825; Levy Yelventon, bm.

Pitman, Joseph & Elizabeth Raper, 11 Mar 1845; Joseph Raper, bm.

Pitman, William H. & Sally Watkins, 5 Jan 1850; Thomas Pitmon, bm.

Pitmon, Elisha Jr. & Edney Creech, 26 Feb 1855; m 27 Feb 1855 by Jesse Parker, J. P.

Pitmon, Thomas & Charity Pitmond, 5 Jan 1846; Bryan R. Hinnant, bm.

Pittman, Elisha & Polly Batten, 18 Apr 1818; John Battin, bm.

Pittman, Garry & Patsey Fivash, 12 Aug 1816; Elisha Pittman, bm.

Pittman, Harrison & Smithy Eason, 19 Dec 1843; Elisha Pittman, bm.

Pittman, Jeremiah & Elizabeth Davis, 23 Dec 1844; Levy Yelventon, bm.

Pleasant, John & Margaret E. Cutts, 2 Apr 1864; m 3 Apr 1864 at the house of M. C. Cutts, by John T. Coats, J. P.

Pollard, Samuel & Penelope Allen, 13 Jan 1854; m 26 Jan 1854 by Robt. Massingill, J. P.

Pool, Albert J. & Sally Baudoun, 1 Jan 1846; Caswell A. Smith, bm.

Pool, Anderson & Betsy Bedinfield, 24 Nov 1829; John Benningfield, bm.

Pool, Anderson & Polly Ann Penny, 25 Feb 1867; Wilie Jones, bm.

Pool, Anderson S. & Louisa Jones, 16 Mar 1859; m 17 Mar 1859 by J. F. Ellington.

Pool, George & Edny Godwin, 12 Apr 1848; Jesse Parker, bm.

Pool, Gilman K. C. & Polly Pool, 7 Mar 1812; Hardy Pool, bm.

Pool, Hardy & Nancy Thorp, 12 Oct 1816; Neill L. Buie, bm.

Pool, Hardy & Mary Baucom, 27 Dec 1837; Johnathan Pool, bm.

Pool, Henry & Rebecca Wellons, 22 Jun 1809; Zachariah Wellons, bm.

Pool, Henry & Nancy Ellis, 12 Jan 1842; Samuel M. Turly, bm.

Pool, James & Patsey Tharp, 23 Dec 1813; Hardy Pool, bm.

Pool, John & Anney Avera, 1 Mar 1794; Hardy Bryan, bm.

Pool, John Jr. & Nancy Britt, 20 Apr 1805; Benjamin Farmer, bm.

Pool, John W. & Margaret A. Peacock, 23 Oct 1858; m 26 Oct 1858 by Jno. H. Kennedy.

Pool, Jonathan & Polly Ellington, 22 Dec 1834; Hardy Pool, bm.

Pool, Lewis & Elizabeth Taltch, 25 Dec 1837; Lovet Spivy, bm.

Pool, Ransom & Elizabeth Simons, m 25 Sept 1858 at Smithfield by J. A. Stevens, J. P.

Pool, William & Rhoda Pearce, 5 Apr 1807; Lamuel Pearce, bm.

Pool, William & Sally Johnson, 10 Mar 1812; Pennul Penny, bm.

Pope, Bryant & Aquilla Selavant, m 5 Aug 1853 by Jesse Parker, J. P.

Pope, Daniel (colored) & Lucinda Lockart, 31 Dec 1866; m 9 Jan 1867 by M. R. Grantham, J. P.

Pope, Henry & Polly Lee, 28 Dec 1823; John Tiner, bm.

Pope, John & Aney Ballance, 17 Feb 1848; Iredell Peacock, bm.

Pope, Simon & Patsey Cole, 17 May 1817; William Todd, bm.

Pope, William & Anne Dew, 24 Jan 1803; Edward Lee, bm.

Pope, William & Polly Fisher, 4 Feb 1807; Jonathan Pullen, bm.

Pope, William & Elizabeth Temple, 25 Oct 1847; Barzilla Blackmon, bm.

Porch, Eaton & Nelly Price, 29 May 1832; Thomas D. Bridges, bm.

Porch, Eaton & Patience Batetn, 26 _____ ___, Dixon Price, bm.

Pornner, James & Eadith Guin, 24 Dec 1791; Andrew Collins, bm.

Porter, Allen & Elizur Hollandsworth, 9 Feb 1853; m 10 Feb 1853 by D. Peacock.

Porter, Nathan & Elizabeth Ivey, 16 Nov 1822; William Ryals, bm.

Powell, A. & Sukey Guy, _____; M. Goman, bm.

Powell, Adin & Mary Williams, 5 Jan 1828; Harmon Cordell, bm.

Powell, Erastus E. & Nancy Jane Barham, m 30 May 1854.

Powell, Gains B. & Sarah A. Keneday, m 26 Mar 1861 at the residnece of J. H. Keneday, by R. D. Lunceford, J. P.

Powell, Kenean & Betsy Adams, 8 Sept 1827; Cidney Adams, bm.

Powell, Nathan & Nancy Ingram, 16 Jun 1790; Jeremiah Powell, bm.

Powell, Stephen & Charlotte Harrell, 19 Nov 1796; Hugh Cravy, bm.

Powell, William & Sarah Pearce, 12 Aug 1808; Enos Powell, bm.

Powell, William & Sarah Ingram, 14 May 1821; Jno. B. Allen, bm.

Powell, William S. & Martha Penny, 16 Oct 1844; Augustus G. Jones, bm.

Powers, David & Susan Jones, 14 Oct 1859; m 20 Oct 1859 at Samuel Jones's, by D. H. Holland, J. P.

Powers, Rodham & Lucy Snipes, 14 Mar 1805; Isham Stevens, bm.

Poyner, Thomas & Elizabeth Guion, 9 Sept 1789; Jeremiah Powell, bm.

Prescut, Aaron & Betsey Snipes, 12 Mar 1822; Nathan Brady, bm.

Previt, William Riley & Milly Bailey, 18 Oct 1821; Nathan Thomas, bm.

Price, Allen & Patsey Edwards, 25 May 1812; Joseph Boon, Jr., bm.

Price, Ashley & Welthy Ann Barber, 31 Mar 1845; Warren Holland, bm.

Price, Berry & Smithy Wallace, 15 Sept 1834; Tho. Lockart, Sr., bm.

Price, David & Susan Wallace, 11 Jan 1837; Moses Wallace, bm.

Price, David H. & Elizabeth Skeene, 13 Feb 1862; m 20 Feb 1862 at Moses Wallis, by N. G. Gully, J. P.

Price, Dixon & Sally Talton, 6 Dec 1817; Danel Dees, bm.

Price, Edward & Mary Jones, [no date; during Gov. Alexander Martin's term, 1782-6, 1789-92]; Jesse Wall, bm.

Price, Edward & Didemiah Lowrey, 17 Feb 1789; Thomas Price, bm.

Price, Edward & Edith Parker, 6 Oct 1815; Micajah Oneal, bm.

Price, Edward & Edith Parish, 20 Jun 1820; John Duncan, bm.

Price, Edward & Polly Ferrill, 9 Apr 1836; Willis Turner, bm.

Price, Elias & Delilah Narron, 12 Oct 1807; Atline Richardson, bm.

Price, Etheldred & Luvey Bryan, 7 Feb 1790; William Hackney, bm.

Price, George & Dolly Avery, 1 Nov 1840; Elisha Harrison, bm.

Price, George L. & Lucinda Atkinson, 16 Jan 1861; m 17 Jan 1861 at Blake Atkinson, by N. G. Gully, J. P.

Price, Guideon & Patience Parker, 5 Apr 1825; Powell Parker, bm.

Price, Henderson & Celia Hogg, m 7 Apr 1853 by S. Wood, J. P.

Price, Hilliard & Isabel Barber, 4 Oct 1842; Solomon Lockart, bm.

Price, Hilliard G. & Tempy A. Robertson, 16 Jan 1866; m 17 Jan 1866 by H. Hocut, M. G.

Price, Ichabud & Ceely Johnson, 4 Nov 1814; Joel Bryan, bm.

Price, Ichabud & Milly Naaron, 6 Dec 1826; Willie Price, bm.

Price, James & Susanna Rogers, 17 Feb 1789; Edward Price, bm.

Price, James & Nancy Johnson, 18 May 1815; Jno. MacLeod, bm.

Price, James & Ally Blackburn, 28 Dec 1816; Nathaniel H. Johnson, bm.

Price, James T. & Martha Ann R. Ellis, 28 Mar 1866; J. J. Farmer, bm.

Price, John & Nancy Vass, 8 Apr 1809; William Phillips, bm.

Price, John & Betsy Cooper, 6 Oct 1809; Benjamin Smith, bm.

Price, Joseph & Strawdry Batten, 16 Aug 1836; Solomon Lockart, bm.

Price, Joseph & Ulrica Ferrell, 22 Nov 1848; Thos L. Jordan, bm.

Price, Lucous & Mary Oneill, 17 May 1780; Isom Oneil, bm.

Price, Martin & Ceely Price, 13 Nov 1818; Dixon Price, bm.

Price, Micajah & Penelopia Gardner, 1 Mar 1787; Daniel Dees, bm.

Price, N. G. & Nancy Stancell, 2 Mar 1867; Quilly Price, bm.

Price, Nathan & Rachel Wedford, 26 Aug 1817; Wm. B. Hocut, bm.

Price, Needham & Nancy Sanders, 27 Dec 1830; Bennet Boddie, bm.

Price, Needham & Eliza Woodell, m 3 Jan 1857 by B. C. Richason, J. P.

Price, Needham & Nancy Driver, 22 Jun 1860; m 24 Jun 1860 at James Drivers, by S. W. Woody, J. P.

Price, Quilly & Mary Parker, 20 Mar 1858; m 11 Mar 1858 at Powel Parker, by L. G. Boyett, J. P.

Price, Rice & Prudence Holder, 29 Feb 1792; William Hackney, bm.

Price, Rice & Cynthia Price, 7 Jan 1812; Bud Price, bm.

Price, Rice Jr. & Mourning Moore, 24 Feb 1795; Dixon Price, bm.

Price, Royal & Nancy Bateman, 29 Dec 1800; Wm. Davis, bm.

Price, Ryal & Elizabeth Oliver, 12 Aug 1790; John Price, bm.

Price, Simon & Pheriby Pearce, 25 Nov 1788; Henry Hayles, bm.

Price, Sion & Penny Hayles, 1 Mar 1814; Tho. Lockart, Jr., bm.

Price, Stephen & Sally Green, 1 Mar 1825; Jonathan Holliman, bm.

Price, Thomas & Ann Ryals, 23 Jun 1784; Charls Ryals, bm.

Price, Thomas & Sarah Dodd, 4 Jun 1800; Pennel Peney, bm.

Price, Thomas & Penny Parish, 5 Feb 1815; Philip Johnson, bm.

Price, Thomas & Temperence Price, 24 Aug 1819; Henry Lewis, bm.

Price, William & Winefred Porch, 24 Jun 1809; William Teal, bm.

Price, William Hinton & Nancy Wilson, 5 Jan 1843; Matthew Wilder, bm.

Price, Zachariah & Molly Moore, 1 Dec 1784; Thomas Gray, bm.

Price, Zachariah & Lydia Sharp, 18 Feb 1800; John Sims, bm.

Pridgen, Hardy & Betsy Peacock, 31 Jan 1838; Arthur Thompson, bm.

Prince, Richard & Molley Rains, 9 Aug 1791; John Snipes, Jr., bm.

Proctor, Henry & Amy Lee, 1 Apr 1798; James Carrell, bm.

Pugh, William & Rhoda Thomas, 27 Nov 1820; Russell Sillivant, bm.

Pulley, Allen (colored) & Violet Richardson, 23 Feb 1867; Bryant Pulley, bm; m 23 Feb 1867 at Calvin Richardsons, by Wm. C. Nowell.

Pulley, Josiah & Willy Richardson, 18 Nov 1858; m 21 Nov 1858 at Calvin Richardsons, by B. Woodard, J. P.

Pulley, Matthew T. & Nancy Earp, 3 Jan 1838; James Wm. Wilder, bm.

Purvis, James & Rhodes Roberts, 14 Aug 1786; Benjamin Sellars, bm.

Racoch, John & Unity Pearce, 26 Sept 1805; William Hinnant, bm.

Radford, Christopher & Mary Ann Upchurch, 6 Nov 1860; m 7 Nov 1860 by B. A. Wellons, J. P.

Radford, Levi & Anny Edwards, 29 Sept 1846; Wilie Holt, bm; m by Willie Holt, J. P.

Radford, Robert & Prissilla Sharp, 27 Feb 1806; Jeremiah Gurley, bm.

Ragsdale, Thomas L. & Delany Hinton, 5 Jul 1824; Wm. Hinton, bm.

Raiford, Isaac & Civil Raiford, 19 May 1817; Philip Raiford, bm.

Raiford, James & Esther Whitley, 13 Dec 1828; Benjamin Stevens, bm.

Raiford, John & Cherry Honeycutt, 28 Aug 1805; Philip Raiford, bm.

Raiford, Philip & Elizabeth Rains, 27 Feb 1821; Jesse Whitley, bm.

Raiford, Reddin & Eliza Oliver, 21 Oct 1823; Levi Oliver, bm.

Rainer, James & Bersheba Holmes, 27 Nov 1837; James G. Rainer, bm.

Raines, Henry & Nancy Raeford, 27 Feb 1821; Philip Raiford, Jesse Whitley, bm.

Raines, Jackson & F. D. Perry, 15 May 1865; R. G. Rains, bm.

Raines, John G. & Elizabeth Beasley, 15 Feb 1859; m 20 Feb 1859 by Wm. F. Hall, Elder.

Raines, William & Terresse Joyner, 2 Jan 1841; Henry Raines, bm.

Raines, William Jr. & Betsey Jane Creech, 22 Nov 1858; m 23 Nov 1858 by Jesse Parker, J. P.

Rains, Edwin & Sally Revell, 30 Jan 1828; Isaac Boothe, bm.

Rains, Henry & Hannah Hawkins, 12 Apr 1810; Simon Pearce, bm.

Rains, Henry & Willey Gerrald, 11 Feb 1836; William Rains, bm.

Rains, John & Elizabeth Peoples, 1 Apr 1806; Jarrot Jelks, bm.

Rains, John H. & Catharine Howell, 17 Sept 1842; Wilie Holt, bm; m by Willie Holt, J. P.

Rains, John H. & Rindy Spivy, 13 Jun 1846; Dixion Spivy, bm.

Rains, L. J. & Zilpha Cammell, 16 Dec 1862; m 22 Dec 1862 by Jesse Parker, J. P.

Rains, Oliver & Elizabeth Pearce, 6 Feb 1804; John Rains, bm.

Rains, Oliver & Martha Sasser, 24 Aug 1847; Henry Rains, bm.

Rains, William G. & Gilly Oneal, 22 Mar 1836; Hopkins Oneal, bm.

Rainwater, William & Molly Reaves, 16 Nov 1787; Samuel Baldwin, bm.

Raiper, Calvin & Elizabeth Saluvan, 15 Feb 1853; m 17 Feb 1853 by Stanly Kirby, J. P.

Rand, John B. & Charity Baucum, 10 Dec 1860.

Raper, Henry & Anny Johnson, 21 Nov 1844; Perry Renfrow, bm.

Raper, John & Betsy Sasser, 7 Feb 1814; John Sasser, bm.

Raper, John & Nancy Moore, 15 Sept 1845; Williamson Hinnant, bm.

Raper, Joseph & Sally Wellons, 16 Feb 1848; Joshua Creech, bm.

Raper, Roberson & Martha Hinnant, 28 Mar 1855; m 29 Mar 1855 by Jesse Parker, J. P.

Raper, Robert & Nancy Watson, 16 Jan 1849; James H. Hinnant, bm.

Raper, William & _____, 28 Feb 1843; Silas Lamb, bm.

Rasberry, Richard & Rachel Edwards, 29 Dec 1852; m 30 Dec 1852 by Willie Holt, J. P.

Rayner, James Jr. & Jane E. Beasley, 11 Aug 1856; m 13 Aug 1856 at K. M. C. Beasley's, by John C. Hood, J. P.

Reaves, G. W. & Winney Wheeler, 12 Apr 1858; m 13 Apr 1858 by W. F. Hall, Elder.

Reaves, Hudson & Elizabeth Holloman, 17 Jun 1817; Henry Parnold, bm.

Reaves, James B. & Nancy E. Hicks, 14 Nov 1857; A. G. Lee, bm; m 1 Dec 1857 by Robt. N. Gully, J. P:.

Reaves, Levi & Betsy Norris, 23 Aug 1802; Eleck Sanders, Edwin Smith, bm.

Redden, Elisha & Aggy Wright, 5 Dec 1810; Rigdon Johnson, bm.

Reddin, Elisha & Betsy Dowdy, 6 Aug 1820; John Lee, bm.

Redford, Richard & Celia Ann Smith, 29 May 1866; G. W. Redford, J. T. Pike, bm; m 31 May 1866 at Selah Smiths, by J. T. Pike, J. P.

Reding, Elisha & Lucy Hinnant, 4 Oct 1825; James Hilliard, bm.

Reed, James, of Chatham Co., & Charlotte James, 22 Oct 1807; David Stevens, bm.

Reid, Elijah & Phereby Standen, 14 Nov 1849; Willie Holt, bm; m by Willie Holt.

Reid, J. J. & Harriet Ann Millinder, 29 Oct 1859; m 8 Nov 1859 at the residence of H. Millinder, by R. D. Lunceford, J. P.

Ren, Sherod & Jane Massingill, 21 Oct 1815; Zachariah Gower, bm.

Renfroe, Jacob & Martha Simms, 11 Nov 1794; Stephen Grice, bm.

Renfroe, Josiah & Polly Godwin, 11 Apr 1814; Bannister Grizzel, bm.

Renfroe, William & Mary Pelt, 25 Feb 1805; Stephen Grice, bm.

Renfrow, James J. & Mary Boykin, 6 Nov 1866; H. W. Edwards, bm; m 11 Nov 1866 by S. W. Woody, J. P.

Rentfroe, Braswell & Polly Williamson, 3 Jun 1836; Nelson Kent, bm.

Rentfrow, Hinnant & Zilpha Watson, 13 Nov 1852; m 15 Mar 1852 by Noel Barnes, J. P.

Rentfrow, James & Polly Thorn, 9 Oct 1813; Jesse Syllavent, bm.

Rentfrow, James & Rainey Morris, 13 Mar 1855; m 15 Mar 1855 by Noel Barnes, J. P.

Rentfrow, Mabry & Seney Atkinson, 28 Aug 1844; Jesse Parker, bm.

Rentfrow, Merrit & Zilpha Barnes, 20 Sept 1845; Griffin W. Godwin, bm.

Rentfrow, Perry & Lucinda Hawkins Atkinson, 29 Dec 1841; Thos. S. Christenberry, bm.

Rentfrow, Stephen & Patsey Hare, 18 Jan 1842; Pery Rentfrow, bm.

Rentfrow, Willie & Athy Evans, 9 Oct 1828; Jesse Sellavent, bm.

Revel, John & Elizabeth Godwin, 20 Jan 1853; m 25 Jan 1853 by Stanly Kirby, J. P.

Revell, Hardy & Elizabeth Cowell, 10 May 1814; Noah Nichols, bm.

Revil, Hardy & Elizabeth Hinnant, 11 Sept [1811]; Wm. Hinnant, Sr., bm.

Reynolds, Michael & Polly Chambers, 16 May 1783; Joseph Edwards, bm.

Rhodes, Atlas J. K. & Spicey West, 4 Oct 1846; George Keen, bm.

Rhodes, Eden & Joanna Joyner, m 23 Dec 1859 by Ransom Lee, J. P.

Rhodes, Edin & Betsey Brent, 20 Aug 1819; Joshua Daniel, bm.

Rhodes, John & Sarah Moore, 3 Jan 1813; King Vann, bm.

Rhodes, John & Charlotte Brunt, 14 Sept 1814; Allen S. Ballenger, bm.

Rhodes, John F. S. & Mary E. Crocker, m 4 Oct 1856, at James Rhodes.

Rhodes, Joseph E. & Polly Beck, 9 Aug 1804; Isaac Williams, bm.

Rhodes, Moses & Pherube Lee, 25 Jan 1820; Brian Lee, bm.

Rhodes, Nathan & Patsey Jones, 4 Aug 1840; Bural Barber, bm.

Rials, Thomas & Lotty Porter, 13 Jan 1819; James Ryals, bm.

Rice, Thomas & Cloe Bulls, 14 Dec 1814; Jno. Eason, Jr., bm.

Rice, Thomas & Patsy Turner, 11 Sept 1817; Jno. Sanders, Jr., bm.

Richardson, A. W. & Celia Whitley, 24 Jan 1841; John B. Green, bm.

Richardson, Applewhite & Willy Houlder, 22 Nov 1819; Simon Pope, bm.

Richardson, Bertie & Harriet Earp, 2 Jan 1818; Sampson Morgan, bm.

Richardson, Calvin & Mary Hall, m 23 Jan 1861 near Earpsboro, by W. Earp, J. P.

Richardson, Elias & Sarah Pearce, 28 May 1827; Jonathan Hinnant, bm.

Richardson, Hardy & Beady Godwin, 18 Oct 1803; Daniel Evan, bm.

Richardson, James & Aley Woodward, 9 Aug 1805; Joseph Richardson, bm.

Richardson, James & Nicy Talton, 19 Sept 1841; Henry Sasser, bm.

Richardson, James (colored) & Olive Talton, 29 Aug 1866; William Richardson, bm.

Richardson, Joe (colored) & Gilley Richardson, 2 Feb 1867; Jesse Hinnant, bm; m 2 Feb 1867 by W. C. Sowell.

Richardson, John & Polly Hayls, 24 Feb 1809; Jacob Flowers, bm.

Richardson, John & Penny Price, 23 May 1820; Hillary Wilder, bm.

Richardson, Joseph & Martha Hackney, 30 May 1798; Joseph Richardson, bm.

Richardson, King (colored) & Nicey Richardson, 2 Feb 1867; Jeses Hinnant, bm; m 2 Feb 1867 by W. C. Nowell.

Richardson, Lunceford & Laurinda Vinson, 13 Dec 1836; Wm. H. Watson, bm.

Richardson, Pharoah & Mary Vinson, 23 Nov 1839; William H. Morning, bm.

Richardson, Ransom & Lucinda Oneal, 2 Oct 1833; Richardson Oneal, bm.

Richardson, Ransom (colored) & Sally Ann Watson, 1 Dec 1866; McNab Earp, bm; m 2 Feb 1866 by McNab Earp, J. P.

Richardson, Samuel & Celah Hackney, 23 Dec 1807; John High, bm.

Richardson, William & Emeline Earp, 20 Jan 1847; Jacob A. Richardson, bm.

Richardson, William & Mary E. Atkinson, 22 Jun 1866; M. C. Richardson, bm; m 27 Jun 1866 at Thomas Atkinsons, by Joseph Wheeler, M. G.

Ridgely, Loyed G. & Pameser Helms, 7 Jan 1846; Wm. H. Morning, bm.

Rithinson, Thomas & Milbury Heeth, 10 Jul 1802; William Hinnant, Sr., bm.

Ritter, Henry & Polly Pettis, 30 Jan 1821; Henry Whitman, bm.

Rivers, William & Elizabeth Pool, 20 Sept 1788; Richard Rivers, bm.

Rivers, William & Mary Ann Hinton, 14 Apr 1813; William Rivers, bm.

Roads, James H. & Phereby Tompson, m 5 Feb 1852 by E. Atkinson, bm.

Roads, William & Mary Searls, 2 Oct 1797; Abraham Weib, bm.

Robbards, William & Sally Griffith, 28 Jul 1841; Isaac Beasly, bm.

Roberds, John & Elizabeth Boddery, 4 Dec 1815; Ephraim Overby, bm.

Roberson, Needham & Patience Richardson, 13 Jan 1808; Noah Nichols, bm.

Roberts, Adin & Sophia Stevens, 20 May 1824; Bythan Bryan, bm.

Roberts, David & Drusilla Hughes, 6 Nov 1840; Upton Powell, bm.

Roberts, Elbert & Polly Allen, 5 May 1836; Joseph Gurley, bm.

Roberts, Elbert & Polly Alley, 14 May 1836; Henry O. Stallings, bm.

Roberts, James & Nancy Bodiery, 5 May 1816; Britain Roberts, bm.

Roberts, James & Nicey Milliner, 24 Nov 1838; Elbert W. Roberts, bm.

Roberts, John & Polly Snipes, 6 Feb 1816; Meed Gully, bm.

Roberts, Joseph & Mary Futrell, 26 Nov 1840; Jno. P. Williams, bm.

Roberts, Linsey & _____ Brady, 10 Sept 1793; James Langford, bm.

Roberts, Thomas & Winnowfred Buzby, 29 May 1764; Thomas Busby, Jeremiah Hendrick, bm.

Roberts, William & Margaret Tucker, 20 Aug 1782; Charles Parish, bm.

Roberts, William & Polly Massingill, 28 Dec 1808; Samuel Strickland, Jr., bm.

Roberts, William & Chilly Howell, 9 Jan 1825; Wm. Strickland, bm.

Roberts, William Jr. & Betsey Reaves, 12 Oct 1793; Thomas Roberts, bm.

Robertson, Harbard & Edith Hinton, 13 Apr 1789; George Hinton, bm.

Robertson, James B. & Julia Ellington, 9 May 1863; m 12 May 1863 at the house of Elder John Ellington, by M. G. Todd.

Robertson, John W. & Serena J. O'neal, 6 Mar 1860; m 8 Mar 1860 at the house of William H. O'neal, by M. G. Todd.

Robertson, William & Morning Houlder, 9 Dec 1824; John T. Hayles, bm.

Rodgers, Chesly & Peggy Bowler, 17 Jul 1829; James Jones, bm.

Rodgers, Ezikiel & Martha O. Lockart, m 15 May 1851 by James B. Jackson, M. G.

Roe, Ann & Sally Edwards, 22 Mar 1817; James Peeden, bm.

Roe, William & Mary Garner, 27 Nov 1826; Simon Cockerall, bm.

Roe, William & Elizabeth Ann Wall, 17 Dec 1838; Seawell Hall, bm.

Rogers, Daniel & Betsy Garner, 27 Nov 1792; William Smith, bm.

Rogers, Daniel & Lydia Garner, 23 Nov 1797; Robert Rogers, bm.

Rogers, Green & Tabbitha Upchurch, 16 Jan 1786; James Baucom, bm.

Rogers, John & Polly Kelly, 11 May 1797; Danel Rogers, bm.

Rogers, John & Celah Kelly, 19 Jan 1804; John Kelly, bm.

Rogers, Reubin & Tempia James, 9 Dec 1767; James Wooten, bm.

Rogers, Sampson & Polly Watkins, 27 Nov 1798; Daniel Rogers, Jr., bm.

Rolin, Lewis & Roda Bagget, 15 Feb 1797; Charles Rials, bm.

Rollins, Richard & Polly Braddy, 9 Aug 1816; Jesse Wellons, bm.

Roper, Robertson & Clara Moore, 16 Jul 1840; Garry Sillavent, bm.

Rose, A. H. & Elizabeth Eldridge, 7 Jun 1859; m 9 Jun 1859 by John Harper, J. P.

Rose, Bardin & Polly Daivis, 27 Jul 1844; Pitts Kirby, bm.

Rose, Ben B. & Lizzy Eldridge, 10 May 1841; Jeremiah L. George, bm.

Rose, George P. & Nancy Brunt, 19 Oct 1852; m 21 Oct 1852 by Powel Blackman, J. P.

Rose, Haris & Zilpa Holland, 8 Dec 1846; Josiah Hinnant, Jr., bm.

Rose, Henry & Nancy Edwards, 3 Dec 1827; James Peeden, bm.

Rose, Henry C. & Sarah Fulghum, 27 Mar 1866; C. B. Hicks, bm.

Rose, James & Jerusha McGlawhon, 18 Dec 1798; Joseph Langston, bm.

Rose, James & Delpha Sasser, 27 SEpt 1837; Jesse Hinnant, bm.

Rose, John & Milly Johnson, 12 Feb 1830; Warren Johnston, bm.

Rose, John & Catharine Gay, m 3 May 1853 by Jas. Faulk, J. P.

Rose, Jordan & Alsey Kern, 19 Nov 1819; H. Sasser, bm.

Rose, Larry & Elizabeth Gay, 9 May 1855; m 20 May 1855 at Henry Bagleys, by S. Bagley, J. P.

Rose, Larry & Susan Starling, m 8 Oct 1865 by P. Godwin, J. P.

Rose, Mark & Sally Keen, 26 Feb 1816; Henry Sasser, bm.

Rose, Thomas R. & Mary Allen, 12 Jul 1847; Ransom G. Allen, bm.

Rose, Thomas R. & Leacy Allen, 16 Nov 1857; Vine H. Adams, bm; m 18 Nov 1857 by R. Masingill, J. P.

Rose, Thomas W. & Nancy Ryals, 24 Apr 1861; m 25 Apr 1861 at the residents of R. Ryals, by Wm. F. Hall, Elder.

Rose, Tobias & Sally Parish, 2 Jun 1849; Henry Bagley, bm.

Rose, William N. & Pherebee Lee, 22 Dec 1847; Sir William Blackman, bm.

Ross, James Jr. & Levina Vinson, 13 Dec 1792; Hardy Bryan, bm.

Rosser, Isaac & Elisabeth Vinson, 13 Mar 1802; Lewis Mth. Moore, bm.

Rosser, John & Elizabeth Pearce, 28 Jan 1804; John Sanders, Jr., bm.

Row, David & Xexey Sasser, 26 Feb 1848; Mottamer Cullom, bm.

Russel, Charles & Pressey Barker, 27 Mar 1791; William Giles, bm.

Ryals, Alfred & Rebecca Moore, m 24 Dec 1851 by Powel Blackman, J. P.

Ryals, Britain & Sarah Cross, 27 Feb 1838; Merrel Ryals, bm.

Ryals, Charles & Alsey Bagget, 8 Sept 1790; Edward Penny, bm.

Ryals, James A. & Phebee Woodall, 23 Apr 1859; m 28 Apr 1859 by Wm. F. Hall, Elder.

Ryals, Merrell & Brazzilla Woodall, 16 Jun 1821; Lamuel Peebles, bm.

Ryals, Ramon & Elizabeth Dixon, 28 May 1844; Robert W. Stevens, bm.

Ryals, Ransom & Emily Woodall, 29 Oct 1857; James A. Godwin, bm; m 2 Oct 1857 by B. Godwin, J. P.

Ryals, Right & Susan Creech, 26 Sept 1826; John Allen, bm.

Ryals, William & Edith Chiles, 20 Mar 1790; Isom Oneil, bm.

Ryals, Young & Susan Canada, 28 May 1833; Right Byrd, bm.

Salmon, William & Athey Wallace, 3 Feb 1847; Robert Masingill, bm.

Sampson, Isaac (colored) & Kiziah Peedin, 21 Sept 1865; Isaac Reid, bm.

Sampson, William & Mary Ann Raiford, 5 Oct 1848; A. D. Northam, bm.

Sanders, Alexander & Betsy Massengill, 9 Feb 1819; Etheldred Bell, bm.

Sanders, Alexander & Pherebe Johnson, 2 Mar 1839; Robert T. Massingill, bm.

Sanders, Alexander (colored) & Harriet Sanders, 16 May 1867; Henry Sanders, bm.

Sanders, Baldy & Delia H. Sanders, 21 Mar 1822; John Eason, bm.

Sanders, Bryan S. & Mary Earp, 10 Mar 1847; Aaron Martin, bm.

Sanders, Bythan (colored) & Tempy Hinton, 22 Dec 1866; Dillan Avera, bm; m 25 Dec 1866 by Jethro Thain, J. P.

Sanders, Claudius B. & Zilla E. Whitley, m 4 Jan 1854 by J. Tillett.

Sanders, Daniel (colored) & Cherry Eldridge, 24 Mar 1866; J. W. Eason, bm.

Sanders, Henderson & Lydia Sanders, 21 Apr 1866; Reubin Sanders, bm.

Sanders, John & Mimme Jones, 14 Mar 1797; Nahon Norris, bm.

Sanders, Jordan & Emeline Massengill, 5 May 1849; Allen Johnson, bm.

Sanders, Julius (colored) & Violet Tomlinson, 5 Jan 1867; Gillis Turner, bm; m 8 Jan 1867 by A. R. Duncan, J. P.

Sanders, Lynn B., of Virginia, & Polly Ann Sanders, 22 Nov 1843; Ashly Sanders, bm.

Sanders, Ransom & Jemima J. Sanders, 27 Jul 1826; William McCullers, bm.

Sanders, Ransom (colored) & Mary Grantham, 31 Dec 1866; Theo. Whitfield, bm.

Sanders, Reuben & Keran Smith, 16 Nov 1793; R. Sanders, Hardy Bryan, bm.

Sanders, Reuben T. & Eliza C. Boon, 30 Mar 1832; John B. Watson, bm.

Sanders, William & Mary Bryan, 8 Sept 1785; William Bryan, bm.

Sanders, William & Selah Cockrell, 27 Nov 1810; Simon Cockrell, bm.

Sanders, William B. & Candace E. Stallings, 1 Jun 1846; Robert A. Sanders, bm.

Sanders, William H. & Louensa Avera, 7 Sept 1855; Thos. Rice, bm.

Sanders, Willis H. & Lucinda Smith, 19 Sept 1844; Wm. B. Sanders, bm.

Saser, William & Marian Gerrald, 18 Aug 1823; John Saser, bm.

Sasser, Asa L. & Elizabeth D. Holt, 26 Nov 1856; m 2 Dec 1856 at Willie Colts, by T. W. Whitley, J. P.

Sasser, Eli & Peggy Ann Garne, 5 Mar 1846; Raford Gurly, bm.

Sasser, Ely & Elizer Garne, 20 Jan 1849; Banajah Williams, bm.

Sasser, Henry & Nancy Kirby, 26 Feb 1812; Ichabud Balkcon, bm.

Sasser, Henry & Patsey Bagley, 3 Mar 1838; Clark Gerald, bm.

Sasser, John & Delany Hall, 20 Apr 1816; Enos Gerald, bm.

Sasser, John & Kizia Stallings, 24 Nov 1838; Alsey Perry, bm.

Sasser, John & Betsey Sellers, 9 Dec 1846; William Hollomon, bm.

Sasser, John H. & Patience Ann Rains, 12 Apr 1866; John McC. Guy, bm.

Sasser, Joseph & Lucy Hollingsworth, 12 Jun 1837; Julius A. Stevens, bm.

Sasser, Josiah & Elizabeth Bryan, 10 Dec 1770; William Bryan, bm.

Sasser, Josiah & Sally Beard, 13 Dec 1825; James Frelick, bm.

Sasser, Olin & Nancy Scott, 23 Nov 1824; Chs. Crawford, bm.

Sasser, William & Martha Watson, 29 Jan 1848; Jas. Davis, bm.

Sasser, Willie & Polly Raiford, 10 Nov 1826; O. C. Sasser, bm.

Sauls, Eton & Sally Pool, 30 Mar 1818; Wm. Jones, bm.

Sauls, William & Elizabeth Young, 11 Feb 1825; James Hilliard, bm.

Sauls, William & Joanna Pamelia Kate, m 24 Jun 1862 at the house of Wm. Saules, by John R. Coats, J. P.

Scarborough, Enos & Luvey Ward, 19 Nov 1796; Hugh Cravy, David Drake, bm.

Schambly, Freeman & Reldy Oneal, 26 Aug 1834; Hutson Bailey, bm.

Scott, Britain & Nancy Raines, 4 Jul 1817; Jesse Whitley, bm.

Scott, Green H. & Polly Hinton, 28 Oct 1817; M. A. Britt, bm.

Scott, Henry & Charlotte J. Barefoot, 26 Aug 1858; m 29 Aug 1858 by John C. Hood, J. P.

Scott, Irven & Lucy Ingram, 24 Jul 1844; Nicholas Lee, bm.

Scott, John & Silvy Ivy, 2 Sept 1806; E. Sanders, bm.

Scott, William J., of Sampson Co., & Dicy Evans, 8 Nov 1843; Evans Chance, bm.

Seaberry, Rufus & Della Mitchner, 29 Apr 1867; m 1 May 1867 by J. A. Ellis, J. P.

Seacy, Asa & Elizabeth Johnson, 27 Feb 1805; Jno. Searcy, bm.

Seals, Benjamin & Elizabeth Crawford, 2 Mar 1797; Willis Cole, bm.

Searcy, John & Mary Averae, 2 Feb 1789; Aaron Vinson, bm.

Searcy, John & Betsy Langston, 12 Nov 1806; Thomas Barber, bm.

Searcy, John & Lucy Temple, 19 Dec 1795; Salathiel Holton, bm.

Seberry, Willis & Nancy Powell, m 4 Dec 1859 at Martilly Powels, by Ransom Lee, J. P.

Sellers, Alsey & Cintha Milliner, 13 Jun 1846; Bryan Sanders, bm.

Sellers, Benjamin & Sally Taylor, 5 Aug 1820; Adin Powell, bm.

Sellers, Daniel A. & Patsey Jane Peeden, 22 Jun 1859; m 30 Jun 1859 at the residence of H. Peeden, by Wilie Wellons, J. P.

Sellers, James & Elizabeth Collens, 13 Aug 1819; Etheldred Holt, bm.

Sellers, Richard W. & Elizabeth Hedgepeth, 16 May 1855; m 17 May 1855 at Benjamin Sellers's, by Wm. H. Sellers, J. P.

Sellers, William H. & Harriet E. Raiford, 21 Dec 1853; m 29 Dec 1853 by Elder Dixon Phililips.

Sellivant, Russell & Isabel Pugh, 22 Feb 1820; Jessee Bailey, bm.

Sharp, Henry & Keziah Gurley, 26 May 1801; Jeremiah Gurley, bm.

Shaw, Clement & Betsy Earp, 25 Jan 1825; Lucas Hayles, bm.

Shaw, Hugh V. & Mary Jernigan, 10 May 1784; Joseph Owen, bm.

Shaw, Joseph & Pherebe Newby, 16 Dec 1817; John Nowell, bm.

Shaw, William, of Orange Co., & Katharine Shaw, 15 Feb 1792; Edward Lee, bm.

Shaw, William & Polly Nowell, 9 Oct 1818; George Todd, bm.

Sheperd, Jonathan & Polly Dodd, 15 Feb 1823; Thomas Price, bm.

Shepherd, John & Anna Baker, 15 Aug 1823; Nicholas Rose, bm.

Short, Starling & Polly Smith, 3 Sept 1806; William Johnson, bm.

Silevent, Henry & Elizabeth Broughten, 25 Sept 1844; S. P. Horton, bm.

Silivent, Jonathan & Ann Batten, 28 Nov 1821; Wilie Gerald, bm.

Sillavant, Garry & Nancy Ann Jones, 9 Nov 1851; m 20 Nov 1851 by Kinchen Crumpler, M. G.

Sillaven, Jesse & Precilla Watson, 26 Feb 1811; Henry Sasser, bm.

Sills, Barham & Lucy Morgan, 11 Nov 1806; David Ivy, Sr., bm.

Sills, James & Polly Lee, 24 Dec 1809; Harriss Tomlinson, bm.

Simmons, Stephen (colored) & Sylla Langston, 8 Oct 1866; Geo. Martin, bm; m 9 Oct 1866 by Bryant Williams, J. P.

Simons, Henry & Polly Smith, 6 Aug 1818; William Smith, bm.

Simpkins, Benjamin & Rachel Blackman, 25 Mar 1814; Jeremiah Blackman, bm.

Simpkins, Calvin & Joanna Rhodes, m 10 Aug 1862 by Needham Bryan, J. P.

Simpkins, Thomas & Winefred Johnson, 12 Feb 1814; Thomas Price, bm.

Sims, Benjamin & Anne Tyner, 26 Aug 1788; Wm. Stevens, bm.

Sims, Jacob & Charllotte Jernigan, 24 May 1803; Edmond Sims, bm.

Sims, Jeremiah & Elly Stevens, 6 May 1818; Hartwill Ivy, bm.

Sims, Marke & Elizabeth Watson, 3 Nov 1767; James Wooten, bm.

Sims, Zachariah & Syndaralugh Page, 27 Oct 1820; James G. Woodall, bm.

Skene, William & Elizabeth Wallace, 2 Nov 1852; m 10 Nov 1852 by C. J. Bingham, J. P.

Skinner, Nathan & Nancy Bennet, 25 Feb 1817; Henry Stevens, bm.

Slocumb, Junius G. & Louisa Boon, 9 Apr 1838; H. W. Husted, bm.

Smith, Aaron & Winifred Vinson, 12 Jun 1798; Daniel Avery, bm.

Smith, Aaron & Fereby Pool, 31 Jan 1809; John Smith, Jr., bm.

Smith, Abraham & Sarah Rosser, 17 Jan 1787; John Eason, bm.

Smith, Alexander Jr. & Peggy Averyt, 16 Feb 1803; William Ryals, Jr., bm.

Smith, Alexander Sr. & Sarah Talton, 24 May 1815; Larkin Smith, bm.

Smith, B. V. & Jane E. Atkinson, 5 Mar 1864; m 6 Mar 1864 by W. A. Smith, J. P.

Smith, Benjamin & Mary Oliver, 4 Jan 1853; m 6 Jan 1853 by Wm. Rains, J. P.

Smith, Benjamin A. & Caron Gower, 10 Jun 1847; W. T. Roberts, bm.

Smith, Benjamin H. & Elizabeth Youngblood, 1 Jan 1838; James R. Ellis, bm.

Smith, Britain & Sally Bulls, 16 Jul 1808; Thos. Avera, bm.

Smith, Briton & Martha Price, 8 Dec 1813; John Smith, bm.

Smith, Britton & Sally Ann Norris, 3 Mar 1855; m 4 Mar 1855 by R. W. Stevens, J. P.

Smith, Bryan & Mary Whitley, 16 Nov 1843; Sam'l S. Turner, bm.

Smith, Bryant H. & Sarah F. Coats, 19 May 1866; W. G. Smith, bm.

Smith, Bud & Peney Johnson, 25 Apr 1828; Noel West, bm.

Smith, Calvin & Dolly Carrell, 17 Mar 1820; Levi Ferrell, of Wake Co., bm.

Smith, Clayton & Tamsey Bailey, 1 Mar 1791; John Driver, John Thomas, bm.

Smith, Daniel & Lugeenia Cross, 5 Dec 1848; Wm. H. Morning, bm.

Smith, David & Sally Ingram, 28 Apr 1808; Bryan Smith, bm.

Smith, David & Keron Ann Sanders, 8 Apr 1846; Bryan Smith,, bm.

Smith, Edmond (colored) & Mary Smith, 2 Feb 1867; Eli Morgan, bm.

Smith, Edwin & Elizabeth McCullers, 12 Mar 1811; Wm. W. Bryan, bm.

Smith, Elam & Cynthia Green, 28 Mar 1809; Briton Deloach, bm.

Smith, Felps & Barshaby Cobb, 12 May 1778; Benj. Wilkerson, bm.

Smith, George & Sarah Mitchener, 13 Jan 1866 Julius Smith, bm.

Smith, Henry & Dorcass Johnson, 1 Apr 1806; Ambrose Ingram, bm.

Smith, Henry & Nancy Ingram, 24 Feb 1841; Joel Lee, bm.

Smith, Isaac & Sarah Oneil, 26 Jul 1798; Samuel Godwin, bm.

Smith, James & Jane Lee, 14 Oct 1797; Samuel Lee, Jr., bm.

Smith, James A. & Martha Byrd, 11 Jul 1852; m 13 Jul 1852 by C. J. Bingham, J. P.

Smith, James H. & Nancy Bryan, 8 Aug 1825; A. Smith, bm.

Smith, James H. & Martha Ann Stephenson, 4 Dec 1856; R. M. Stephenson, bm; m 5 Dec 1866 by John R. Coats, J. P.

Smith, Joab & Mary Johnson, 26 Jan 1825; Allen S. Ballinger, bm.

Smith, Joel & Rachael Watson, 25 Feb 1834; Riddick Warren, bm.

Smith, John & Edith Avera, 23 Jun 1778; John Smith, bm.

Smith, John & Polly Auston, 24 Nov 1819; John Auston, bm.

Smith, John & Edith Bryan, 10 Oct 1823; Simon Bryan, bm.

Smith, John Sr. & Winifred Gilmore, 24 Sept 1821; Jessee Holleman, bm.

Smith, John Jr. & Betsy Rivers, 18 Feb 1804; Redden Johnston, bm.

Smith, John A. & Louezur Johnson, 11 Oct 1853; m 13 Oct 1853 by H. H. Finch, J. P.

Smith, John A. & Martha E. Beasley, 29 Sept 1857; Thomas Tart, bm; m 22 Oct 1857 by John C. Hood, J. P.

Smith, Joseph M. & Julie Ingram, 24 Jul 1845; John W. Ferrell, bm.

Smith, Matthew & Edith Lynch, 26 May 1801; Joseph Langston, bm.

Smith, McCallam & Mazallane Smith, m 26 Mar 1850 by A. J. Leach, J. P.

Smith, Nathan (colored) & Ann Heath, 13 Oct 1866; Adam J. Heath, bm; m 13 Oct 1866 by A. J. Heath, J. P.

Smith, Nehemiah & Lurana Avera, 9 Jan 1787; Nahor Norriss, bm.

Smith, Reuben & Milly Godwin, 26 May 1807; John Byrd, bm.

Smith, Richard & Cady Ferrell, 18 Feb 1805; Alexander Penny, bm.

Smith, Samuel & Patience Chamblee, 7 Feb 1848; Bryan Hocut, bm.

Smith, Samuel G. & Nancy Bryan, 27 Jul 1833; Irvin Parnell, bm.

Smith, Sidney A. & Mary E. Williams, 16 Jul 1855; m 17 Jul 1855 by Paul J. Carraway, M. G.

Smith, William & Siddy Beal, 26 Feb 1844; Needham G. Gulley, bm.

Smith, William & Renda Smith, 22 Jun 1857; m 23 Jun 1857 by J. F. Ellington.

Snead, George P. & Mary R. Sanders, m 11 Nov 1860 by J. F. Ellington.

Snead, Thomas D. & Elizabeth J. Sanders, 1 Dec 1852; m 2 Dec 1852 by J. B. Jackson, M. G.

Sneed, Robert & Mary Eldridge, 25 Nov 1828; Richd. Washington, bm.

Sneed, Stephen & Matilda V. Ennis, 24 Nov 1852; m 25 Nov 1852 by Pharoh Richardson, J. P.

Snipes, Britain & Aley Martin, 30 Aug 1800; Joseph Brown, bm.

Snipes, Jackson & Martha Wall, 1 Mar 1848; Wm. H. Lassester, bm.

Snipes, Jesse & Sally Roberts, 27 Aug 1802; Edward Price, bm.

Snipes, John & Jean Killinsgworth, 6 Jul 1785; Samuel Baldwin, bm.

Snipes, Nathan & Margarett Bridgers, 6 Sept 1789; John Isler, bm.

Snipes, Needam & Pherebe Turner, 14 Mar 1796; Phil Johnson, bm.

Snipes, Needham & Tempy A. Wall, 8 Jan 1850; Needham J. Whitley, bm.

Snips, Drury & Unity Houlder, 6 Aug 1822; John S. Whitley, bm.

Solomon, Elijah & Letty Durham, 23 Oct 1797; Edmund Tomlinson, bm.

Southard, Jackson & Ann Smith, 10 Jun 1859; m 12 Jun 1859 by Jesse Parker, J. P.

Sowell, Clayton & Sarah Adams, 6 Mar 1788; Howell Adams, bm.

Speed, Robert & Nancy Ryal, 29 Sept 1812; Jessee Adams, bm.

Spell, Dempsy & Zilpha Horn, 11 Oct 1815; Lewis Caudle, bm.

Spell, Reddich & Elizabeth Worly, 18 Nov 1811; Hilbert Starling, bm.

Spell, Thomas & Cresy Gouvin, 5 Nov 1808; Thomas Taylor, Jonathan Stansell, bm.

Spence, Elisha & Nancy Wood Jr., 25 Nov 1823; William W. Nichols, bm.

Spence, James & Nancy Pate, 1 Jan 1825; Elisha Spence, bm.

Spencer, D. C. & Patsey N. Watson, 30 Mar 1859; m 31 Mar 1859 by Wilie Wellons, J. P.

Spencer, James R. & Harriet Renfrow, m 8 Jan 1861 by Ray Phillips, J. P.

Spencer, John & Polly Stallings, 24 Mar 1821; William Spencer, bm.

Spencer, William & Peggy Massey, 15 Mar 1819; Isaiah Massey, bm.

Spencer, William J. & Edith Oliver, m 22 Jan 1856 at John Peedens, by Wm. H. Sellers, J. P.

Spicer, James & Peguila Price, 30 Mar 1784; Joseph Spicer, bm.

Spivey, Lovet & Lizy Avera, 20 Jul 1821; Isaac Stalling, bm.

Spivy, Dickson & Scarby Slaughter, 1 Oct 1804; Cullen Talton, bm.

Spivy, Larkin & Rildy Talton, 22 Jun 1849; Jennett Holland, bm.

Spivy, William & Nancy Pool, 12 Apr 1794; Reuben Wilkinson, bm.

Spivy, William & Polly Langley, 22 Apr 1815; Isaac Langley, bm.

Stackrock, David O. & Betsy Sanders, 15 May 1827; J. Sanders, bm.

Stafford, Jesse & Patsy Forehand, 28 Dec 1813; Lewis Forehand, bm.

Stafford, Joseph & Chelly A. Denning, 30 Nov 1853; m by E. S. Jones, J. P.

Stallings, Caleb & Zilpha Hartly, 5 Feb 1866; Jerry Holt, bm.

Stallings, Callin & Polly Massey, 17 Jan 1825; Allen S. Ballinger, bm.

Stallings, Ezekiel & Elizabeth Wilder, 11 Apr 1818; Jesse Creech, bm.

Stallings, Henry O. & Aquilla Hughs, 6 Oct 1838; Needham Oliver, bm.

Stallings, Isaac & Sally Jinkins, 30 Apr 1825; Edwin Spivy, bm.

Stallings, Isaac & Mourning Sellers, 12 Apr 1854; m 13 Apr 1854 by Ransom Kirby, J. P.

Stallings, Jacob & Edith Avera, 13 Apr 1784; Isaac Stallings, bm.

Stallings, James & Ulrica Bryan, 2 Apr 1818; Isaac Stallings, bm.

Stallings, James & Nancy Creech, 29 Apr 1824; Jno. Spencer, bm.

Stallings, James & Fanny Legon, 9 Dec 1848; Richard Stallings, bm.

Stallings, James B. & Elizabeth Jones, 15 Dec 1847; Wm. H. McCullers, bm.

Stallings, John & Nancy Oniel, 30 Dec 1812; Aron Solomon, bm.

Stallings, Richard & Polly Simpkins, 12 Mar 1814; Joseph Brown, bm.

Stallings, Zadok & Anne Avera, 15 Apr 1785; Jacob Stallings, bm.

Stancell, Allen S. & Elizabeth Selivent, 22 Dec 1858; m 24 Dec 1858 at Williams Stancill, by L. Y. Boyett, J. P.

Stancell, Elias & Elizabeth Stancell, 16 Feb 1867; Gaston Stansell, bm.

Stancell, John C. & Eliza Ann Creech, 29 Sept 1866; John D. Massey, bm; m 30 Sept 1866 at the Union Church, by W. P. Phillips, J. P.

Stancell, Moses & Emily Massingill, 10 Dec 1866; John W. Avera, bm; m 11 Dec 1866 at Mrs. Wiley Massingill, by Parrot Creech.

Stancell, Reddic & Polly Creech, m 31 Jan 1867 at Barna Creech, by Wilie F. Gerald, J. P.

Stancell, Robertson & Mary Stancell, 25 Feb 1866; Ransom Hare, bm.

Stancil, Jesse & Rhody Price, 10 Dec 1835; Hudson Reves, bm.

Stancil, Joseph & Sarah Godwin, 13 Mar 1867; m 15 Mar 1867 by J. F. Ellington, M. G.

Stancil, Young A. & Susan C. Godwin, 19 Aug 1858; m 22 Aug 1858 by B. Godwin, J. P.

Standley, Jesse & Ame Baker, 13 Jul 1802; Wm. Standley, bm.

Standly, Lewis & Ridley Kean, 4 Nov 1846; Gideon Keen, bm.

Stanly, Eli & Susan Emily Stanly, 7 Mar 1854; m 8 Mar 1854 by R. Masingill, J. P.

Stanly, Elijah & Nancy Dunn, 29 Dec 1823; Ezekiel Creech, bm.

Stanly, Elijah & Jensey Stanly, 12 Jul 1856; m 13 Jul 1856 by George Keen, J. P.

Stanly, Elisha & Precilla Dun, 11 Sept 1810; John Carter, bm.

Stanly, Elisha & Rainy Peoples, 20 May 1843; Amos Johnson, bm.

Stanly, Giddy & Pherebee Pope, 15 Aug 1846; William Stanly, bm.

Stanly, James & Lelah Black, 9 Mar 1809; Jesse Stanly, bm.

Stanly, James & Nicey Adams, 20 Mar 1833; George Dunn, bm.

Stanly, Jesse Jr. & Barthsheba Stanly, 25 Aug 1841; Silas Webb, bm.

Stanly, John & Sealy Corbet, 2 Jan 1816; James Stanly, bm.

Stanly, John W. & Charlotte Stricklin, 13 Oct 1862; Sir William Stanly, bm.

Stanly, John W. M. & Nannie Stanly, 11 Dec 1860; m 13 Dec 1860 by Jas. M. Adams, J. P.

Stanly, Lewis & Milly Joiner, 17 Dec 1816; John Owen, bm.

Stanly, Lewis & Trecy Kean, 1 Dec 1837; Silas Webb, bm.

Stanly, William & Polly Web, 9 Aug 1809; Elijah Baker, bm.

Stanly, Sir William & Rebecca Strickland, 17 Jan 1843; Jno. W. Stanly, bm.

Stanly, William Jr. & Nancy Webb, 4 Jan 1826.

Stansel, Godfrey & Raney Godwin, 7 Sept 1838; John G. Stansell, bm.

Stansel, John G. & Rhoda Jones, 1 Sept 1848; Jno. B. Beckwith, bm.

Stansel, Thomas & Delaney Sasser, 4 Jul 1860; m 15 Jul 1860 at Oliver Rains's, by Ray Phillips, J. P.

Stansell, Alexander & Celia Barber, 20 Jan 1835; James G. Woodall, bm.

Stansell, John & Polley Worley, 27 Sept 1818; Stephen Barnes, bm.

Stansell, John Jr. & Zilpha Grice, 29 Aug 1785; Benjamin Oneil, bm.

Stansell, Samuel & Patsey Rentfrow, 20 Jul 1838; Austin Hatcher, bm.

Stansell, Willie P. & Martha Stansell, 10 Apr 1852; m 20 Apr 1852 by S. Bagley, J. P.

Stansill, Nathan & Clary Taylor, 17 Feb 1797; John Stansell, bm.

Stansill, Nathan & Nancy Pender, 27 Feb 1799; Freadrick Homes, bm.

Starlin, Elisha & Prissy Parker, 30 Sept 1817; Abraham Batten, bm.

Starling, Daniel & Sephrona Peeden, 1 Feb 1867; Joseph Jones, bm; m 10 Dec 1867 at Drusiller Peedens, by Wilie F. Gerald, J. P.

Starling, David & Nancy Johnson, 31 Jan 1824; Exum Wellons, bm.

Starling, Elisha & Margarett Milliner, 17 Jan 1839; James Peeden, Sr., bm.

Starling, Graphin & Anny Hearne, 28 Feb 1810; Samuel Batten, bm.

Starling, Hilliard & Winey Worley, 22 Jan 1803; Jesse Creach, bm.

Starling, Jesse & Winnefred Gay, 27 Aug 1822; Henry Parnel, bm.

Steaphens, David & Any Johnson, 13 Mar 1793; Uriah Johnson, bm.

Steavens, John & Pheareby Fail, 19 Apr 1792; Thos. Fail, bm.

Stephenson, Alfred & Winefred M. Dodd, 14 Sept 1861; m 15 Sept 1861 at Mathew Dodd's, by John M. Stephenson, J. P.

Stephenson, Amos & Sally Parish, 5 Apr 1848; Ransom M. Stephenson, bm; m 5 Apr 1848 by John M. Stephenson, J. P.

Stephenson, Britton & Martha Blalock, 17 Apr 1854; m 20 Apr 1854 by A. J. Leach, J. P.

Stephenson, David & Ann Clifton, 24 Feb 1824; Simon P. Parrish, bm.

Stephenson, Elbridge & Sarah Lee, 19 Dec 1866; Jno. D. Massey, bm; m 20 Dec 1866 at Quary Stephensons, by H. A. Clifton, bm.

Stephenson, George & Penny Woodall, 14 Feb 1835; Moor Stephens, bm.

Stephenson, George & Mary Lasiter, 5 Aug 1853; m 11 Aug 1853 by J. H. Keneday, B. M.

Stephenson, James H. & Lucindy Coats, m 29 May 1853 by J. T. Leach, J. P.

Stephenson, Jesse & Lotty Stephenson, 1 Oct 1841; Allen Stephenson, bm;

Stephenson, John & Sarah Pleasant, 30 Dec 1816; James Whitenton, bm.

Stephenson, Kimon & _____ Whiggs, 12 Sept 1850.

Stephenson, L. D. & Arabella W. Mitchener, 4 Mar 1861; m 5 Mar 1861 by Thos. G. Whitaker, M. G.

Stephenson, Moore & Zilla Coats, 3 Nov 1832; Joshua Stephenson, bm.

Stephenson, Nazree & Chilly Johnson, 25 Sept 1862; m 27 Sept 1862 at Jas. H. Johnsons, by R. W. Stevens, J. P.

Stephenson, Quinton & Maryann Elizabeth Creech, m 3 Dec 1851 by H. H. Finch, J. P.

Stephenson, Solomon & Creecy Johnson, 4 Feb 1817; Barnabas Johnson, bm.

Stephenson, William & Mary E. Griffin, 14 Feb 1860; m 15 Feb 1860 by C. J. Bingham, J. P.

Stephenson, William Rufus & Martha A. Mitchener, 6 Feb 1858; m 10 Feb 1858 by Wm. E. Pell.

Sterling, Henry & Cemantha Pain, 26 Feb 1844; James Hinannt, bm; m 26 Feb 1844 by James Hinnant, J. P.

Sterling, Isaac & Louisa Oliver, 27 Aug 1836; Henry O. Stallings, bm.

Sterling, Nicholas & Elizabeth Pope, 23 Nov 1847; George Dunn, bm.

Sterling, William & Susan Blackman, 13 Dec 1848; Wm. Gay, bm.

Stevens, A. T. & Mary Ann Ogburn, 16 Sept 1863; m 24 Sept 1863 at Mr. Calvin Ogburn's, by Aldridge Partin.

Stevens, Augustus W. & Sarah Bryan, 14 Dec 1839; Thos. W. Stevens, bm.

Stevens, Benjamin & Peggy Cross, 26 Nov 1822; James Godwin, bm.

Stevens, Benjamin & Keran Thomson, 17 Apr 1839; M. C. Comes, bm.

Stevens, Burt & Pency Villia Jones, 4 May 1817; Alexr. Smith, Jr., bm.

Stevens, Charles & Mary Holliman, 6 Oct 1795; Frederick Hollemon, bm.

Stevens, Charles & Elizabeth Ingram, 14 May 1800; Matthias Handy, bm.

Stevens, Charles & Edith Farmer, 12 Oct 1805; Will Guy, bm.

Stevens, Charles & Betsy Farmer, 25 Sept 1821; Adin Powell, bm.

Stevens, E. P. & Elisabeth Stancell, 20 Jun 1849; Stephen H. Stansell, bm.

Stevens, Edward & Drusillah Howard, 18 Sept 1822; Absalem P. Woodall, bm.

Stevens, Edward Jr. & Talitha Rivers, 19 Dec 1791; Richard Rivers, bm.

Stevens, Everitt P. & Nicy Steevns, 18 Aug 1848; Wm. H. Oneal, bm.

Stevens, Everright P. & Rhoda Houlder, 28 Dec 1819; Jacob Stevens, bm.

Stevens, Henry & Sally White, 13 May 1794; William Coats, bm.

Stevens, Henry & Betsey Bass, 23 Apr 1807; Jno. Stevens, Jr., bm.

Stevens, Irby & Betsey A. Spence, 14 Dec 1850.

Stevens, Jacob & Elizabeth Boon, 30 May 1793; Joseph Boon, bm.

Stevens, Jacob & Patience Pearce, 22 May 1797; Jno. Stevens, Jr., bm.

Stevens, Jacob A. & Elizabeth L. Irby, 15 Sept 1857; m 16 Sept 1857 at the residence of H. Irby, by B. Lane, J. P.

Stevens, James & Sarah Cole, 15 Oct 1825; Josiah Cole, bm.

Stevens, John Jr. & Elizabeth Allen, 11 Oct 1804; John A. Smith, bm.

Stevens, John P. & Bartillie Holland, 11 Dec 1866; Calvin Darmon, bm; m 24 Dec 1866 at Jesse Hollands, by H. A. Clifton, J. P.

Stevens, Josiah & Kizzy C. Alford, 25 Feb 1867; N. B. Toler, bm.

Stevens, Julius A. & Rebecca A. Bulls, 4 Aug 1838; Alexander H. Thornton, bm.

Stevens, Levy & Sarah Carrell, 28 Jun 1836; Haywood Martin, bm.

Stevens, Needham & Elizabeth Mitchener, 11 Jan 1830; Saml. S. Turner, bm.

Stevens, Needham & Emily Stevens, 24 Mar 1830; Henry Stevens, bm.

Stevens, Richard & Lizzie Johnston, 23 Jul 1818; Jeremiah Sims, bm.

Stevens, Robert W. & Susannah Barber, 29 Mar 1837; Haywood Martin, bm.

Stevens, Simeon & Keziah J. Kilgo, 2 Jan 1808; Berry Wooten, bm.

Stevens, Simon & Emily Scott, 4 Dec 1832; Joseph Matthews, bm.

Stevens, Whitly & Betsy Killingsworth, 2 Jan 1806; Wm. B. Raiford, bm.

Stevens, William H. & Elizabeth S. Allen, 20 Dec 1834; William A. Bass, bm.

Stevens, William H. & Sarah Martin, 23 Oct 1858; m 28 Oct 1858 at Abraham Martins, by T. W. Whitley, J. P.

Stevens, Williamson & Emily Trawick, 27 Feb 1838; Benjamin Whitley, bm.

Stevens, Zacheriah & Susanna Rivers, 19 Jan 1791; Richard Rivers, bm.

Stevenson, Britten & Nancy Grimes, m 28 Dec 1850 by A. J. Leach, J. P.

Stevenson, Edward & Louisa Holland, 2 Sept 1846; Jesse Stephenson, bm.

Stevenson, Henry & Delilah Daniel, 23 May 1798; James Johnson, bm.

Stevenson, James & Charlotte Lee, 24 Dec 1845; Josiah Evans, bm.

Stevenson, Jerrel & Olive Johnson, 27 Feb 1816; David Stevens, bm.

Stevenson, John & Sally Cooper, 18 Oct 1824; Harris Tomlinson, bm.

Stevenson, Joshua & Isbel Powell, 8 Jun 1832; Moor Stephenson, bm.

Stevenson, Osbern & M. Pleasant, 4 May 1847; Solomon Stephenson, bm.

Stevenson, Ransom M. & Matilda Holland, 22 Oct 1847; Amos Stevenson, bm; m 22 Oct 1847 by A. J. Leach, J. P.

Stevenson, Solomon & Nancy Langdon, 18 Dec 1822; Simon P. Parish, bm.

Stevons, William & Mary Sasser, 28 Oct 1792; Jno. Atkinson, bm.

Stewart, Charles & Sally Woodall, 29 Oct 1821; Terry Barber, bm.

Stewart, Eldridg & Delaney Matthews, 13 Jun 1846; Robert W. Stevens, bm.

Stewart, James & Harriet Woodall, 9 Dec 1840; James G. Woodall, bm.

Stewart, Jesse & Sally McLane, 21 Dec 1847; Wm. A. Stewart, bm.

Stewart, William & Mary Jernigan, 26 Sept 1848; John C. Hood, bm.

Stillwell, Thomas & Nelly Rains Worley, 23 Aug 1819; John Rains, bm.

Stimson, Erasmus & Patience Ford, 10 Dec 1813; William Hawkins, bm.

Stott, Alsey & Polly Stansel, 25 Dec 1837; Godfrey Stansell, bm.

Stricklan, Nathan & Rebecca Lee, 20 Apr 1833; Robert W. Sneed, bm.

Strickland, Aden & Betsy Strickland, 20 Mar 1827; Riddick Warren, bm.

Strickland, Bennet B. & Caroline Allen, 8 Apr 1842; Sir Wm. Stanly, bm.

Strickland, Bythan E. & Salina H. Johnson, 13 Mar 1867; J. W. Strickland, bm; m 14 Mar 1867 at H. R. Stricklin, by George Keen, J. P.

Strickland, Calvin & Anne Oneal, 14 Sept 1835; John Bryan, bm.

Strickland, David & Sophia Stevens, 30 Sept 1834; D. H. Bryan, bm.

Strickland, Eli & Susan O'neal, 5 Mar 1828; Richardson Oneal, bm.

Strickland, Ely & Cornelia Oneal, 4 Nov 1844; Larkin Leigh, bm.

Strickland, Hartney & Catharin Baily, 6 May 1847; Griffin Bailey, bm.

Strickland, Henderson & Patsy ONeal, 9 Nov 1838; Hillard Strickland, bm.

Strickland, Hillmon & Patience Price, 27 Sept 1836; Applewhite W. Richardson, bm.

Strickland, Hillyard & Nancy Richardsn, 24 Feb 1842; A. J. Taylor, bm.

Strickland, Jackson & Sarrah H. Hocutt, 24 Nov 1860; m 2 Dec 1860 by S. W. Woody, J. P.

Strickland, Jacob & Sally Holt, 15 Jan 1847; Pelick Massey, bm.

Strickland, James & Elizabeth B. Wall, 25 Oct 1836; Robert N. Gulley, bm.

Strickland, Jeremiah & Elizabeth Gurley, 1 Apr 1783; Benjamin Strickland, bm.

Strickland, Jeremiah & Reley Price, 10 Oct 1825; Samuel Strickland, bm.

Strickland, Jesse B. & Sally Ann Wiggins, 20 Dec 1851; m 22 Dec 1851 by R. Massingill, J. P.

Strickland, John T. & Susan Britt, 18 Mar 1867; m 19 Mar 1867 at B. A. Cores, by George Keen, J. P.

Strickland, Jonathan & Mary Daniel, 23 Feb 1836; Young Eldredge, bm.

Strickland, Levi & Winnifred Braddy, 27 Mar 1824; Abner Brady, bm.

Strickland, Lewis & Elizabeth Thornton, 5 Sept 1833; Henry Ingram, bm.

Strickland, Nathan & Edith Smith, 29 Feb 1804; Sam'l. Lee, Jr., bm.

Strickland, Samuel & Sarah Hocutt, 30 Nov 1790; Applewhite Richardson, bm.

Strickland, Samuel & Sally Thompson, 25 Aug 1803; John Herring, bm.

Strickland, Samuel & Delilah Pope, 15 Mar 1821; Henry Jordan, bm.

Strickland, Samuel & Susan Stanly, 18 Jul 1835; Elijah Baker, bm.

Strickland, William & Lany Creech, 30 Nov 1813; Joshua Creech, Jr., bm.

Strickland, William R. & Sarah A. George, 7 Apr 1866; Thos. D. Snead, bm.

Strickland, Wright & Susan Tailor, 23 May 1836; J. A. Stevens, bm.

Stricklin, James & Celah Horn, 31 Jul 1815; Jno. C. Guy, bm.

Stricklin, Nathan & Elizabeth Harrell, 28 May 1793; John Stricklin, bm.

Stricklin, Henry Wright & Elizabeth Baker, 24 Sept 1842; John Stanly, bm.

Studevant, Calvin & Martha Baucumb, 3 Jan 1836; Thomas Busbee, bm.

Sturdervant, _____ & Eleanor Lockart, 18 Mar 1840; David Thomson, bm.

Sturdivent, Holm & Esther Perry, 28 Feb 1801; Alexander Peney, Elick Sanders, bm.

Sugg, Joshua & Martha Martin, 17 Oct 1829; John H. Martin, bm.

Suggs, Rigdon & Sylvear Martin, 28 Feb 1825; Lazarus Matthews, bm.

Sugs, Aquila & Mary Barber, 19 Aug 1848; Young A. Barber, bm.

Sullavent, Ruffin & Sarah Sillavent, 9 Nov 1851; m 28 Nov 1861 by Stanly Kirby, J. P.

Sulliven, William & Tabitha Lee, 19 Feb 1772; Jno. Smith, John Pope, bm.

Sumner, Joseph J. & Winefred Rivers, 12 Aug 1814; William Rivers, bm.

Surles, James H. & Francess Wheeler, 24 Dec 1858; m 30 Dec 1858 by W. F. Hall, Elder.

Surles, W. B. & Sarah M. Byrd, 25 Oct 1851; m 20 Nov 1851 by N. L. Phillips, J. P.

Surls, Thomas & Penny Johnson, 13 Jan 1836; John Wood, bm.

Swanson, Philip & Sarah Parish, 12 Nov 1792; Uriah Johnson, bm.

Sweaney, Miles & Jane Dodd, 7 Mar 1795; John Dodd, bm.

Swiney, William & Zilphia Price, 12 Mar 1818; Tho. Lockart, Jr., bm.

Syllavent, Garry & Patience Odam, 9 Mar 1838; Jesse Hinnant, bm.

Sympkins, Calvin & Elizabeth Hinton, 24 Sept 1825; Edwin Spivy, bm.

Taborn, Westley & Smiethey Hogan, 12 Jun 1847; Exum Holland, bm.

Talton, Arthur & Unity Pearce, 31 May 1791; William Talton, bm.

Talton, Cullom & Lewcy Clark, 7 Jun 1806; Jonathan Talton, bm.

Talton, Curtis & Lucy Ann Edwards, 1 Apr 1851; m 3 Apr 1851 by W. Holt, J. P.

Talton, James & Sarrah Almonds, 5 Feb 1799; Wm. Farmer, bm.

Talton, James & Nancy Spivy, 21 Mar 1807; Reuben Wilkerson, bm.

Talton, James & Sally Talton, 1 Sept 1840; John H. Rains, bm.

Talton, Jesse A. & Lydia Lewis, 9 Sept 1817; James Clark, bm.

Talton, Jonathan & Polly Taylor, 15 Jul 1809; Needham Talton, bm.

Talton, Ransom & Evaline Deanes, 8 Jun 1866; Ransom Hare, bm.

Talton, W. J. & Mary Yelvington, 15 Oct 1860; m 17 Oct 1860 at Jethro Yelvingtons, by John W. Hodges, J. P.

Talton, William & Judith Stallings, 16 Dec 1779; Zadok Stallings, bm.

Talton, William & Elizabeth Hobbs, 11 Jan 1866; Willie Starling, bm.

Tant, John & Winefred Lee, 15 Mar 1849; Young G. Lee, bm.

Tapley, Adam & Anne Brannan, 16 Feb 1786; William Hobbs, bm.

Tart, John & Susan Ingram, 26 Feb 1844; Westbrook Lee, bm.

Tart, Lee S. & Mary Wood, 9 Feb 1867; Wm. T. Tart, bm.

Tart, Nathaniel & Avy Barefoot, 21 Mar 1842; William Tart, bm.

Tartt, Thomas Jr. & Purny Jane Smith, 28 May 1838; Joel Lee, bm.

Tartt, William & Winnefred Smith, 17 Mar 1838; Harry Johnson, bm.

Taylor, Benjamin & Alsey Pritchet, 17 Feb 1787; David Bell, bm.

Taylor, John & Diannah Baily, 8 Mar 1789; William Baily, bm.

Taylor, Ransom & Esther Nowell, 7 Feb 1835; Thomas Turley, bm.

Taylor, Ransom & Nancy Lee, 16 Jun 1838; John Lee, bm.

Taylor, Thomas & Charlotty Spivey, 15 Apr 1805; Simon Pearce, bm.

Taylor, Willis & Tempi Hamby, 25 Nov 1839; Roberson Rosser, bm.

Teal, Lewis & Edney Lankford, 19 Apr 1800; Barnaby Bulls, bm.

Teal, William & Rachel Bulls, 6 Apr 1791; Nathan Powell, bm.

Tedder, Thomas & Celia Holloman, 6 Nov 1816; Reuben Dodd, bm.

Teder, Stephen & Elizabeth Simpson, 16 Feb 1819; Tharris H. Hawley, bm.

Teele, William & Patience Daugherty, 24 Feb 1819; Isaiah Massey, bm.

Telfair, Alexander & Julia A. Boon, 17 Nov 1838; Wm. H. Morning, bm.

Temple, Burwell & Elizabeth Whitley, 13 Nov 1853.

Temple, Burwell W. & Martha T. Blackman, 18 Feb 1854; m 26 Feb 1854 by Robt. Massingill, bm.

Temple, Caswell & Mary Hawkins Massingill, 23 Mar 1860; m 25 Mar 1860 at Warren Masser, by George Keen, J. P.

Temple, P. R. & Penelope Massingill, 14 Jan 1857; m 15 Jan 1857 by W. H. Massingill, J. P.

Temple, Peter R. & Mary Woodall, 8 Jan 1848; R. H. Blackman, bm.

Temple, Peter R. & Evaline Price, 7 Jun 1866; A. Knox, bm.

Temple, Ransom H. & Nancy Allen, 1 Nov 1837; Starling W. Temple, bm.

Temple, Sterling & Naoma Massingill, 20 May 1808; George Masingill, bm.

Thain, Jethro & Amanda Allen, 3 Sept 1839; m 6i Sept 1859 at the house of J. A. Stephens, by R. D. Lunceford, J. P.

Thane, Samuel B. & Pasha Elisar Woodard, 17 Dec 1862; m 4 Jan 1863 at the house of Joseph Woodard, by Wms. Brown, Elder.

Thane, Thomas & Francis Avera, m 12 Sept 1855 at Mrs. Lucinda Averas, by Edwin Boykin, J. P.

Thane, William & Julia Ann Cullum, m 15 Nov 1855 at the residence of Henry Cullum, by Edwin Boykin, J. P.

Tharp, Henry H. & Amanda M. Utley, 14 Jan 1851; m 15 Jan 1851 by Wm. H. Morning, J. P., "in the presence of Willis H. Sanders, Norflett Bell, David Avera Jnr, and others."

Thomas, Alexander & Polley Murphy, 22 Mar 1805; Elisha Thomas, bm.

Thomas, Elisha & Lucy Massey, 16 Feb 1764; Drury Vinson, Benjamin Scott, bm.

Thomas, Elisha & Edith Lockart, 7 Sept 1802; Stephen Lockhart, bm.

Thomas, James H. & Mariah Stanly, 21 Dec 1846; George Keen, bm.

Thomas, James H. & Mariah Stanly, 9 Sept 1848; William Stanly, bm.

Thomas, Jesse & Polly Stafford, 10 Apr 1813; Joseph Thomas, bm.

Thomas, Joseph & Polly Smith, 24 Feb 1808; Simon Pearce, bm.

Thomas, Micajah & Patsy Long, 25 Jan 1825; Jno. MacLeod, bm.

Thomas, Solomon & Ridley Bryan, 25 Feb 1792; Isaac Hinton, bm.

Thompson, David & Sally McCullers, 10 Nov 1818; Ray Helme, bm.

Thompson, Elijah & Nancy Braswell, 20 Dec 1814; Sam Strickland, bm.

Thompson, Elijah Y. & Sarah A. Oliver, 28 Jan 1860; m 31 Jan 1860 at Haywood Creech's, by Williams Brown.

Thompson, Jarrett & Susanna Chambers, 19 Sept 1791; Michal Reynolds, bm.

Thompson, John & Barbara Caps, 19 May 1798; Barnaby Bulls, bm.

Thompson, John W. & Sarah P. Peedin, 29 Jan 1862; m 30 Jan 1862 at Wm. J. Peedin's, by William Brown.

Thompson, Lewis & Heron Strickland, 4 Aug 1810; William Thompson, bm.

Thompson, Nicholas & Betsy Hays, 11 Jan 1793; Elijah Thompson, bm.

Thompson, Nickey & Susan Lee, 18 Aug 1845; Dempsey Grant, bm.

Thompson, Steven G. & Harriet Narion, 27 Aug 1844; Zadock Peacock, bm.

Thompson, Uriah & Louisa Wallace, 5 Dec 1866; Calvin J. Wallace, bm; m 6 Dec 1866 at Elisha Wallace, by B. A. Wellons, J. P.

Thompson, William & Fereby Roberts, 29 Aug 1802; Needham Warren, bm.

Thompson, William B. & Clary Hollimon, 10 Feb 1843; Stephen Thompson, bm.

Thomson, Britton & Matilda Worley, 23 Jan 1841; Jno. P. Williams, bm.

Thomson, David & Mrs. Phereby Helme, 9 Jan 1837; Thos. Rice, bm.

Thomson, Devereux D. & Lucy Edwards, 18 Dec 1840; Elijah Thomson, bm.

Thomson, Harry & Milly Collins, 2 Mar 1835; Lewis Thomson, bm.

Thomson, Jesse R. & Harriet Spencer, 8 Jan 1842; Deverich D. Thomson, bm.

Thomson, John R. & Martha J. Peeden, 8 Jan 1849; Devereux D. Thomson, bm.

Thomson, Lewis & Sophia Rhodes, 7 Apr 1840; Jno. P. Williams, bm.

Thornton, David & Nancy Ingram, 27 Jan 1807; Saml. Lee, Jr., bm.

Thornton, Harrod & Zilpha Blackmon, 24 Aug 1803; Saml. Lee, bm.

Thornton, Herod & Pherebe Clenny, 23 May 1820; Saml. Lee, bm.

Thornton, Michael S. & Martha Nowls, 26 Apr 1841; William Bundy, bm.

Thornton, Owen & Joannah Bryan, 12 Oct 1810; Harrod Thornton, bm.

Thornton, Thomas & Nancy Jordan, 1 Dec 1851; John Eason, bm.

Thornton, Thomas H. & Rhabeca L. Hays, 27 Jul 1844; Daniel Labon, bm.

Thornton, William & Mary Bell, 3 Feb 1846.

Thornton, William E. & Penney Harriett Creech, 20 Mar 1852; m 21 Mar 1852 by C. Langdon, J. P.

Thurston, William J. Y. & Zilpha Gulley, 26 Apr 1864; m 3 May 1864 at John G. Gully's, by J. F. Ellington.

Tigh, John & Sally Cobb, 15 Sept 1793; Saml. Oneal, bm.

Tiner, Jacob & Caty Benson, 28 May 1805; William Holt, Jr., bm.

Tiner, James & Winefred Thomson, 8 Jun 1835; Lewis Thomson, bm.

Tiner, Jesse & Sally Myatt, 26 Nov 1812.

Tiner, Lindsay & Sarah A. E. Thompson, 22 Dec 1860; m 23 Dec 1860 at Nickolas Thompsons, by W. A. Smith, J. P.

Tiner, Ransom & Mary Ann Allen, 1 Aug 1840; James H. Corbit, bm.

Tiner, Willis & Parthena Jernigan, 12 Apr 1799; Jesse Tiner, bm.

Tippitt, William D. & Elizier Ann Hinton, 25 Mar 1856; m 2 Apr 1856 at Freeman Chamly, by S. M. Woody, J. P.

Tisdale, E. S. & Emiline Pulley, 19 Nov 1861; m 21 Nov 1861 at Bryant Pulleys, by J. R. Brown.

Tisdell, Edwin S. & Lucinda Oneal, 21 Dec 1857; m 22 Dec 1857 at Hopson Oneals, by W. Earp, J. P.

Tisdale, Elisha & Polly Oneal, 25 Sept 1810; Isom Onel, bm.

Tisdale, Elisha & Nancy Oneal, 5 May 1845; Evrett P. Stevens, bm.

Tisdale, Joel & Elizabeth Bayley, 22 Feb 1847; Richardson Oneal, bm.

Tisdale, Kelly & Sallie Ann Thompson, 2 Apr 1866; Wm. H. Pilkinton, bm; m 3 Apr 1866 at Mrs. Aney Kornegays, by W. H. Sellers, J. P.

Tolar, Nathan B. & Disey Stevens, 1 May 1857; Barna Lane, bm.

Toler, Sanders & Adalne Tiner, 20 Aug 1866; Ashley Creech, bm.

Toler, Stephen & Catty Brent, 23 Nov 1819; Benjamin Dunn, bm.

Toller, Stephen & Polly Gully, 28 Sept 1818; William Holt, bm.

Tomlinson, Brazel & Salina G. Renfrow, 28 Apr 1866; W. B. Jones, bm.

Tomlinson, Edmund & Delilah McKoy, 28 May 1794; Nahor Norris, bm.

Tomlinson, Edmund & Sally Coats, 25 Jul 1809; Harriss Tomlinson, bm.

Tomlinson, Harriss & Edith Lockhart, 29 Sept 1802; John Sanders, bm.

Tomlinson, James & Mary Bridgers, 27 Sept 1836; Jackson A. Leach, bm.

Tomlinson, Thomas & Sarah Penny, 17 Apr 1818; Harriss Tomlinson, bm.

Tomlinson, William & Sarah Horn, 15 Feb 1837; William Tomlinson, bm.

Tomlinson, William H. & Martha Ellington, 23 Apr 1853; m 27 Apr 1853 by J. B. Jackson.

Tool, Jonathan & Edith Lee, 17 Nov 1834; John R. Evans, bm.

Tool, Lodwick & Sally Lee, 28 Dec 1843; Barna Guin, bm.

Toole, Frederick & Rhoda Joiner, 24 Aug 1807; Saml. Lee, Jr., Francis Harrell, Jr., bm.

Traywick, Othniel & Sarah Eason, 6 May 1797; George Traywick, bm.

Tucker, William & Salley Meredith, 19 Nov 1807; David Sauls, John Kelley, Sr., bm.

Tucker, William & Nelly Wilder, 6 Feb 1816; Caron Brannon, bm.

Turley, Richard & Mary Peal, 25 Aug 1788; Wm. Ward, bm.

Turley, Richard & Eliza Farrar, 29 Jun 1822; Thomas Turley, bm.

Turley, Samuel M. & Livly Ellis, 11 Jan 1834; J. G. Gully, bm.

119

Turley, Thomas & Patience Brady, 24 Feb 1819; Etheldred Holt, bm.

Turley, Thomas & Ridley Ellis, 13 Jan 1858; Samuel M. Turley, bm; m 15 Jan 1858 by J. F. Ellington.

Turnell, James & Elizabeth Talton, 29 Nov 1825; Wilie Gerald, bm.

Turner, Atlas & Edith Simpkins, 22 Mar 1836; William Jones, bm.

Turner, David & Jane Bridgers, 27 Oct 1803; William Turner, bm.

Turner, David S. & Alice C. Mitchner, 8 May 1866; R. D. Lunceford, bm.

Turner, James & Dicy Dodd, 13 Jan 1808; Rigdan Johnson, bm.

Turner, James & Edith Smith, 2 Feb 1814; Philip Johnson, bm.

Turner, John & Polly Avera, 22 Dec 1796; Tadok Stallings, bm.

Turner, John B. & Sophia G. Powell, 27 Sept 1831; Wm. H. Watson, bm.

Turner, Kinchen & Sarah Watts, 21 Dec 1801; John Turner, bm.

Turner, Samuel S. & Edith Mitchner, 22 Jul 1835; Britain S. Utley, bm.

Turner, Thomas & Elizabeth Ferrell, 26 Jul 1837; William G. Parish, bm.

Turner, Thomas & Phereba Dodd, 6 Feb 1861; m 7 Feb 1861 by J. F. Ellington.

Turner, William & Edith Smith, 9 Oct 1812; Dd. Turner, bm.

Turner, Willis & Mary Bedngfield, 8 Nov 1836; Edward Price, bm.

Tyner, Uriah & Tranquilla Griffis, 21 Dec 1839; Wm. Munden, bm.

Underdew, James & Mary I. Scott, 10 Nov 1858; m 11 Nov 1858 at Levy Boothes, by John C. Hood, J. P.

Underwood, Thomas & Sarah Thornton, 10 Mar 1783; John Whitley, bm.

Underwood, Wright & Elizabeth Baker, 9 May 1866; E. D. Snead, bm.

Utley, Mike (colored) & Minerva Gay, 1 Mar 1867; Young Hathcock, bm; m 1 Mar 1867 at Smithfield, by Seth Woodall, J. P.

Uzzell, Isham & Nancy Blackman, 6 Feb 1790; Wm. Blackman, Jesse Purvis, bm.

Vann, Rufus & Edith Bryan, 3 Feb 1960; m 9 Feb 1860 by John C. Hood, J. P.

Vaughn, Stephen & Mary Hinson, 15 Aug [1780]; Arthur Bryan, bm.

Vick, Jesse & Molley Robertson, 12 Feb 1788; Thomas Robertson, John Gaerald, bm.

Vincent, John C. & Emily W. Eason, 8 May 1848; A. A. McDugold, bm.

Vincent, Thomas L. & Sarah A. E. Eason, 25 Nov 1846; Needham B. Stevens, bm.

Vincent, William & Winefred Averytt, 30 Jan 1814; Jonathan Averyt, bm.

Vining, Shadrach & Phereby Ratcliff, 13 Apr 1778; Porter Ratcliff, bm.

Vinson, Addison & Sarah Baines, _____ ; Jno. Vinson, Jr., bm.

Vinson, Archbald & Ruth Smith, 31 Mar 1797; William Bryan, bm.

Vinson, Calvin (colored) & Ellen Richardson, 16 Feb 1867; Haywood Vinson, bm; m 17 Feb 1867 by Ray Phillips, J. P.

Vinson, Drury & Nancy Brown, 18 Oct 1802; S. Brown, bm.

Vinson, Drury & Anne Durham, 2 Dec 1804; Samuel Avera, bm.

Vinson, Haywood (colored) & Isabella Watson, 17 Oct 1866; Theo. Whitfield (colored), bm; m 18 Oct 1866 by McNab Earp, J. P.

Vinson, Hinton & Patsy Bryan, 7 Feb 1817; Noah Nichols, bm.

Vinson, Hinton & Phereby Allen, 1 May 1823; S. T. Sanders, bm.

Vinson, James & Elizabeth Barnes, 6 Apr 1805; Harman Hobby, bm.

Vinson, James & Betsey Bridgers, 12 Feb 1822; Abner Vinson, bm.

Vinson, John Jr. & Sarah Allen, 21 Nov 1822; Hinton Vinson, bm.

Vinson, Needham & Caroline Evans, 27 Apr 1846; Young Bridgers, bm.

Vinson, Paton & Nancy Harper, 25 Mar 1796; Drury Vinson, bm.

Vinson, William & Jane Ford, 27 Dec 1849; John Ford, bm.

Waddell, John & Emily Bird, 25 Jan 1847; E. A. Bryan, bm.

Wade, Mark & Lidy Messer, 28 Mar 1863; R. W. Stevens, bm.

Wadel, Everet & Sally Longley, 25 Mar 1845; James Hinnant, bm.

Wadford, Hardy & Susanna Price, 3 Dec 1818; Moses Jordan, bm.

Wadkins, Winsor & Phereby Harper, 24 Oct 1818; Westley F. Wellons, bm.

Walker, David & Phenelah Silks, 19 Oct 1785; Clement Armstrong, bm.

Walker, Jacob & Luvey Gardner, 1 Nov 1790; John Moore, bm.

Walker, Jacob & Saley Batten, 22 Jan 1822; John Brown, bm.

Walker, John & Carien Woodall, 28 May 1821; Absalom P. Woodall, bm.

Walker, Jones & Betsey Powell, 29 Aug 1853; m 1 Sept 1853 by Nathan Williams, J. P.

Walker, William & Nancy Lee, 11 Jul 1844; William Price, bm.

Wall, Aaron & Zilpha Gully, 11 Mar 1826; David Thomson, bm.

Wall, Bennet & Sally Murphrey, 1 Feb 1823; Aaron Wall, bm.

Wall, Bennett & Rixy Carroll, 1 Jul 1859; Thos. D. Snead, bm; m 3 Jul 1859 at Malachi Walls, by R. N. Gully, J. P.

Wall, Jacob R. & Grizzy Ann Boyette, 12 Nov 1866; J. H. Ennis, bm; m 15 Nov 1866 by Jesse Hinnant, J. P.

Wall, James D. & Nancy E. Broughton, m 24 Jul 1858 by R. N. Gully, J. P.

Wall, James M. & Mary Broughton, 6 Jan 1858; J. R. Wall, bm; m 6 Jan 1858 at John R. Walls, by Robt. N. Gully, J. P.

Wall, Jarot B. & Sally Hinnant, 28 Sept 1830; Robert N. Gully, bm.

Wall, Jesse & Mary Perry, 2 Mar 1798; Robt. Gulley, Jr., bm.

Wall, Jesse & Polly Devall, 20 Jan 1809; Jacob Brooks, bm.

Wall, John & Polly Gulley, 2 Jan 1798; William Wall, bm.

Wall, Johnson B. & Luvina Gay, 6 Mar 1854; m 11 May 1854 by A. G. Lee, J. P.

Wall, Jonathan & Phereby Murphrey, 23 Nov 1824; Aaron Wall, bm.

Wall, Jonathan T. & Polly Hayles, 12 May 1836; Hutson Earp, bm.

Wall, Mabry T. & Louiza J. Talton, 20 Apr 1855; m 22 Apr 1855 at Asa Taltons, by Perry Godwin.

Wall, Malacai & Minda Battin, 27 Oct 1851; m 29 Oct 1851 by S. P. Horton, J. P.

Wall, Malichi & Mary Ginnet, 11 Jul 1849; John Murphrey, bm.

Wall, Perry & Aby Johnson, 27 Aug 1822; Jno. Boon, bm.

Wall, William B. & Mary Ann Hinton, 10 Jan 1827; Robt. N. Gully, bm.

Wall, William H. & Appy Batten, m 15 Nov 1855 by B. C. Richardson, J. P.

Wall, William H. & Rutha Ellen Batten, 21 Feb 1866; Stephen Sneed, bm.

Wallace, Aron & Nancy Stanley, 8 Mar 1837; Barnaba Dunn, bm.

Wallace, Calvin & Avey Peebles, 1 Feb 1848; Elisha Wallace, bm.

Wallace, Calvin R. & Milly Crocker, 15 Jan 1846; David H. Price, bm.

Wallace, John & Siorty Stanly, 16 May 1809; John Owens, bm.

Wallace, Lewis & Ganzada Hughs, 15 Aug 1845; Calvin Simpkins, bm.

Wallace, Moses & Rutha Price, 25 Jan 1849; Ashley Price, bm.

Wallace, Ransom & Elizabeth Stanly, m 26 Feb 1863 at James Standleys, by R. Masingill, J. P.

Wallis, Elisha & Rebecca Adams, 24 Feb 1835; Lewis Blackman, bm.

Wallis, James & Thena Crocker, 8 Oct 1840; Young Bridgers, bm.

Wallis, Jarret & Nancy Crocker, 4 Oct 1843; Berry Price, bm.

Wallis, Moses & Elizabeth Griffin, 2 Apr 1816; Abraham Webb, bm.

Wallis, Reuben & Ammy Austin, 16 Jan 1854; m 27 Jan 1854 by J. T. Leach, J. P.

Walston, Benjamin & Elizabeth Lee, 16 Feb 1828; Clem Barker, bm.

Walton, Andrew & Mary C. Honeycutt, 22 Dec 1866; A. J. Honeycutt, bm; m 23 Dec 1866 at Abner(?) Honeycutts, by Jno. R. Coates, J. P.

Walton, Avera & Cynthia Pate, 9 Oct 1821; Joseph Wright, bm.

Walton, James & Jane E. Bridgers, 15 Mar 1841; Ransom Sanders, bm.

Walton, Samuel, of Wake Co., & Cynthia Avera, 18 Nov 1800; Etheldred Smith, bm.

Walton, Samuel & Julia Pate, 24 Jan 1843; Ruffin W. Tomlinson, bm.

Walton, Timothy & Nancy Leach, 2 Jan 1792; Elleck Sanders, bm.

Walton, Timothy & Elizabeth Jones, 24 Jun 1822; Wm. A. Walton, bm.

Walton, William & Elizabeth Smith, 28 Nov 1767; David Smith, bm.

Walton, William & Sally Avera, 21 Apr 1798; Aventon Avera, bm.

Ward, Absalom & Rhoda Watkins, 24 Feb 1835; Tigal Ballance, bm.

Ward, Asa Jr. & Patsey Richardson, 26 Jan 1840; Asa Ward, bm.

Warren, Elijah & Polley Ingram, 16 Oct 1779; Richard Warren, bm.

Warren, George & Mary Blackman, 15 May 1783; Richard Warren, bm.

Warren, John (colored) & Catharine Turner, 21 Nov 1866; P. H. Oliver, bm; m 22 Nov 1866 by James Hay, J. P.

Warren, Richard Sr. & Polly Turley, 23 Aug 1801; Needham Warren, bm.

Warrick, John & Zilpha Jones, 29 Aug 1813; Micajah Cox, bm.

Warring, William & Elsie Talton, 24 Nov 1812; P. Raeford, bm.

Warwick, Hezekiah & Martha Stevens, 3 Dec 1866; Georg Martin, bm; m 6 Dec 1866 at Ezekiel Stephens, by Bryant Williams, J. P.

Watford, David & Patsy Price, 12 Feb 1824; Hardy Watford, bm.

Watford, Willie & Willey Lipperd, 6 Aug 1824; John Richardson, bm.

Watkins, Allen & Rhode Godwin, 14 Aug 1795; James Kirby, John Pearce, bm.

Watkins, Amos & Lucy Evans, 14 Oct 1799; James Kirby, bm.

Watkins, Burden & Cintha Horn, 23 Jul 1855; m 24 Jul 1855 at Milly Horns, by S. Bagley, J. P.

Watkins, David & Fany Sellars, 26 Feb 1812; James Bryan, bm.

Watkins, Incel & Fanny Ballance, 31 May 1823; Cullen Talton, bm.

Watkins, James & Molly Kerby, 3 Jan 1826; Jesse Kerby, bm.

Watkins, Pearce & Patsy Pearce, 20 Jan 1817; Loverd Pearce, bm.

Watkins, Peter & Delilah Grice, 25 May 1789; Stephen Grice, bm.

Watkins, Robert & Celah Bryan, 16 Jan 1790; Barnaby Lane, of Wake Co., bm.

Watkins, Simon & Bedy Flowers, 28 May 1833; Gaston Lockart, bm.

Watkins, Wiley & Alcey Johnson, 16 Mar 1795; Aron Johnson, Hardy Bryan, bm.

Watly, Stephen H. & Clarkey Richardson, 9 Sept 1848; Thos. H. Ligon, bm.

Watson, Allen & Decy Parish, 27 Dec 1805; Isham Watson, bm.

Watson, Baalam & Mary Downing, 25 Feb 1794; Archelus Barnes, of Johnston Co., Jesse Barnes, of Wayne Co., bm.

Watson, Bridgers & Milly Starling, 24 May 1825; Etheldred Futrell, bm.

Watson, David & Kiddy Roe, 25 Apr 1808; Wm. Guy, bm.

Watson, Dempsey & Edith Pope, 25 Feb 1835; Stephen Hicks, bm.

Watson, Elick (colored) & Susan Whitley, 1 Sept 1866; W. H. Whitley, bm.

Watson, Giles (colored) & Maria Atkinson, 25 Jun 1866; J. B. Alford, bm.

Watson, Giles (colored) & Senora Victoria Robertson, 6 Feb 1867; J. W. B. Watson, bm; m 7 Feb 1867 by James Jeffreys, J. P.

Watson, Harrias & Penny Privett, 13 Nov 1818; William Watson, bm.

Watson, Henry L. & Annie E. Moore, 10 Dec 1866; H. B. Turner, bm; m 20 Dec 1866 at Dr. E. D. Sneads, by W. B. Jones, M. G.

Watson, Jesse & Sally Hinnant, 10 Sept 1820; Jesse Sillavent, bm.

Watson, John B. & Mary Cooper, 20 Aug 1817; Nathan V. Boddie, bm.

Watson, Joseph & Martha Kirby, 27 Aug 1849; Robert Roper, bm.

Watson, Labon & Sally Watson, 24 Feb 1795; David Watson, bm.

Watson, Leavan & Priscillia Odam, 29 Nov 1785; William Fish, bm.

Watson, Littleton & Zelia Keen, 27 Aug 1821; Garry Price, bm.

Watson, Nathan (colored) & Gracy Watson, 25 Jan 1867; J. B. Alford, bm; m 26 Jan 1867 by W. D. Holt, J. P.

Watson, Riddick & Milley Watson, 27 Feb 1792; David Watson, bm.

Watson, Robert & Sally Ann Peeden, 16 Feb 1848; Garry Crumple, bm.

Watson, Stephen & Betsey Watson, 10 Mar 1812; Jesse Sillivent, bm.

Watson, Solomon & Harriet Hooks, 25 Dec 1830; B. R. Hinnant, bm.

Watson, Solomon & Hepsebah Jane Hinnant, 14 Jan 1834; Hardy Pilkinton, bm.

Watson, Solomon (colored) & Minerva Ruffin, 11 Apr 1866; W. M. Murphey, bm.

Watson, Thomas & Seany Peele, 24 Mar 1866; Harris Lamon, bm.

Watson, Toddy (colored) & Louisa Watson, 9 Feb 1867; A. J. Heath, bm; m 15 Feb 1867 by A. J. Heath, J. P.

Watson, William, son of Jas. Watson, & Elizabeth Tarver, 20 Oct 1763; James Watson, Henry Mains, David Holliman, bm.

Watson, William & Nancy Bryan, 23 Oct 1810; Willis Watson, bm.

Watson, William & Patience Williamson, 25 May 1818; Henry Sasser, bm.

Watson, William & Penelope Kerby, m 8 Jan 1853 by Stanly Kirby, J. P.

Watson, Willie & Harriet Boyett, 2 Jan 1846; Stanley Kirby, bm.

Watson, Willis & Rachel Herring, 28 Jan 1802; M. Handy, bm.

Watson, Willis & Betsy Bulls, 4 Jun 1807; Ellick Sanders, bm.

Watson, Zadock & Padeath Johnson, 30 Jul 1792; James Faulk, bm.

Wayne, Frederick & Martha E. Graham, 29 Feb 1864; m 10 Mar 1864, at Henderson Grantham.

Weaver, Asa & Betsy Weaver, 16 Aug 1820; Lewis Fail, bm.

Weaver, Reubin & Kezziah Ann Ingram, 29 Nov 1860; m 2 Dec 1860 at Elizabeth Ingram's, by John Harper.

Weaver, William Henry & Elizabeth Lee, 10 Feb 1852; m 12 Feb 1852 by Powel Blackmon, J. P.

Webb, Bennet & Lecy Ellis, 31 Oct 1835; Henry Guin, bm.

Webb, John & Susan Baker, 4 Oct 1854; m 5 Oct 1854 by Robt. Massingill, J. P.

Webb, Meredith & Creecy Moore, 22 Aug 1811; James Webb, bm.

Webb, Reddin & Betsy Blackwell, 29 Nov 1825; James Ivy, bm.

Webb, Seawell R. & Anna Beasley, 26 Dec 1838; Jesse Beasley, bm.

Webb, Silas & Louisa Creech, 13 Jan 1838; William Standley, Sr., bm.

Webb, William & Lucinda Young, 24 Oct 1855; m 11 Dec 1855 by Right Ryals, J. P.

Webb, William H. & Elizabeth E. Flowers, m 13 Jul 1859 at James Rhodes's, by N. Buzram, J. P.

Weddin, James P. & Julia M. Terry, m 15 Jun 1854 by Edwin Boykin, J. P.

Weeks, Garry & Susan Eldridge, 15 Feb 1867; John Weeks, bm; m 19 Feb 1867 at Abigail Eldridgs, by Bryant Williams, J. P.

Wellons, Benjamin & Sarah Barnes, 29 Mar 1849; Ezekil Rogers, K. M. C. Williamson, bm.

Wellons, Charles & Nancy Godwin, 18 Nov 1815; Thos. Sasser, bm.

Wellons, Charles & Bethaney Jones, 12 Mar 1834; Jas. A. Turnel, bm.

Wellons, Clinton & Nancy Dodd, 19 Feb 1842; Zachariah Jones, bm.

Wellons, Curtis H. & Harriet King, 4 Feb 1839; Dixon Pearce, bm.

Wellons, Exum & Edith Godwin, 14 Aug 1822; Jess A. Talton, bm.

Wellons, James & Cynthia Sanders, 13 Feb 1820; Willie N. White, bm.

Wellons, James D. T. & Alice Blackman, 8 Mar 1858; m 9 Mar 1858 by John C. Hood, J. P.

Wellons, Jesse & Druzella Shepherd, 23 Jan 1856; m 24 Jan 1856 at the residence of J. Sheperd, by H. H. Finch, J. P.

Wellons, Jessee & Nancy Johnson, 29 Nov 1823; James Wellons, bm.

Wellons, John & Anna Midgett, 27 Sept 1817; James Wellons, bm.

Wellons, Marmaduke & Polly Warren, _____ 18__; E. Starling, bm.

Wellons, Westley F. & Elizabeth Pearce, 3 Nov 1812; Kader Pearce, bm.

Wellons, William & Elizabeth Roberts, 11 Sept 1820; James Wellons, bm.

Wellons, Willie & Zilpha E. Oliver, 12 May 1853; m 19 Mar 1853 by Wm. Rains, J. P.

Wellons, Zacheriah & Eliza Lockhart, 6 Feb 1817; Bryan Smith, bm.

West, Allen & Lucy Baker, 28 Mar 1843; Starling Massingill, bm.

West, Charles & Charlotte Martin, 26 Feb 1844; Robert W. Stevens, bm.

West, Handy W. & Tranquilla Johnson, 18 May 1839; Noel West, Jr., bm.

West, John E. & Sarah E. Rose, 1 Feb 1867; G. R. Britt, bm; m 14 Feb 1867 at Benjamin Roses, by Bryant Williams, J. P.

West, Loyed & Martha Morgan, 16 Oct 1846; Zachariah Tiner, bm.

West, Noel & Winifred Johnston, 19 Dec 1806; John Wood, bm.

West, Venson & Levina Hayse, 10 Jan 1798; Adams Alexander, bm.

West, William Henry & Tempe Lee, 22 May 1852; m 17 Mar 1852 by Powel Blackman, J. P.

Westbrook, Joseph T. & Pherebee Eldridge, 1 May 1852; m 6 May 1852 by Powel Blackman, J. P.

Westbrook, William T. & Pennina Smith, 17 Nov 1860; m 29 Nov 1860 at Pinny Smith, by Powel Blackman, J. P.

Wever, Moses & Elizabeth Hayles, 1 Nov 1845; R. W. Stevens, bm.

Wheeler, Jesse & Rulany Johnson, 11 Apr 1827; Joseph Wheeler, bm.

Wheeler, Jesse & Catherine Johnson, 22 Jun 1857; m 2 Jul 1857 by T. Garrard.

Wheeler, Joseph & Fanny Johnson, 26 Sept 1827; Henry Jordan, bm.

Wheeler, Zerabal & Elizabeth Deem, 14 Dec 1847; Noah Wheeler, bm.

Whitaker, Samuel & Lydia Stallings, 15 Jun 1837; Isaac Stalling, bm.

White, John & Temperance Utley, 26 Oct 1839; William B. Sanders, bm.

White, Jonathan & Nancy Cordell, 1 Mar 1820; David Parrish, bm.

White, Solley & Sarah Johnson, 27 Sept 1792; Isaac Johnson, bm.

White, Thomas & Bedy Hall, 25 Aug 1841; Bryant Pulley, bm.

White, Willie N. & Mary Eason, 16 Sept 1819; L. Smith, bm.

Whitefield, George W. & Catharine Hart, 4 Feb 1828; Wimberley Hinton, bm.

Whitfield, Lewis & Patsey Bryan, 9 Nov 1816; S. Mitchner, bm.

Whitfield, Theophilus & Bettie Brown, 18 Apr 1866; Thomas Morgan, bm.

Whitfield, Sir William & Betsy Wimberly, 17 Dec 1808; Willis Watson, bm.

Whitington, Solomon & Sally Lasseter, 18 Nov 1806; William Wilder, bm.

Whitley, A. T. & Minerva Ann Smith, 22 Sept 1857; m 23 Sept 1857 by J. F. Ellington.

Whitley, Bryant & Nancy Thomas, 23 Dec 1824; Willie Whitley, bm.

Whitley, Cane (colored) & Adlade Watson, 25 Sept 1866; Joseph Jernigan, b; m 29 Sept 1866 by Elisha Holland, M. G.

Whitley, Daniel & Sarah Wooten, 26 Dec 1825; Tho. Lockart, Jr., bm.

Whitley, Dennis (colored) & Lou Eatman, 7 Dec 1866; Jesse Hinnant, bm; m 8 Dec 1866 by Jesse Hinnant, J. P.

Whitley, Enoch & Elizabeth Gully, 20 Dec 1792; Nathan Gulley, bm.

Whitley, Evrett D. & Catharine Richardson, 6 Jun 1848; Josiah H. Whitley, bm.

Whitley, Harris H. & Marseline Vinson, 9 Sept 1849; Thomas T. Grice, bm.

Whitley, Haywood W. & Esther Jernigan, 16 Oct 1839.

Whitley, James H. & Rhoda E. Richardson, 13 Jul 1863; m 16 Jul 1863 at A. W. Richardson's, by M. G. Todd, M. G.

Whitley, James K. & Nancy Woodard, 1 Jan 1866; Willie H. Whitley, bm; m 3 Jan 1866 at Berry Woodard's, by Wm. Himan, J. P.

Whitley, James M. & Nancy Raiford, 24 Aug 1842; T. W. Whitley, bm.

Whitley, Joe & Winifred Barnett, 22 Feb 1866; Owen Whitley, bm.

Whitley, John & Esther Bulls, 15 May 1806; Willis Watson, bm.

Whitley, John & Sally Green, 11 Dec 1816; Enoch Whitly, bm.

Whitley, John & Nancy Wilder, 16 Apr 1825; Richard Taylor, bm.

Whitley, John Jr. & Esther Bulls, 24 Jan 1814; Alfred Whitley, bm.

Whitley, K. B. & Martha Heath, 23 Jun 1849; B. Smith, bm.

Whitley, Meritt & Adlade Evans, 21 Dec 1865; Wesley Whitley, bm.

Whitley, N. R. & Martha Richardson, 27 Nov 1849; William Hilliard, bm.

Whitley, Needham & Zilpha Williamson, 22 Jan 1828; Wm. Green, bm.

Whitley, Pobe (colored) & Mary Watson, 9 Feb 1867; A. J. Heath, bm; m 15 Feb 1867 by A. J. Heath, J. P.

Whitley, Thadeus & S. C. Fillom, 25 Sept 1840; Wm. Hastings, bm.

Whitley, Wesley & Easter Godwin, 6 Dec 1865; Rober Smith, bm.

Whitley, William & Nancy Pope, 23 Dec 1807; Kedar Whitley, bm.

Whitley, William & Celah Holder, 1 Mar 1820; Jno. Sanders, Jr., bm.

Whitley, William R. & Rexey Chamblee, 15 Apr 1854; m 18 Apr 1854 by B. ONeal, J. P.

Whitley, Willie & Betsy Williamson, 25 May 1824; Aaron Wall, bm.

Whitmon, William & Susana Martin, 3 Apr 1829; Rigdon Suggs, bm.

Whittenton, Jonathan & Sally Allen, 25 Nov 1816; James Whitenton, bm.

Whittington, John & Amy Messer, 22 Apr 1815; Whitmell Johnson, bm.

Whittington, Jonathan & Clary Green, 13 Jul 1813; Wm. Whitinton, bm.

Whittington, William & Sally Eason, 5 Dec 1810; Etheldred Bell, bm.

Whittington, William & Elizabeth Barber, 28 Sept 1813; John Barber, bm.

Wiggins, Archibald & Elizabeth Wallis, 23 Feb 1819; Hardy Adams, bm.

Wiggins, William & Wealthy Bartley, 12 Aug 1813; Jesse Standley, bm.

Wiggins, Willis & Mourning Stevens, 17 Dec 1779; Jacob Stevens, bm.

Wiggs, Arthur & Elizabeth Stevens, 10 Mar 1851; m 11 May 1851 by E. Atkinson, J. P.

Wiggs, Arthur & Martha Casey, 13 Sept 1853; m 22 Sept 1853 by E. Atkinson.

Wiggs, Henry & Linda Pearce, 18 Nov 1842; Wm. Massey, bm; m by Willie Holt, J. P.

Wiggs, Isaiah & Amy Collins, 22 Oct 1847; Stephen Bagley, bm; m by Willie Holt.

Wiggs, John & Penelope Broughton, 31 Dec 1855; m 1 Jan 1856 at the residents of J. Broughton, by B. Lane, J. P.

Wiggs, John T. & Penelope Stephenson, 1 Feb 1856; m 7 Feb 1856 by Morris Stephenson, Elder.

Wiggs, Martin & Martha Ellis, 24 May 1814; James Ross, bm.

Wiggs, W. H. & Sarah Ann Edgerton, 15 May 1865; Jesse Parker, bm.

Wilburn, Lewis & Mary Garland, 13 Feb 1804; Sampson Rogers, Jn. Sanders, Jr., bm.

Wilder, Cullen & Nelly Brannon, 1 Oct 1799; William Branan, bm.

Wilder, Irwin & Winey Avera, 28 Mar 1801; John Wilder, bm.

Wilder, Isham & Casanda Wise, 14 Oct 1832; Geo. S. Gully, bm.

Wilder, Isham & Willy Hopkins, 20 Oct 1849; Samuel W. Smith, bm.

Wilder, James H. & Kesiah C. Barnes, m 9 Aug 1855 at her fathers Elias Barnes', by R. N. Gulley, J. P.

Wilder, John Jr. & Katharine Killingsworth, 17 Feb 1798; Samuel Wilder, bm.

Wilder, Matthew & Milla O'Neal, 14 Aug 1810; Hardy Avera, bm.

Wilder, Matthew & Martha Avera, 22 Apr 1836; Solomon Lockart, bm.

Wilder, Matthew & Jane Avera, 6 Feb 1843; George Price, bm.

Wilder, Reuben & Olive Wilder, 29 Jul 1817; Thomas Branan, bm.

Wilder, Reuben & Catharine Holder, 7 Jan 1826; Saml Mitchner, bm.

Wilder, Reuben & Nancy Whitley, 16 Aug 1847; Wm. T. Robertson, bm.

Wilder, Samuel & Mary Green, 26 Aug 1794; Joseph Irwin, bm.

Wilder, Till & Esther Avera, 14 Nov 1803; David Wilder, bm.

Wilder, William, of Wake Co., & Elizabeth Lee, 22 Mar 1794; John Moore, bm.

Wilder, William & Mary Whitington, 2 Nov 1795; James Langdon, bm.

Wilder, William & Polly Richardson, 29 Jul 1818; Etheldred Bell, bm.

Wilder, William & Nancy Green, 14 May 1825; William Green, bm.

Wilder, William G. & Milly Jane Hinton, 8 Jun 1860; m 20 Jun 1860 by S. W. Woody, J. P.

Wilkenson, Cary & Edith Stancell, 31 Dec 1819; Benjamin Hatcher, bm.

Wilkerson, Charles & Alece Brewer, 26 May 1823; Hardy Bailey, bm.

Wilkerson, Elkany & Patience Rogers, 17 Dec 1784; Charles Wilkerson, bm.

Wilkerson, James & Cinda Parnell, 31 Jan 1856; m 3 Feb 1856 at Jerry Parnells, by Wm. H. Sellers, J. P.

Wilkerson, William & Elizabeth Oliver, 8 Sept 1860; m 13 Sept 1860 at Jeremiah Parnels, by Jesse Parker, J. P.

Wilkins, Elie & Evaline Hill, 19 Jul 1853; m 21 Jul 1853 by D. H. Whitley, J. P.

Wilkins, John & Marinda Bains, 18 Mar 1851; m 20 Mar 1851 by Wilie Holt.

Wilkins, Owen & Rebecca Johnson, 24 Nov 1857; John Wilkins, bm; m 26 Nov 1857 by Jas. H. Sasser.

Wilkins, Phililp & Martha Ann Evans, 27 Jul 1856; Owen Wilkins, bm.

Wilkins, Philip & Julia Ann Davis, 13 Aug 1860; m 14 Aug 1860 at the residence of John Davis, by J. A. Stevens, J. P.

Wilkins, Pinkney & Phebe McLamb, 10 Jul 1858; m 11 Jul 1858 by Right Ryals, J. P.

Wilkinson, Berry & Beedy Oneal, 17 Nov 1815; Wm. Hinnant, bm.

Wilkinson, Calvin & Nancy Cockrell, 1 Jan ____; Levy Yelventon, bm.

Wilkinson, Micajah & Matilda Jerald, 15 Jul 1815; Elisha Pitman, bm.

Wilkinson, Nathan & Sweeten Parnold, 1 Mar 1796; Benjami Wilkinson, bm.

Wilkinson, Reuben & Reldy Parnell, 27 Nov 1833; John Jackson, bm.

Wilkinson, Roland & Senith Yelventon, 15 Dec 1792; Reuben Wilkinson, bm.

Willeford, John P. & Sally Roberts, 28 Apr 1853; m 28 Apr 1853 by U. Bradley, J. P.

Williams, Benajah & Sally Lewis, 22 Jul 1853; m 24 Jul 1853 by E. Atkinson.

Williams, Brant & Betsy E. Ingram, 28 Oct 1848; B. C. Blackman, bm.

Williams, Bright & Mary Ann Stanley, 19 Jun 1860; m 12 Aug 1860 at William Stanleys, by Jas. H. Adams, J. P.

Williams, Frederick, of Montgomery Co., & Polly Gower, 24 Sept 1802; John Matthews, bm.

Williams, Herod & Fathy Brewer, 15 Apr 1788; Jesse Wootten, bm.

Williams, Iredel & Gilly Parker, _____ ; Beary Lewis, bm.

Williams, Isaac & Susan Lee, 7 Dec 1816; Jno. Sanders, Jr., bm.

Williams, Jackson & Charlotte Ogburn, 17 Jan 1840; Thomas Barber, bm.

Williams, James & _____ , 28 ____ 1799; William Williams, of Wake Co., bm.

Williams, James B. & Mary P. Williford, 30 Jun 1860; m 3 Jul 1860 at Joseph Willifords, by Perry Godwin.

Williams, James C. & Theny Eldridge, 1 Mar 1859; m 3 Mar 1859 by John C. Hood, J. P.

Williams, John & Polly Allen, 13 Sept 1804; Jno. Saunders, Jr., bm.

Williams, John & Nancy Pate, 1 May 1812; Bolling Green Hobbs, bm.

Williams, K. M. C. & Sarah McKiney, 16 Jun 1849; Edwin Boykin, bm.

Williams, Peter & Lydia Carter, 1 Nov 1794; Irvin Carter, bm.

Williams, Rowland & Nancy Ren, 9 Feb 1792; Thomas Leach, bm.

Williams, Samuel & Fereba McCullers, 22 Dec 1779; Samuel Smith, bm.

Williams, William & Sally Ann Debnam, 15 Aug 1839; Augustus W. Stevens, bm.

Williams, William & Betsy Adams, 29 Aug 1826; Gideon Woodall, bm.

Williamson, Raiford & Charlotte Pearce, 6 Feb 1836; Allen S. Ballinger, bm.

Willis, John & Riley Price, 15 Aug 1825; John D. Talton, bm.

Willis, John & Matilda Simpkins, 21 Jun 1836; John G. Gully, bm.

Willoby, Cader & Susanna Moody, 8 Dec 1805; James Moody, bm.

Willoughby, Solomon & Martha Clarke, 1 Jan 1785; James Hardcasle, bm.

Wilson, Arther & Mary Lee, 27 Jul 1844; William McLain, bm.

Wilson, Edmund & Polly Blalock, 4 Jan 1854; m 5 Jan 1854 by J. T. Leach, J. P.

Wilson, John & Patty Davis, 14 Sept 1785; Jacob Davis, bm.

Wilson, John & Sally Hobby, 11 Sept 1800; John J. Briggs, bm.

Wilson, Starling & Martha Capps, 6 Jul 1865; Blake Barfield, bm.

Wilson, William & Sally Hicks, 10 Nov 1818; Etheldred Holt, bm.

Wimberley, George & Phereby Hinton, 11 Feb 1790; George Hinton, bm.

Wimberly, Malachi & Charity Horn, 10 Oct 1778; Richard Horn, bm.

Winburn, John & Elizabeth Fulgham, m 14 Apr 1852 by Revd. Ellen Macon.

Winburn, Thomas & Patsy Pope, 23 Apr 1810; Wm. Hinton, bm.

Windham, D. D. & Lydia Barber, 11 Nov 1857; Gaston Johnson, bm; m 12 Nov 1857 by A. Coats, J. P.

Windham, John & Polly Carter, 20 Jul 1814; T. J. Walton, bm.

Windham, John & Sarah Stevenson, 26 Feb 1833; Joseph Carter, bm.

Windham, Rufus M. & Dorcas Benson, 19 Nov 1860; m 22 Nov 1860 by B. A. Woodall, J. P.

Wise, James & Ruth Warren, 6 Feb 1780; Richard Warren, bm.

Wise, Rigdon & Christian Lockamy, 27 Mar 1848; N. B. Stevens, bm.

Wise, Thomas & Hester Sims, 13 Dec 1785; Benjamin Sims, bm.

Wood, Henderson & Selina Ellis, 20 Jul 1857; E. D. Nichols, bm.

Wood, John & Dorcass Johnson, 23 Dec 1792; Etheldred Johnson, bm.

Wood, John S. & Penny Wall, 1 Dec 1852; m 2 Dec 1852 by L. Dodd, J. P.

Wood, John S. & Nancy J. Parker, 31 May 1860; m 28 Oct 1860 at the residence of E. Parker, by John C. Hood, Sr., J. P.

Wood, Thomas & Penny Massingill, 7 Jan 1858; James Tart, bm; m 9 Jan 1858 at Henry Masingill, by R. Masingill, J. P.

Wood, Whitfield & Betsey Tart, 17 Mar 1832; Asa Thomson, bm.

Wood, William & Zilpha Evans, 26 Dec 1815; John Johnson, bm.

Wood, William & Pherebe Barefoot, 16 Sept 1840; James T. Jackson, bm.

Wood, William & Avey Ann Parker, 16 Jan 1862; m 6 Feb 1862 at Joseph B. Parkers, by R. Masingill, J. P.

Wood, William D. & Mary Johnson, 23 Feb 1857; J. H. Daniel, bm; m by Linn B. Sanders, J. P.

Wood, William D. & Mary Penny, m 7 Aug 1840; Willie Johnson, bm.

Woodall, Abner & Sarah Lee, 22 Sept 1852; m 23 Sept 1852 by Harry Johnson, J. P.

Woodall, Absalom & Caty Parish, 24 Dec 1788; Ryal Jenings, bm.

Woodall, Absalom Jr. & Pheba Johnson, 28 Jul 1819; Allen Johnson, bm.

Woodall, Clement & Sally Messer, 10 Feb 1822; James A. Woodall, bm.

Woodall, Gideon & Mary Lassiter, 26 Sept 1826; James Lassiter, bm.

Woodall, Gideon & Tabetha Dixon, 16 Feb 1848; Robert W. Stevens, bm.

Woodall, Isham & Rebecca E. Draughon, 19 Oct 1860; m 31 Oct 1860 by B. A. Wellons, J. P.

Woodall, Jacob & Phereby Gower, 16 Dec 1789; Absalom Woodall, bm.

Woodall, Jacob & Thena Massengale, 9 May 1820; James Woodall, bm.

Woodall, Jacob & Penny Lasseter, 29 Aug 1826; Gideon Woodall, bm.

Woodall, James & Mary Jenings, 28 Jan 1789; Ryal Jenings, bm.

Woodall, James & Mary Allen, 26 Jan 1792; Absalom Woodall, bm.

Woodall, James & Sally Barber, 10 Aug 1821; Plyer Barber, bm.

Woodall, James Jr. & Polly Johnson, 10 Jul 1819; Abslom Woodall, bm.

Woodall, James A. & Elizabeth Whitley, 27 Feb 1866; Iredell Godwin, bm.

Woodall, James A. Jr. & Mary Dixon, 9 Sept 1847; Wm. W. Morgan, bm.

Woodall, James D. & Sarah Hill, 7 Nov 1816; Payten Ivey, bm.

Woodall, John & Mildred Speed, 15 Nov 1815; James Woodall, Jr., bm.

Woodall, John A. & Lucy Johnson, 22 Jan 1867; James A. Ryals, bm; m 24 Jan 1867 by N. B. Barber, M. G.

Woodall, Martin & Judith Gibs, _____; Jacob Woodall, bm.

Woodall, Merrit & Harriet Nelms, 4 Aug 1843; Robt. W. Stevens, bm.

Woodall, Seth & Mary Tomlinson, 29 Oct 1853; m 8 Nov 1853 by J. T. Leach, J. P.

Woodall, Simeon & Harret Mace, 8 Dec 1841; John Barber, bm.

Woodall, Simeon & Mary Moore, 20 Oct 1843; Aleaxnder Stansel, bm.

Woodall, Troy W. & Emily W. Bizzelle, 7 Dec 1858; m 14 Dec 1858 by J. J. Hobby.

Woodall, William & Edith Barber, 6 May 1819; T. Barber, bm.

Woodall, William & Peney Johnson, 21 Jan 1825; James Woodall, Sr., bm.

Woodard, Benjamin & Polly Davis, 17 Feb 1798; Jacob Edwards, bm.

Woodard, Benjamin & Emma Phillips, 17 Feb 1838; Henry Woodard, bm.

Woodard, Berry & Cary Tucker, 10 May 1825; Irven Wilder, bm.

Woodard, Bertie & Polly Bailey, 7 Aug 1840; Warren W. Bailey, bm.

Woodard, Elisha & Nancy Earp, 7 Jan 1819; Tobias Hollimon, bm.

Woodard, Erasmus & Julia Ivy, 21 Oct 1835; Needham Oliver, bm.

Woodard, Henry & Sally Massy, 23 Feb 1835.

Woodard, Jacob & Polly Hawley, 26 Apr 1844; Gary Sillavent, bm.

Woodard, James & Fereby Holiman, 6 Jun 1800; West Woodard, bm.

Woodard, Jepha & Sally Hatcher, 19 Mar 1811; Benjamin Hatcher, bm.

Woodard, Jesse & Edney Hollaman, 1 Jan 1818; James Richardson, bm.

Woodard, Jessee & Redby Adams, 17 Feb 1826; James Adams, bm.

Woodard, Jethro & Betsey Woodard, 24 Aug 1841; Tobias Woodard, bm.

Woodard, John & Sarah Hocut, 30 Nov 1794; William Hocut, bm.

Woodard, John & Delany Edwards, 18 Mar 1839; Jeses Holt, bm.

Woodard, John & Mariah Tiner, 18 Jun 1845; Joseph Woodard, Green H. Holland, bm.

Woodard, Jonathan & Judy B. Johnson, 29 Jul 1822; Solomon Johnson, bm.

Woodard, Joseph & Patience Daughtery, 13 Dec 1813; John Pearce, bm.

Woodard, Joseph & Elvy Edwards, 27 Sept 1847; Henry Hamilton, bm.

Woodard, Joseph & Anna Wiggs, 23 Dec 1863; m 24 Dec 1863 by Willie Holt.

Woodard, Matthew & Phebe Bryan, 14 Aug 1818; Allen Richardson, bm.

Woodard, Micajah & Chloe Liles, 26 Aug 1794; Micajah Liles, bm.

Woodard, Samuel & Nancy Rivenbark, 23 May 1836; William Benson, bm.

Woodard, Warren & Sally Hamilton, 10 Apr 1816; Wm. Hen. Guy, bm.

Woodard, William & Eliza Moore, 15 Feb 1847; Williamson Hinnant, bm.

Woodard, William A. & Rebecca A. Johnson, 4 Feb 1860; m 5 Feb 1860 by J. F. Ellington.

Woodard, William H. & Rebecca Capps, 28 Jan 1861; m 30 Jan1861 by W. A. Smith, J. P.

Woodard, Willis & Edith Phillips, 13 Nov 1812; Warren Woodard, bm.

Woodell, Charles & Maiden Searcy, 21 Jan 1797; Richard Holt, bm.

Woodley, Thomas A. (Dr.) & George Anna Higgins, 27 Mar 1866; Frederich Loops, bm.

Woods, James & Elizabeth Jones, 27 Nov 1866; J. J. Farmer, bm; m 30 Nov 1866 by J. F. Ellington, M. G.

Woodward, Berry & Temperance Wilder, 23 Aug 1825; Reuben Wilder, bm.

Woodward, Matthew & Leathy Smith, 29 Sept 1803; John Smith, bm.

Woodward, West & Betsey Smith, 29 Sept 1803; John Smith, bm.

Woody, John D. & Mary E. Kenyon, 2 Nov 1866; C. M. Holliman, bm.

Woody, Samuel & Acculy Naron, 4 Jul 1836; Stephen Hicks, bm.

Worley, Benjamin & Sally Price, 28 Feb 1820; Needham Warren, bm.

Worley, Needham & Sally Hicks, 17 Jan 1838; Jesse Overby, bm.

Worley, William & Nanny Edwards, 20 Jan 1800; Joseph Edwards, bm.

Worly, Rosser & Betsy Collins, 20 Jan 1810; Cornelius Linch, bm.

Worly, William & Catharine Crocker, 14 Apr 1866; Alexander Thain, bm.

Wooten, William & Winefred Oneal, 6 Oct 1809; William B. Hocut, bm.

Wren, Calvn & Piety Stevenson 15 Jan 1846; Josiah Evans, bm.

Wright, Joseph & Sally Pate, 2 Sept 1815; Allen Tomlinson, of Wake Co., bm.

Wright, Sion & Ann Meeks, 14 Mar 1785; Wm. Stevens, bm.

Wright, William & Elizabeth Oneal, 13 ____ 1790; Arthur Pope, bm.

Wriley, Peter W., of Wake Co., & Lilly Whitley, 16 Nov 1843; Jacob Johnson, bm.

Yelventon, Asa & Sarah Horn, 25 Feb 1806; Tignal Pugh, bm.

Yelventon, Gideon & Beedy Hatcher, 14 May 1785; John Hatcher, bm.

Yelventon, Jacob & Charity Cammel, 1 Dec 1778; Charles Wilkeson, bm.

Yelventon, Jason & Rebecca Barnes, 14 Jul 1828; Levy Yelventon, bm.

Yelventon, Levy & Patience Hinnant, 28 Oct 1820; Nathaniel Futrell, bm.

Yelvington, Bennet & Nelly Rains, 14 Dec 1841; Levy Yelventon, bm.

Yelvington, Howell & Willey Brown, 11 Oct 1841; Joel Garner, bm.

Yelvington, Jethro & Elizabeth Talton, 12 Apr 1833; Samuel A. Bryan, bm.

Yelvington, Jethro & Elizabeth J. Johnson, 9 Oct 1860; m 16 Oct 1860 at M. Johnsons, by J. W. Hodges, J. P.

Young, Edwin & Elizabeth Fairley, 29 Aug 1862; m 30 Aug 1862 by W. D. Holt, J. P.

Young, Ezekiel & Martha Tomlinson, 2 Apr 1828; B. H. Tomlinson, bm.

Young, Francis & Sally Tomlinson, 30 Jan 1796; Abner Sauls, bm.

Young, Francis & Lucy Ogburn, 20 Oct 1835; Thomas Durham, bm.

Young, Harmon (colored) & Lavina Lockart, 13 Feb 1867; Y. D. Vinson, bm; m 20 Feb 1867 by M. K. Grantham, J. P.

Young, James R. & Martha J. Peacock, m 21 Feb 1856 at William Peacocks, by John C. Hood, J. P.

Young, John B. & Cyntha Bryan, 13 Mar 1838; Thos. Young, bm.

Young, Thomas & Betsy Gainer, 2 Dec 1809; Thomas Page, bm.

Young, Turner & Nancy Ellington, 7 Aug 1825; Hardy Watford, bm.

Youngblood, Icabud & Betsy Rice, 16 Dec 1806; Thos. Folsom, bm.

Youngblood, James & Miriam Lunceford, 27 Aug 1840; H. H. Hobbs, bm.

Youngblood, Thomas R. & Caroline Lunceford, 17 May 1848; James H. Youngblood, bm.

Avera (cont.)
Kedar 64
Lizy 109
Louensa 104
Lucinda (Mrs.) 117
Lucrecy 5
Lueaser 72
Lurana 108
M. 15, 34, 41, 75
Maria 10
Martha 128
Mathew 16
Matthew 5, 52, 75
Nancy 26
Oliver 35
Patience 6
Polley 80
Polly 2, 120
Polly Ann 2
Sally 33, 123
Saml 25
Samuel 121
Sarah 55
Sarah Ann 28
Selah 43
Susan 60
Thos. 106
Viney 60
William H. 4
Winefred 67
Winey 128
Winiford 75
Averae, Mary 105
Averet, Edith 15
Avery, Alexander 5
Daniel 106
Dolly 95
Edith 13
John 69
Patience 33
Polly 14
Averyt, Jonathan 120
Keziah 33
Lizay 91
Peggy 106
Sally 83
Winefred 120
Averytt, Edith 9
Jonathan 120
Winefred 120
Aycock, Berry 55
William H. 6
Zilphia 4
Babcock, Phebe T. 81
Baggell, Josiah 42
Bagget, Alsey 103
Edith 91
Roda 102
Baggley, Ann 64
Bagley, Edney 28
Harriet 53
Henry 102
Jane 6
Joanny 6
Patsey 104
Penelope 28
S. 8, 15, 42, 44, 52,
67, 102, 111, 123
Sarah A. C. 48
Stephen 128
T. 1
Theny 26
Theohpilus 52
Theophilus 7, 48
Tho. 34
Thomas 42
Trecenda 52
Bagly, Henry 87

Bagly (cont.)
Micagah 12
Bagwell, Mary 18
Bailey, (?) 82
Anna 42
Arthur 6, 7
Baldy G. 62
Catharin 114
Celah 36
David 62
Elizabeth 62, 83
Gilly 82
Griffin 114
Hardy 62, 129
Hutson 104
J. Hudson 20
Jesse 46
Jessee 105
John 24
L. D. 49
Leasy 84
Lunford 80
Matilda 46
Milly 95
Nancy 36, 49
Olief 1
Pherebee 77
Phereby 85, 87
Piety 50
Polly 132
Richard 52
Ruth 74
Sarah 66
Susan W. 62
Tamsey 107
Warren 6
Warren W. 132
Baily, Caroline 4
Catharin 114
Charity 77
Delsey 82
Diannah 116
Griffin 114
Jesse 7
Mary 7
Nicy 7
William 116
Bains, Marinda 129
Baker, Ame 110
Amy 78
Anna 105
Clem M. 54
Clement 7
Deliah 22
Elijah 110, 115
Elizabeth 49, 115, 120
Hannor 7
James 7
Lucy 126
Lusenda 7
Martha I. 7
Nanny 1
Rhoda 46
Sukey 70
Susan 125
William 30
Baldwin, Samuel 98, 108
Balkcon, Ichabud 104
Balkcum, Ichabard 12
Ballance, Aney 94
Fanny 123
Harriet 89
Teagle 6
Tigal 123
Ballenger, Allen S. 99
Apsabeth 3
John 8
Mariah 92

Ballenger (cont.)
William 3, 72
William T. 37
Ballinger, Allen S. 39,
47, 49, 65, 75, 76,
79, 89, 107, 109,
130
Bevely D. 60
Elizabeth 39
W. S. 57
William S. 2
Banks, Coria A. 38
John L. 33
Barbee, Plyer 86
Susan 51
Barber, Absalum (Sr.) 61
Adaline 18
Alcinda 9
Amanda 80
Amy 67
Angeline 81
Ann 67
Apslaur 22
Ashley 10
Ashly 49
Aurelia 44
Bailie 9
Brazilla 9
Bural 99
Burwell 9, 10, 67
Carnan 8
Casanda 9
Cassie 9
Catherine 10
Celia 111
Edith 132
Elizabeth 9, 22, 23,
43, 67, 68, 128
Elizabeth A. 10
Elizur 82
Emeline C. 66
Eveline S. 44
G. 67
Gastin 23
Geo. 62
George 8, 9
Hardy 9, 77
Haukins 35
Isabel 95
James K. 43
John 9, 128, 132
Julia 48
L. H. 8
Larkin 8, 66
Luquinay 57
Lusey 9
Lydia 131
Maria 67
Mary 115
Matilda 16
N. B. 9, 132
Nathaniel 8
Nathaniel B. 66
Owein 46
Owen 8, 57, 67
P. A. 8
Patsy 48, 77
Penellope 81
Penny 85
Phir 79
Plyer 8, 9, 47, 68,
83, 132
Plyer (Jr.) 40
Polley 79
R. M. 10
Reuben 8, 9
Reuben (Jr.) 9
Rildey 22

Barber (cont.)
Romulus 8
Rosie F. 10
Sally 132
Sarah 14, 32
Susannah 113
T. 132
Tempy E. 71
Terry 9, 10, 43, 114
Theophilus 8
Theterson 26
Thomas 8, 12, 42, 44, 79, 105, 130
Thos. 70
Welthy Ann 95
William G. 44
Young A. 75, 115
Barefoot, Avy 116
Charlotte J. 105
Clarkey 60
Esther A. 10
Fanney 50
Handy 76
Jane 76
John 82
Pherebe 131
Rebecca 81
Sally 87
Susan 25, 64
Thomas 64
Wiley 10
Wm. (Sir) 74
Barfield, Blake 130
Barfoot, John 10
Barham, Benjamin A. 26
Joseph E. 2
Nancy Jane 94
Barker, Clem 122
Elijah 44
Pressey 103
Barnes, Archelus 124
Bethany 14
Cherry 52
Cynthie 52
Edith 61
Elias 64, 80, 128
Elizabeth 121
H. L. 42
Henderson 84
Jacob 10
Jesse 124
Joanna 2
John I. 52
Joseph 11
Kesiah C. 128
Kiddy 5
Mary A. 52
Noel 53, 80, 99
Patience 65
Patsey 80
Polly 67
Rebecca 134
Sarah 125
Sarah E. 66
Solomon 66
Stephen 31, 43, 58, 111
Stevens 31
Zilpah 46
Zilpha 99
Barnett, Winifred 127
Barney, J. J. 5
Barnhill, Unity Jane 14
Barns, Patience 5
Bartley, Wealthy 128
Bass, Andrew 33
Betsey 112
Katy 49

Bass (cont.)
Sally 61, 75
William A. 113
Basses, Aron 88
Bateman, Nancy 96
Batetn, Patience 94
Battan, John 11
Batten, Abraham 11, 111
Amos 11
Ann 106
Appy 122
Catharine 70
Cinthy 86
Edwin 17
Elizabeth 12
Joanna 35
John 12, 19
Louiza 12
Lucinda 17
Martha 11
Nancy M. 36
Patsey 42
Pleasant 12
Polly 93
Rutha 15
Rutha Ellen 122
Saley 121
Samuel 11, 42, 111
Starling 15
Strawdry 96
Winefred 78
Wm. H. 36
Zilphey 86
Battin, Dolly 12
James 12
John 93
Minda 122
Nancy 19
Baucom, Bennet 12
James 101
Mary 93
Baucum, Charity 98
Baucumb, Martha 115
Baudoun, Sally 93
Bawes, Catharine 28
Bayley, Elizabeth 119
Beal, Elizabeth 81
John 81
Siddy 108
Beaman, Isaac 27, 47
Jacob 44
Welthy 27
Beard, Counsel J. 14
Sally 104
Bearfoot, Miles 13
Beasley, Anna 125
Celia Ann 80
E. A. 8
E. O. 20
Elizabeth 97
Jane E. 98
Jesse 125
Juda C. 76
Judith 14
K. M. C. 98
Martha E. 107
Mary M. 49
Beasly, Harriet 63
Isaac 101
Mary Ann 56
Nancy A. 63
Beck, Polly 99
Beckwith, Anne 51
Jno. B. 111
Bedinfield, Betsy 93
Bedingfield, Disa 61
John 53
Keron 56

Bedingfield (cont.)
Lucy 53
Bedngfield, Mary 120
Beel, Edna 10
Nancy 18
Bell, Ann Mariah 5
Benjamin 65
D. 13
David 40, 116
Elizabeth 48, 68
Etheldred 9, 13, 103, 128, 129
H. J. 70
Henry J. 66
Martilla 4
Mary 40, 118
Mary E. 76
Norflett 117
Patsey 76
Bennet, Nancy 106
Bennett, Philemon 13
Benningfield, John 93
Benson, Caty 118
Dorcas 131
Mary 67
Nancy 49
W. C. 9, 14, 64
William 133
William C. 14
Benton, Charlotte 3
Betten, James H. 86
Bingham, C. J. 26, 57, 63, 88, 106, 107, 112
Bird, Emily 121
Rachel 63
Bizzelle, Emily W. 132
Black, Lelah 110
Blackburn, Ally 96
Blackkmond, Zilpha 40
Blackman, Alice 125
B. 65
B. C. 129
Barzella 2
Barzilla 14
Brazilla 14
Edith 73
Elina V. 61
Eliza 59
Elizabeth 77
Esther 77
Ichabod 14, 15, 35, 73
Jeremiah 59, 106
John 7, 77
John Clarrissa 19
Josiah 69
Lewis 122
Martha J. 78
Martha T. 117
Mary 38, 71, 123
Nancy 3, 120
Patsey 81
Polly 28, 46
Powel 14, 19, 71, 102, 103, 126
Powell 14
R. H. 78, 117
R. L. 73
Rachel 106
Rhoda 78
S. W. 57, 72
Sally 34
Sarah 69
Susan 112
Tabitha 59
William 14
William (Sir) 43, 102
Winny 38

Blackman (cont.)
Wm. 120
Blackmon, Barzilla 72, 94
Elizabeth 39
Harry 14
Powel 15, 125
Powell 32
Sally 2
Zilpha 118
Blackwell, Betsy 125
Blackwood, Jeremiah 73
N. H. 38
Blalock, Martha 111
Polly 130
Ritter Jane 69
Blaman, S. W. 72
Blanchet, Sally 13
Blaneford, Winiford 7
Blanketship, Lynchia 12
Blow, Wright 15, 82
Blunt, Benjamin 26
William 77
Wm. 41
Boddery, Elizabeth 101
Boddie, Bennet 96
Nathan V. 124
Bodie, J. E. 15
Bodiery, Nancy 101
Bolten, Wm. 43
Bolton, Betsey 19
Bools, Gethrow 37
Boon, Allice K. 15
C. 34
Eliza 60
Eliza C. 104
Elizabeth 113
Emeline C. 34
Evelina V. 14
Jno. 122
Jno. Westly 68
Joseph 16, 45, 113
Joseph (Jr.) 95
Julia A. 116
Louisa 106
Nancy 68
Patsy 28
Sally 25, 58
Willie S. 34
Boothe, Isaac 80, 97
Boothes, Levy 120
Borcum, Eliza 75
Borden, Abram G. 49
Borham, Bettie 54
Bosweth, Cathran A. 84
Bowes, Sally 44
Bowler, Peggy 101
Boyet, Ferreby 83
Boyett, Chason 40
Harriet 124
Isaac 16, 69
L. G. 52, 54, 96
L. Y. 109
Patsy 18
Penelope 51
T. G. 29
Zilpha 31
Boyette, Grizzy Ann 121
L. G. 11
Boykin, Christion 30
Edwin 3, 28, 29, 32, 39, 47, 56, 57, 81, 83, 84, 90, 117, 125, 130
J. S. 16
Jesse 16
Mary 99
Milbry 16

Boykins, Edwin 26
Jonathan 16
Boyland, Peggy 39
Boyt, Nanny 58
Patsey 58
Boyte, Cally 66
Braddy, Abner 114
Polly 102
Sally 30
Winnifred 114
Bradley, H. 30
U. 129
W. 43
Brady, (?) 101
Abner 114
Betsy 58
Blake 2
Grace 25
John 16, 60
Nathan 95
Patience 120
Winifred 70
Winnifred 114
Wm. 70
Branan, Olive 40
Thomas 128
William 128
Brannan, Anne 116
Martha 66
Wiley 17
William 17
Brannon, Betsy 38
Cador 17
Caron 119
Nelly 128
Sally 35
William 17
Branswell, David 46
Brantly, Sarah 28
Brasier, Mary Ann 46
Brassel, Jacob 17
Brassell, Polly 37
Brasswell, Polly 84
Braswell, Betsey 32
Betsy 51
David 32
George W. 3
Leucy 37
Levi 72
Martha 72
Nancy 117
Sally 37
William 77
Braswill, Laney 75
Bratcher, Tabithey 22
Breech, Bennet 67
Brent, Betsey 99
Catty 119
Brewer, Alece 129
Fathy 130
J. G. 16
Jenny 39
Bridgers, B. 17
Betsey 121
Braswell 50
Caroline 45
Charity 32
Francis 47
J. T. 89
Jane 49, 120
Jane E. 122
Margarett 108
Martha 34
Mary 119
Polly 32
Ransom 5, 10
Sally 17, 47
Tom D. 17, 52, 56

Bridgers (cont.)
Young 2, 5, 33, 50, 121, 122
Bridges, Laura L. 8
Maryan 43
Thomas D. 94
Briggs, John J. 130
Brigrow, Needham 14
Britt, Cynthia 23
Elizabeth 83
G. R. 126
Jonathan 4, 33
M. A. 104
Martha W. 34
Nancy 94
Patience Ann 70
Patsy J. 73
Rachael 80
Rebecca Mariah 46
Susan 114
Winifred 33
Broadrib, Elizabeth 41
Broadstreet, Allana 32
Caroline 45
Edith 76
Edny 75
Jeany 49
Milley 91
Broadwell, John 12, 35, 36
Brogden, Cuzzy 88
Bronson, Benj. B. 37
Brooks, Charity W. 5
J. R. 45
Jacob 122
Jno. R. 31, 46
Jno. W. 18
John R. 16
Nicy 79
Broughten, Elizabeth 105
Broughton, Betsy 36
Elizabeth 16
J. 128
Jesse 18
John 29
Joseph L. 82
Mary 29, 121
Nancy E. 121
Penelope 128
Sally 36
Stephen 18
Brower, W. M. S. 31
Brown, Ann 46
Betsey 41
Bettie 126
Celia 12
Elizabeth 36, 87
J. R. 19, 119
John 19, 42, 121
Joseph 19, 47, 54, 108, 109
Lucinda 12
Mildred 49
N. L. 19
Nancy 49, 121
Obedince 11
S. 121
Sally 42
Stephen 18, 41
Susan 79
Thomas 19, 56
Vicy 18
W. M. S. 36
Willey 134
William 12, 17, 29, 31, 37, 117
Williams 117
Wm. 67

Brown (cont.)
Wm. S. 22, 29
Wms. 37, 48, 89, 90,
  117
Brunt, Charlotte 99
  Elizabeth 15
  Nancy 41, 102
Bryan, Aby 2
  Arthur 120
  Asptil 56
  Benjamin 2
  Buthan 35
  Bythan 50, 76, 101
  Cathrin Caroline 73
  Celah 123
  Charlotte 88
  Cyntha 134
  D. H. 114
  David H. 39
  E. A. 68, 121
  Earbia 20
  Edith 107, 120
  Elizabeth 39, 48, 104
  Eny 13
  Hardy 17, 35, 43, 75,
    94, 102, 104, 123
  Hary 19
  James 20, 123
  James B. 62
  Jane 10
  Jas. H. 29, 38, 57
  Joannah 118
  Joel 95
  John 88, 114
  John (Jr.) 80
  John H. 45
  John L. 59
  L. A. 65
  Larry 54
  Lisba 43
  Luvey 95
  Margaret E. 73
  Mary 104
  Nancy 107, 108, 124
  Needham 5, 9, 19, 23,
    66, 72, 75, 106
  Needham G. 60
  Needham W. 20
  Patsey 126
  Patsy 121
  Phebe 133
  Ridley 117
  Robert 35
  Samuel A. 134
  Seny 61
  Simon 20, 61, 73, 107
  Susan 112
  Susannah 21
  Ulrica 109
  William 43, 45, 104,
    121
  William W. 5
  Willliam 17
  Wily 51
  Wm. 5
  Wm. W. 46, 107
Bryant, Asha 73
  Larkey 16
  Nicholas 10
  Redding 63
  W. H. N. Arthur 2
Buchanan, Wm. H. 18
Bugram, Wm. 81
Buie, Neill 24
  Neill H. 93
Bull, Wm. 27
Bullock, Ann 19
  Elizabeth 11, 75

Bulls, B. 31
  Barnaby 16, 116, 117
  Betsy 125
  Cloe 100
  Elizabeth 13
  Esther 127
  Jethro 20, 87
  Nancy 89
  Nancy J. 32
  Rachel 116
  Rebecca A. 113
  Reve 47
  Sally 106
  Wm. (Jr.) 22
  Zilpah 23
Bundy, William 118
Burden, Tabitha 89
Burket, Mary 74
Burkhead, L. S. 11, 18,
  77, 87, 92
Burnett, Eliza 86
Burtons, John 3
Busbee, Johnson 78
  Nancy 75
  Ranson 21
  Thomas 115
  Wilson 53
Busby, Thomas 101
Butler, James 40
Buzby, Winnowfred 101
Buzram, N. 125
Bynum, Drewry 32, 68
Byrd, Betsy 2
  Elizabeth 91
  George 68
  John 9, 22, 25, 108
  Lemuel (Sr.) 91
  Martha 107
  Mary C. 91
  Marzilla 26
  Nancy 69
  Olive 25
  Peggy 69
  Pherbee 62
  R. 91
  Reding 2
  Redly 13
  Richard 22
  Right 22, 103
  Samuel 10
  Sarah 69
  Sarah M. 115
  Smithey 9
  Susan 21
  Tabitha 71
  Thomas 22
  Unity 67
Byrds, L. S. 21
  Richard 22
CHampion, Henry 25
Calvit, Mary (Mrs.) 51
Cammel, Charity 134
Cammell, Zilpha 98
Canada, Eliza Ann 9
  Susan 103
Capps, Caley 90
  Elijah 57
  Elizabeth 13
  Emely Jane 70
  Esther 31
  Henry 31
  J. T. 27
  Kissiah C. 57
  Martha 130
  Mary F. 21
  Nancy 66
  Patsey 31
  Rebecca 133

Capps (cont.)
  William 13, 23, 29, 48
  William (Sr.) 23
  Wm. 47
Caps, Ann 87
  Barbara 117
  Elijah 23
Capse, Annis 82
  Lucretia 48
  Matthew 82
  Rebeckah 20
Car, Dempsey 83
  Nancy 83
Card, Mary Ann 2
Cardell, John 48
  Sally 48
Carell, John 23
Carer, Harriet C. 43
Carliles, Nancy 75
Carmack, Levi 58
Carraway, P. I. 1
  P. J. 13, 55, 81
  Paul J. 49, 108
Carrel, David 23
Carrell, Aley 82
  Beedy 70
  Benjamin 21, 23, 46,
    62
  Dolly 107
  Gincy 32
  James 12, 22, 24, 25,
    44, 56, 85, 97
  Jane 64
  John 4, 23, 24, 51, 67
  July 41
  Rhoda 78
  Sally 23
  Sarah 113
  Simeon 32
  Sintha 48
  Susanna 46
Carrol, Marry Jane 62
Carroll, Allen 54
  B. G. 82
  Benjamin 58
  Dallas 24
  Delilah 58
  L. T. 23
  Mary 6
  Rixy 121
Carter, Ader 38
  Charlotte 53
  Emily 50
  Emily Jane 43
  Irvin 38
  John 37, 110
  Joseph 131
  Kindred 38
  Lucy 16
  Lydia 130
  Mary 49, 55
  Polly 131
  William M. 84
Carvele, Winefrin 65
Casey, Martha 128
Caudle, Amy 73
  Harmon 24
  Jonathan 24
  Lewis 108
  Pollly 9
  Susan 72
Cellars, Cally 75
Chambe, John 21
Chambers, Polly 99
  Susanna 117
Chamblee, Fremon 25
  Hiram 86
  Patience 108

Chamblee (cont.)
  Rexey 127
Chamly, Freeman 119
Champion, Henry 25, 72
Chance, Evans 105
Chiles, Edith 103
Chirstmon, Mary J. 47
Christenberry, Thos. S.
  99
Christophers, C. 61
Cimbrel, Martha 57
Claney, Pherebe 85
Clark, Abisha 50
  Arebella 57
  Civil 51
  Emily 30
  Gracy 72
  Harris 15
  Helen Mariah 13
  James 116
  Lewcy 116
  Susannah 64
Clarke, Ann 70
  John 54
  Martha 130
Clemmons, Peggy 87
Clenny, Mary 66
  Pherebe 118
Clifton, Acriel P. 73
  Ann 111
  Candies 73
  Elizabeth 66
  Emily M. 3
  H. A. 55, 111, 113
  Henry A. 26
  J. 36
  Jo 25
  Joel 26, 64, 86
  Joel (Sr.) 25
  Joseph 26, 38
  Thurston 26
  William 25
Coalts, Ann 91
Coates, Jno. R. 38, 46,
  122
Coats, A. 8, 24, 65, 79,
  131
  Amy Ann 22
  Cyntha 5
  D. A. 23
  Emily 65
  Jno. R. 39
  John 40
  John R. 46, 104, 107
  John T. 93
  Lucindy 111
  Nancy 63
  Penny 40
  Polly Ann 61
  Sally 119
  Sarah F. 107
  W. H. 24
  William 6, 112
  William H. 65
  Wm. H. 26, 40
  Zilla 112
Cobb, Barshaby 107
  John Petty 54
  Sally 118
Coble, Samantha 66
Cockerall, Simon 101
Cockerell, Simon 26
Cockrel, Thomas 43
Cockrell, Ervin 26
  Mary 42
  Nancy 129
  Sam'l 26
  Sarah 42

Cockrell (cont.)
  Selah 104
  Simen 55
  Simon 104
  Thmas 50
Cockwell, Thomas 66
Cole, Betsy 57
  Elizabeth 34
  Josiah 113
  Nancy 62
  Patsey 94
  Rebeckah 17
  Sally 74
  Sarah 113
  Thomas 77
  Thos. 81
  Willis 49, 59, 105
Collens, Elizabeth 105
Collier, Elwood 11
  Mary Ann 11
  Mezaney 32
Collins, Amy 128
  Andrew 94
  Betsy 133
  D. G. 27
  Deal 27, 30, 61
  Dial 25
  Frances 59
  George 38, 88
  Milly 118
  Nancy 39
  Patiance 38
  Patty 37
  Polly 29, 70
Colts, Willie 104
Comes, M. C. 112
Cook, Jno. P. 30, 83
Cooke, Patsy 91
Cooper, Ann 46
  Betsy 96
  Betty 92
  John 45, 56
  Mary 124
  Sally 53, 113
  Tabethy 47
Copeland, Charles 65, 66
  Charles (Sr.) 28
  Elizabeth 52
  Joanna 52
Cops, Edith 91
Corbet, Nancy 58
  Sealy 110
Corbin, Mary 11
Corbit, James 28
  James H. 60, 118
  James M. 19
  Loderick A. 28
  Mary J. 52
  Nancy 30
  Susannah 17
  Viney 30
Cordal, Martha 25
Cordell, Abby 57
  Harmon 94
  John 22, 48, 67
  Nancy 126
  Polly 24
  Sally 48
Core, Penelope 32
Cores, B. A. 114
Correll, Dallas 24
Corts, A. 79
Cotton, Ally 61
  Leanna 63
  Polly 77
  Thena H. 71
Courdell, Candiss 57
Cowell, Elizabeth 99

Cowell (cont.)
  Jordan 76
Cox, Mary 11
  Micajah 123
Crafford, Anny 31
  Polly 47
  Winifred 61
Cravy, Hugh 94, 104
Crawford, Alley (Mrs.)
  29
  Catharine 46
  Celia 39
  Charles 55
  Chs. 104
  Elizabeth 105
  Jesse 29
  Julia 21
  Sarah 74
Creach, Jesse 111
  Joannah 84
  Joshua 28
  Rebecca 30
  Willy 26
Creech, Alvin 29
  Apsabeth 37
  Ashley 119
  Barna 27, 110
  Betsey Jane 97
  Catharain 23
  Catherine 29
  Edney 93
  Eliza Ann 110
  Elizabeth 29, 90
  Ezekiel 29, 78, 110
  Hawood 29
  Haywood 117
  Isakiah 29
  James 29
  Jesse 12, 109
  Joshau (Jr.) 37
  Joshua 28, 29, 51, 98
  Joshua (Jr.) 29, 115
  Kedar 30, 31
  Lany 115
  Larkin 29
  Louisa 78, 125
  Margaret 67
  Mary L. H. 87
  Maryann Elizabeth 112
  Nancy 91, 109
  Noah 87
  P. 14, 39
  P. (Rev.) 39
  Parrot 39, 110
  Parrot (Rev.) 8
  Penney Harriett 118
  Polly 110
  Robert (Rev.) 10
  Sally 28
  Stanford 29, 89
  Susan 30, 103
  Tempy 37
  W. H. 29
  Winny 53
  Wm. M. 38
  Worley 48
Crocker, (?) (Mrs.) 83
  Catharine 133
  Catty 42
  Elizabeth H. 73
  Harriet 83
  James 42, 90
  Joseph 18
  Linsey (Mrs.) 90
  Martha 28
  Mary E. 99
  Milly 122
  Morning 88

141

Eason (cont.)
John 5, 10, 20, 87,
103, 106, 118
Madalena 72
Margaret 69
Marsaline 18
Mary 2, 126
Nancy 4
Olive 47
Penny 17
Sally 128
Sarah 119
Sarah A. E. 120
Shadrach 69
Smithy 93
Temperance 75
Theaney 88
Thos. 76
Viney 87
Winifred 48
Eatman, Cresy 7
Delilah 20
Lou 127
Thomas 6
Eatmon, Eastly 55
Martha 38
Nancy 48
Eavens, Betsey C. 24
Polly 15
Edgerton, Sarah Ann 128
Edward, David 50
Patsy 80
Edwards, Anny 97
Apsabeth 42
Benjamin 37
Carolin 37
Celia 31
Delany 133
Edith 49, 74
Elizabeth 2, 31
Elvy 133
Emily 80
H. W. 99
Jacob 132
John 37
Jos. 27
Joseph 51, 85, 90, 99,
133
Joseph (Jr.) 17
Lucy 118
Lucy Ann 116
Marcy Ann E. 90
Martha 52
Mary 37
Micajah 90
Nancy 29, 102
Nanny 133
Newsom 37
Patsey 95
Patty 91
Peity 48
Polly 22, 90
Rachel 98
Raiford 24
Rebecca 31
Robert 28
Sally 101
Sampson 37, 59
Sarah 28, 84, 93
Sarah (Mrs.) 83
Sarah M. 83
Stephen 37
Thos. (Sr.) 48
Wm. B. T. 36
Eldredge, Elizabeth 51
Loverd 15
Susan 71
Young 114

Eldridg, Abigail 125
Betsy 59
Eldridge, Abigail 125
Ann 74
Betsey 73
Cherry 103
Elizabeth 102
L. 57, 88
Lizzy 102
Loverd 73, 88
Mary 10, 108
Pherebee 126
Susan 125
Theny 130
Wm. S. 71
Eliot, John 91
Ellen, Nancy 23
Nancy Flu 79
Ellenton, Sally 57
Ellice, Winnyford 78
Ellington, Adlade C. 40
Bennett 76
Betsy 21
Edith 86
J. F. 5, 15, 18, 28,
33, 34, 40, 41, 45,
46, 48, 50, 66, 67,
69, 93, 108, 110,
118, 120, 127, 133
J. H. 66
John 101
John F. 89
Jos. C. 67
Julia 101
Kindred C. 72
Martha 119
Nancy 134
Polly 94
Elliot, Sally 12
Ellis, Betsey 38
Edny 12, 21
Elizabeth 20
F. F. 21, 91
Gearmon 21
Haywood 28, 76
J. A. 105
James R. 38, 106
Jno. I. 38
John 12, 40, 46, 86
John Lacy 38
Lecy 125
Lively 119
Martha 128
Martha Ann R. 96
Nancey 66
Nancy 93
Ridley 120
Selina 131
Telitha C. 63
W. A. 38
William 10
Ennis, J. H. 121
John 38
Maria 32
Mary 46
Matilda V. 108
Milly 46
Nancy 14
Nancy Emiline 57
Ramon 38
Raymond 46
Sarah L. 50
William 32
Winnifred 38
Errant, Betsy 85
Eskridge, Luvey 24
Etheredge, Lucy J. 1
W. R. 39

Ethridge, Jency 68
Thomas L. 68
Evan, Daniel 100
Evans, Adlade 127
Athy 99
Betsy Ann 72
Caroline 121
Charlotte 73
David 18, 39
Dicy 105
Edith 91
Elenor 46, 89
Joanna 46
John R. 119
Jonathan 89
Josiah 113, 133
Lucy 123
Martha Ann 129
Peggy 25
Sally 64
Zilpha 131
Everytt, William 78
Ezzel, Fannie M. 14
FAulk, James 53
Fail, Ailsey 53
Dixon 72
Edith Ann 48
Elizabeth 27
Jonthan 27
Julia 52
Lewis 125
Maria 75
Mary A. 34
Nancy 29, 71
Needham 66
Patsy 66
Pheareby 111
Pherebee 74
Phereby 39
Polly 72
Sally 75
Sarah 43
Thos. 111
William 20
Faile, Anne 5
Faircloth, Stephen 18
Fairley, Elizabeth 134
Faison, Martha Jane E.
63
Farmer, Benjamin 94
Betsy 112
Edith 112
Harriett 29
J. J. 96, 133
James J. 68
Jinkins 78
Jno. 2, 8, 21
Polly 49
Sally 76
Sarah 78
Susanah 8
William 39, 49
Wm. 116
Farrar, Eliza 119
Farrell, John 61
Farrow, Catharine 16
Faulk, Creck 43
Elizabeth 14, 71
James 6, 28, 53, 125
Jas. 44, 102
Jas. (Jr.) 8
John 40
Thos. 82
Feboash, Morning 69
Fellow, William 91
Fentrell, Mary 29
Ferrell, Betsy 86
Cady 108

Ferrell (cont.)
  Elizabeth 50, 120
  John W. 38, 107
  Leucy 38
  Levi 107
  Mary 38
  Miriam 42
  Nancy 23
  Susannah 15
  Tempy 79
  Thebes 86
  Ulrica 96
  Winefred 23
Ferrells, Harrison 44
Ferrill, Polly 95
Feutral, Elizabeth 44
Field, Lucey 39
Fields, John 32
Fillom, S. C. 127
Finch, H. H. 11, 21, 44,
  45, 59, 67, 78, 107,
  112, 125
  Henry 55
  Patty 55
Finlayson, A. J. 3
Fish, John 27
  Salley 27
  William 124
Fisher, Polly 94
Fivash, Patsey 93
Floid, Aven 53
  Betsey 53
Flours, W. B. 27
Flowers, Bedy 123
  Elizabeth E. 125
  Ellender 64
  Emily 33
  Harriet 44
  Henry 41
  Jacob 70, 100
  Joel 70
  Martha 78
  Mary 27
  Sally 46
  Tempe 41
  Winifred 49
Fluellen, Avy 86
  Sarah 85
Fluellin, Piety 23
Folk, Polly 26
  Thomas 41
Folsom, Thomas 80
  Thos. 83, 134
Ford, Elizabeth 34
  Jane 121
  John 121
  Patience 114
Forehand, Lewis 109
  Patsy 109
Fountain, Mariah 35
Fowler, Pattrick 41
Fralick, Jane 47
Freeman, David 21
  Joseph C. 41
  Mark 88
  Patsey 81
  Rixey 69
Frelick, James 104
Frost, Jesse 5
  Rachel 18
  Rachill 24
  Ryal W. 83
  Sarah 39
Fulgham, Edith 51
  Elizabeth 130
  Jacob B. 74
Fulghum, Sarah 102
Futerals, Jesse 84

Futerell, Sarah 41
Futral, Etheldred 41
Futrel, Etheldred 40
  Nathaniel 42
Futrell, Arcady 84
  Crawford 32
  Drusilla 90
  Etheldred 33, 124
  Exum 30
  G. 48
  L. G. 31
  Mary 79, 101
  Nathaniel 134
  Soloman 84
  Solomon 30, 42
  Wilkerson 90
Gaerald, John 120
Gainas, Penny 39
Gainer, Betsy 134
Gaines, Simon 39
Gale, Clary 65
Game, Samuel 42
Ganer, Eli 42
Gardner, Luvey 121
  Penelopia 96
Garland, Louiza 2
  Mary 128
Garne, Elizer 104
  Peggy Ann 104
Garner, Asa 55
  Bedy 19
  Betsy 11, 101
  Christian 50
  Cintha 17
  Cynthia 55
  Delaney 88
  Dicen 26
  Elisha 70
  Elizabeth 42, 52, 55
  Ely 88
  James 19, 42
  Joel 134
  John 52
  Levi 42
  Lydia 101
  Mary 101
  Nancy 86
  Patsy 26
  Polly 42, 49
  Sally 11
  Sarah 31, 70
  William 42
  Willis 26
  Winefred 43
  Zilpha 8
Garrald, Ann 64
Garrard, T. 10, 35, 126
Gart, Polly 32
Gatlin, Zilpha 1
Gay, Betsey 12
  Catharine 102
  Elizabeth 102
  Josiah 30
  Josial 17
  Laurinda 28
  Lucinda 64
  Lucretia 82
  Luvina 122
  Minerva 120
  Polly 65
  Ranzey 93
  Ruth 30
  Willey 59
  Winnefred 111
  Wm. 112
Gearald, Delany 29
  Patsey 43
Gearold, Edney 42

Gennett, Betsey 29
George, Alice 39
  Betsy 1
  Charity 2
  Isaac L. 15
  Jeremiah L. 102
  Nancy 73
  Sarah A. 115
  Winifred 14
Gerald, Anne 88
  Clark 104
  Enos 88, 104
  Jno. 11
  John 60
  Quilly 12
  W. F. 15, 87
  Wilie 106, 120
  Wilie F. 110, 111
Germillon, Polley 40
Gerrald, Anne 88
  Disey 37
  Enos 88
  John 64
  Marian 104
  Willey 97
Gibbs, Holly 24
Gibs, Judith 132
Giles, Bearshaba 17
  Elisabeth 16
  Nancy 64
  Nathaniel 36
  Sally 56
  Sarrah 54
  William 64, 74, 103
Gilman, Harbard 6, 85
Gilmore, Winifred 107
Ginnet, Mary 122
Gisborn, Catherine 6
Glasgow, E. 6
Glover, Benjamin J. 51
Godawin, B. 1
Godwin, Amanda 50
  B. 10, 22, 29, 32, 33,
  44, 48, 61, 63, 70,
  73, 89, 103, 110
  Beady 100
  Benjamin 77
  Cady 76
  Clany 44
  Clarkey 89
  Cozzey 36
  Easter 127
  Edith 125
  Edney 35
  Edny 93
  Elbert 6
  Elenor 29
  Elijah 44
  Elizabeth 4, 99
  Ephraim 44
  G. W. 80
  Gracy 21
  Griffin W. 99
  H. 12
  Hinton M. 74
  Iredell 15, 132
  James 112
  James A. 103
  Jenny 55
  Martha 5
  Martha H. 88
  Milly 108
  Minton M. 6, 44
  Nancy 30, 125
  P. 11, 12, 25, 32, 50,
  69, 74, 102
  Pereby 89
  Perry 12, 48, 69, 84,

Godwin (cont.)
122, 130
Polly 17, 89, 99
Raney 110
Rhode 123
Samuel 107
Sarah 110
Silvy 12
Simon 7
Smithey A. 9
Stephenson 41, 70
Susan C. 110
Susan H. 14
Unity 56
Wiley 55
Willie 30
Goman, M. 94
Goodrach, Catern 68
Goodrich, Betsy 49
Gordan, Elizabeth 9
Gouvin, Cresy 108
Gower, Araminta 64
Caron 106
Gideon 62, 64
Lydia 25
Phereby 131
Polly 130
Reuben 64
William 45
Zachariah 99
Gowers, Gideon 44
Graham, Martha E. 125
Grant, Dempsey 118
Kinchin 73
Pollie 61
Winny 73
Grantham, Alley 81
Caroline 81
Dicy 58
Henderson 125
M. K. 16, 45, 134
M. R. 91, 94
Mary 104
Sidney 81
Gray, Henry 4, 6, 76
Thomas 85, 96
Grayn, Lotty 20
Green, Betsy 56
Clary 128
Cynthia 107
Darkas 80
Furney 82
Furnifold 46
George 3
Jane 59
John 51
John B. 100
Laban 51
Martha 2
Mary 17, 129
Milly 17
Nancy 20, 45, 47, 129
Polly 82
Rebey 45
Reding 45
Richd. 57
Sally 31, 96, 127
Sion 20, 45
Wiley 45
William 17, 129
Wm. 127
Greene, R. 63
Gregory, James 85
Patty 78
Grice, Delilah 123
G. 4
Garry 49
Jesse 15

Grice (cont.)
Stephen 40, 41, 43,
51, 99, 123
Tempy Ann 50
Thomas T. 127
Zilpha 111
Grier, William 77
Griffin, (?) (Maj.) 90
Caroline 12
Edmond 82
Elizabeth 122
George W. 89
Mary E. 112
Griffis, Margret Jane 62
Tranquilla 120
Griffith, Sally 101
Grimes, Elizabeth 38
Lucy 1
Matilda 40
Nancy 113
Sally 38
Griswe, Sally 16
Griswold, Mary E. 28
Nancy 34
Grizzel, Bannister 99
Grizzell, Mary 85
Guess, John M. 27
Sarah 27
Guin, Barna 119
Dicey A. 72
Eadith 94
Henry 38, 125
Guion, Elizabeth 95
Guley, Betsy 59
Patty 69
Gulley, Any 18
E. H. 52
Elizabeth 127
G. G. 38
Geo. S. 54
J. G. 81
Jno. G. 45
John G. 118
N. G. 18, 43, 64, 68
Nancy L. 69
Nathan 50, 127
Needham G. 108
Polly 122
R. (Jr.) 52
R. N. 52, 128
Robert 4, 19, 46
Robert (Jr.) 5, 27
Robert N. 11, 114
Robt. (Jr.) 122
W. G. 69
Zilpha 118
Gully, Bethana 53
Elizabeth 46, 127
Geo. S. 128
Harriet 36
J. G. 88, 119
J. S. 30
Jno. G. 35
John 90
John G. 22, 118, 130
Martha 74
Meed 101
N. G. 49, 66, 95
Nathan 127
Patsy 47
Polly 119
R. N. 11, 42, 51, 52,
62, 82, 121
Robert (Jr.) 17
Robert N. 10, 122
Robt. (Jr.) 50, 90
Robt. N. 98, 121, 122
Sally 20, 35

Gully (cont.)
Tranquella 51
Zilpha 118, 121
Gurley, Daniel 10
Elizabeth 9, 47, 114
Elizabeth (Mrs.) 31
Jeremiah 31, 37, 59,
97, 105
Joseph 31, 101
Keziah 105
Lydia 47
Mary 31
Mary H. 45
Maurill 78
Meurell 47
Polly 41
Susanah 58
Gurly, Mary Jane 76
Raford 104
Zilpha 81
Guven, Ester 81
Guy, H. 24, 75
Henry 22
Jno. C. 31, 35, 115
Jno. McC. 8
John McC. 104
Nancy 50
Narcissy 69
Sukey 94
Will 112
Wm. 124
Wm. Hen. 60, 80, 133
Wm. Henry 39
Gwin, Barnabas 73
Elizabeth A. 73
Hackney, Celah 100
Martha 100
Piety 58
William 95, 96
Wm. 8, 56, 85
Hadley, Susanna 39
Hails, Chatmon 47
Hain, Jethor 13
Hair, Jethro 65
Haislip, Betsy 22
Haithcock, Sally 21
Hales(?), Susan (Mrs.)
28
Hales, Rildy 6
Hall, Bedy 126
Delany 104
Edith 33
Martin 39
Mary 100
Matthew 73
Pheraby 37
Sally 23
Sarah 24
Seawell 101
Susan 23
W. F. 8, 43, 72, 80,
98, 115
William F. 23
Wm. F. 38, 83, 97,
102, 103
Zilpha 85
Hamby, Tempi 116
Hamilton, Alisor 59
Barnaba 87
Edeth 15
Eliza 27
Henry 47, 133
John 59
Sally 133
Hamontree, Peter 48
Handy, M. 125
Matthew 32, 83
Matthias 112

Hardcastle, James 130
Hardy, Acquilla 47
  Martha 25, 71
  Nelley 75
  Sally 21
  Sarah 13
Hare, Jno. 48
  Martha 30
  Patsey 99
  Ransom 110, 116
  Rebecca 85
  Sally 85
Harman, Rhoda 40
Harp, John 31
Harper, Absalom 48
  Ammy 78
  Banister 33
  Bartlet 49, 78
  Bryan 33
  Corternea V. T. 62
  John 14, 34, 102, 125
  John J. 68
  John R. 48
  Mary 48
  Nancy 121
  Nancy Willey 78
  Phereby 121
  Polly 24
  Wilsey 77
Harrell, Ann 73
  Betsey 34
  Cenith 83
  Charlotte 94
  Elizabeth 16, 115
  Frances 49
  Francis 33, 34, 39,
    49, 70, 73, 75
  Francis (Jr.) 119
  John 56
  Patty 33
  Susan 34
Harrison, Betsy 65
  Della 68
  Elisha 2, 5, 10, 24,
    48, 95
  Elizabeth 5
Hart, Catharine 126
  Polly 54
Hartly, Zilpha 109
Hasting, Wm. 35
Hastings, Julia A. 18
  Wm. 127
Hastins, Wm. 24
Hatcher, Austen 19
  Austin 36, 42, 111
  Beedy 134
  Benj. 22
  Benjamin 19, 26, 50,
    129, 132
  Betsy 90
  Charles 19
  John 49, 134
  John T. 50, 56
  Mary 42
  Polly 26
  Robert 50
  Sally 132
  Sarah 19
Hatchers, John T. 36
Hathcock, Eveline 15
  Nancy 4
  Young 120
Hawkins, Hannah 97
  William 114
Hawley, Polly 132
  Tharris H. 116
Hay, James 18, 43, 44,
    123

Hayles, Anny 36
  Culia 85
  Elizabeth 126
  Elizabeth Hawkins 52
  Gilbert 50
  Henry 48, 96
  John 6
  John T. 101
  Lucas 105
  Penelopia 55
  Pennina 53
  Penny 96
  Polly 122
  William 35, 52
  Zepha 89
Hayls, Polly 100
Hays, Betsy 118
  Lucreacy 69
  Rhabeca L. 118
Hayse, Levina 126
Haywood, Jno. L. 25
  John L. 47
Hearne, Anny 111
  Betsy 83
  Joseph 13
  Mason 83
Heath, A. J. 108, 124,
    127
  Adam J. 16, 108
  Ann 108
  Martha 127
Hedgepeth, Elizabeth 105
Heeth, Milbury 100
Helme, Caroline 32
  Phereby (Mrs.) 118
  Ray 19, 40, 117
  Robert H. 7, 67, 84
  Roy 54
Helms, Pameser 100
Hendrick, Jeremiah 101
Hennant, Cally 50
  Jesse 50
  Morning 10
Henniard, Mary 66
Herring, John 115
  Rachel 125
Hicks, Alsy 68
  C. B. 102
  Emily 75
  Martha Ann 81
  Nancy E. 98
  Nehemiah 44
  Sally 130, 133
  Stephen 51, 124, 133
  Thomas 62
Higdon, John 51
Higgins, George Anne 133
High, Alsey 19
  John 100
  Martha 21
  Winefred 75
Hill, Benjamin 4, 54
  David 43
  Evaline 129
  Green 17, 51
  Rebecca 83
  Sarah 132
  Savel 85
Hillard, Martha 7
Hilliard, James 98, 104
  William 127
Himan, Wm. 127
Hinannt, James 112
Hines, (?) (Mrs.) 56
  Julia Y. 82
  Nannie 56
Hinnant, Amelia 60
  B. R. 6, 31, 124

Hinnant (cont.)
  Bryan H. 47
  Bryan R. 93
  Bryant R. 89
  Calley 53
  Cally 50
  Elizabeth 47, 87, 99
  Gaston 53
  H. H. 18
  Hardy 75
  Henry 29
  Hepsebah Jane 124
  Holly 28
  James 19, 34, 52, 57,
    77, 87, 89, 112, 121
  James H. 17, 98
  Jeses 100
  Jesse 7, 16, 28, 50,
    53, 82, 83, 100,
    102, 115, 121, 127
  Jessee 58
  John 54
  Jonathan 68, 100
  Josiah 46, 47, 52, 84
  Josiah (Jr.) 41, 87,
    102
  Louisa 52
  Lucy 98
  Mabra 7
  Mabry 16
  Martha 98
  Mary A. 25
  Nancy 89
  Patience 89, 134
  Ransom 91
  Rany 90
  Sally 122, 124
  Sarah J. 58
  Sarah R. 8
  Theo 53
  Thomas G. 36
  William 57, 97
  William (Sr.) 30, 66,
    100
  Williamson 98, 133
  Wm. 54, 129
  Wm. (Sr.) 53, 99
  Wm. Q. 53
Hinson, Mary 120
Hinton, Betsy 53
  Delany 97
  Edith 54, 101
  Eliza Jane 46
  Elizabeth 53, 79, 115
  Elizabeth Hawkins 83
  Elizier Ann 119
  Esther 53
  George 101, 130
  Hardy 53
  Harriot 27
  Isaac 117
  Joseph 53
  Kiddy 85
  Lewcy 2
  Lucy M. 13
  Lydia 54
  M. 58
  Malachi 57
  Mary Ann 100, 122
  Matilda 53
  Milly Jane 129
  Phereby 130
  Polly 26, 85, 104
  Ransom 28, 54
  Rene 85
  Salina 76
  Sally 20
  Sarah C. 82

Hinton (cont.)
Tempy 103
William 53
Willy 4
Wimberley 126
Wm. 17, 53, 75, 97,
    131
Hix, Esther 29
Stephen 6
Hleme, R. H. 74
Hobbs, Bolling Green 130
Elizabeth 116
H. H. 134
Henry H. 42, 80
Sally 54
William 33, 116
Hobby, Anna 64
Edney 1
Harman 121
Henry 19
J. J. 132
Mary 74
Patsy 57
Phereba 42
Piety 24
Sally 130
Wm. 69
Hocot, William B. 68
Hocott, Emily 86
Harriet 88
Hocut, (?) 58
Benjamin 85
Betsy 38, 59
Bryan 108
Crecy 32
Elizabeth 85
H. 95
Joanna 80
Mary 52
Nancy 52, 83
Peninnah 36
Rilda 74
Sarah 133
William 133
William B. 133
Wm. B. 54, 96
Hocutt, Delany 86
Sarah 115
Sarrah H. 114
Hodge, Curtis 54
Dellah 30
Elizabeth 39
Wealthy 25
Hodges, J. W. 50, 67,
    134
John W. 9, 116
Hodgsdon, Esebel 32
Hogan, Smiethey 115
Hogg, Celia 95
Sintha 73
Temperance 36
Hoilt, Beddy 46
Holder, B. B. 66
Catharine 128
Celah 127
James 51, 55
John 56
Prudence 56, 96
Holiman, Fereby 132
Hollaand, Elisha 75
Hollaman, Edney 132
Holland, Alfred 60
Bartillie 113
Betsy 55
Bryant 55
Celia 69
Curtis 67
D. H. 9, 44, 64, 95

Holland (cont.)
David H. 15, 44
Eason 55
Elisha 127
Enos 55
Exum 115
Finettie 8
G. H. 89
Green H. 133
Jennett 109
Jesse 1, 113
Louisa 113
Maia 1
Mary 64
Matilda 113
Nancy 55, 60
Susan Ann 88
Tempy 55
Thomas 60
Warren 95
Willy 13
Zilpa 102
Hollands, C. G. 91
Hollandsworth, Elizur 94
Holleman, C. M. 66
Celia 20
Frederick 18
Jessee 107
William 6
Hollemon, Frederick 112
Mary 112
Holliman, C. M. 133
David 56, 124
Frederic 56
Frederick 85, 112
James 27
Jonathan 96
Jos. 45
Josiah 82, 83
Mary 112
Milchey 6
Mildred 55
Seth 75
William 82
Hollimon, Clary 118
David 93
Griffin 52
Larkin 20
Tobias 58, 132
Hollingsworth, Lucy 104
Rebecca 31
Hollinson, Josiah 24
Holloman, Celia 116
Clarky 44
Elizabeth 98
Josiah 45
Mary 43
Ransom 30
Winnifred 56
Hollomon, Garry 56
James 4
John 56
Patsey 41
Patsy 56, 60, 72
Ransom 56
Rhoda 56
William 104
Hollowell, Polly 78
Holmes, Anna 43
Bersheba 97
Chelly 72
Frederick 61
Fredrick 89
Hardy 86
J. B. 83
Jane 83
John 43
Polley 85

Holmes (cont.)
Sallie Ann 83
Sally 89
Warren 72
Holoman, Nancy 54
Holowell, Wili 59
Holt, Amy 5
Delia 72
Eliza Jane 46
Elizabeth D. 104
Elizabeth S. 1
Elteldred 31
Etheldred 4, 5, 16,
    47, 48, 105, 120,
    130
Harriett 44
James 72
Jerry 109
Jeses 133
Jesse 56, 84
John 57, 81
Joseph 87
Louenza 87
Nancy 70
Nancy M. 56
Polly 66
Ransom 56
Richard 133
Sally 114
Sophia 56
W. 116
W. D. 11, 27, 36, 56,
    57, 59, 69, 90, 124,
    134
W. P. 4
Wilie 17, 55, 80, 84,
    97, 129
William 119
William (Jr.) 118
Willie 23, 28, 31, 36,
    48, 59, 80, 89, 90,
    91, 97, 98, 128, 133
Holton, Salathiel 105
Holts, Joseph 5
Homes, Freadrick 66, 111
Fredrick 89
Herom 13
Hiram 56
James 13
Sally 89
Honecutt, Dilley 68
Honeycut, Betty 57
Candis 86
Lucy 63
William 28
William (Jr.) 57
Winefred 83
Honeycutt, A. J. 122
Abner(?) 122
Cherry 97
Hawkins 46
Mary C. 122
Hood, B. Robin 76
Bold Robin 13, 57, 59
Bold Robin (Jr.) 32
Charles A. 35
Eliza Ann 53
Elizabeth T. 80
J. C. 4, 59, 87
Jno. C. (Jr.) 3
John C. 7, 10, 20, 34,
    56, 59, 61, 63, 73,
    81, 87, 98, 105,
    107, 114, 120, 125,
    130, 134
John C. (Sr.) 72, 131
Mary Ann 72
Mary E. 38

Hood (cont.)
  S. H. 67, 76
  Wm. H. (Jr.) 58
Hooks, Harriet 124
Hopkins, Elizabeth 44
  Nancy 68
  Sarah 26
  William W. 79
  Willy 128
  Wm. W. 50
Horn, Benajah 48, 51, 74
  Celah 115
  Charity 130
  Cintha 123
  Emely 51
  Martha Ellen 29
  Mildred 6
  Milly 123
  Polly 19
  Precillar 51
  Richard 130
  Sally 30, 65
  Sarah 119, 134
  Slomney 40
  Zilpha 108
Horne, Candis 76
  Elizabeth H. 18
  Henry 35
  Rixy 41
  S. R. 18, 69
Horten, Sam D. 21
Horton, Bedith 85
  S. P. 53, 105, 122
  S. S. 38
Houghton, Joshua 51
  Thomas 58
Houlder, Edith 68
  Jas. 6
  Joseah 32
  Josiah 5, 80
  Morning 101
  Rhoda 112
  Unity 108
  Willy 100
Houldor, Jas. 17
House, Elizabeth 18
Howard, Drusillah 112
  Polly 77
Howel, Jethro 39
Howell, Absilla 51
  Catharine 97
  Charles 25
  Cherry 47
  Chilly 101
  Edmond 59
  Elizabeth 57
  Jethro 89
  John 83
  John D. 59, 65
  Mary 79
  Nancy 79
  Patience 21
  Pherebee 39
  Ritor 90
  Tilethy 89
  Willie 58
Howels, Dupree 64
Hudson, Benjamin F. 61
  Caroline 9
  J. J. 59
  Joel 25
  John W. 63
  Mary L. 10
  W. P. 59
Hudtson, Mary 43
Hughes, Drusilla 101
  Mary 76
Hughs, Aquilla 109

Hughs (cont.)
  Bengeman 76
  Ganzada 122
  Mary 76
Humphries, Nancy 17
Huneycut, Mary 82
Hunter, Emily J. 40
Husted, H. W. 106
  Hiram W. 60
Hutchins, Isaac 38
Hutson, Joel G. 76
Ingram, Alsy 65
  Ambrose 107
  Ann 72
  Barnaby 59
  Bethania 7
  Betsey 28
  Betsey E. 129
  Betsy 73
  Chilly 11
  Edith 64
  Elizabeth 112, 125
  Ellinder 72
  Esther Ann 87
  Henry 115
  Joanna 74
  Joseph 37
  Julie 107
  Kezziah Ann 125
  Lucy 105
  Nancy 18, 94, 107, 118
  Needham 1, 60, 71, 81
  Polley 123
  Polly 29, 87
  Sally 107
  Sarah 95
  Susan 116
  Theny 2
  William 74
  Winey 84
  Winnifred 3
  Wm. 59
  Zilpha 6
Inman, Mary 62
Irby, Elizabeth L. 113
  H. 113
Irwin, Joseph 55, 87,
    129
Isler, John 108
Iveans, Sally 26
Ives, T. 83
Ivey, Druzila 48
  Eliza 48
  Elizabeth 94
  James 56
  Payten 132
  Reeves 60
Ivy, David (Sr.) 60, 75,
    106
  Hartwill 106
  James 125
  Julia 132
  Silvy 105
Jackson, B. 28
  J. B. 15, 20, 28, 30,
    49, 75, 77, 108, 119
  J. S. 92
  James B. 101
  James T. 131
  John 14, 60, 70, 129
  Kitsey 44
  Sally 37
  William 55
James, Charlotte 98
  Tempia 102
  Wm. 15
Jarrell, Delanie 12
  Isaac 12, 89

Jarrell (cont.)
  Patience 86
Jarroll, Delanie 12
  Isaac 12
Jeffers, Sally 45
Jeffreys, James 124
  Ruffin 60
Jelks, Jarrot 97
Jenergan, Betsey 14
Jenings, Mary 132
  Ryal 131, 132
Jenkins, Jane 17
Jennigan, Polly 13
Jerald, Matilda 129
Jernigan, Alder 14
  Bright 4, 23
  Cader 78
  Charllotte 106
  Elizabeth Ann 37
  Esther 127
  Jemima 14
  Jerusha 32
  Joseph 127
  Lovey 73
  Mary 105, 114
  Nancy 15
  Nancy Ann 78
  Parthena 119
  Zilpah 25
Jinkins, Lewis M. 21
  Lewis W. 45
  Redding 36
  Sally 109
Johnson, A. 71
  Aby 122
  Alcey 123
  Alexander 63
  Alfred 2, 3
  Allen 62, 63, 89, 103,
    131
  Allen (Sr.) 1, 61
  Alsey 64
  Alvin 49
  Amanda 55
  Amos 110
  Amous 65
  Ann 7
  Annatha 15
  Anny 98
  Any 111
  Aquilla 27
  Ara 64
  Aron 123
  Arthur Bailey 87
  Barnabas 112
  Betsey 86
  Betsy 43
  Bettie 49
  Burwell 6, 82, 88
  Carrell 23
  Cary 34
  Catherine 126
  Ceely 95
  Charlottee 64
  Chilly 112
  Creecy 112
  Cula 46
  Culie Ann 88
  Dilitha 63
  Dorcass 107, 131
  Drury 23, 42
  Edith 24, 57, 69, 81,
    84
  Edmund 64
  Eleanor 71
  Elijah B. 61, 73
  Elizabeth 13, 23, 51,
    59, 68, 70, 89, 105

147

Johnson (cont.)
Elizabeth E. 59, 87
Elizabeth J. 134
Emily 64
Emily Elizabeth 2
Emly 35
Esther 2
Etheldred 131
Evaline 11
Fanny 64, 126
Fereby 41
Fred. 65
Gaston 131
H. 28, 55
Harriet 82, 86
Harrot 40
Harry 2, 38, 59, 81,
  116, 131
Henry 4, 13, 51, 63,
  77
Henry C. 64
Henry W. 91
Honor H. 18
Irene 4
Isaac 22, 63, 64, 77,
  126
Isaler(?) 8
Isom 86
Jacob 134
James 62, 113
Jas. H. 112
Jno. W. 62
Jnona. 44
Joel 64
John 131
John B. 61
John W. 38, 40, 63
Jonathan 34
Joshua 70, 87
Judy B. 133
Keziah 90
Leacy 32
Lemuel 8
Lewcy 2
Liddy 40
Littleton 54
Louezur 107
Louisa 71
Luanna 2
Lucy 71, 81, 132
Lucy H. 33
Lurany 35
Luvensy 5
Lydia 63
M. 134
Margaret 1, 64
Margret 22
Martha 33, 64, 81
Martin 63
Mary 8, 65, 86, 107,
  131
Mary Frances 8
Mary Jane 48
McCoy 86
Milly 102
Moses A. 63
Nancy 8, 22, 58, 60,
  95, 111, 125
Nancy H. 63
Nathan 65
Nathaniel 18, 65
Nathaniel H. 96
Noel 63
Olive 113
Padeath 125
Parazadia 65
Patsey 22, 66, 67
Patsy 65

Johnson (cont.)
Peggy 88
Peney 107, 132
Penny 115
Peter 74
Pheba 131
Pherebe 103
Phereby 77, 91
Phil 108
Philip 43, 91, 96, 120
Phillip 50
Polly 57, 77, 81, 86,
  132
Rachel 87
Ransom 55
Rebecca 129
Rebecca A. 18, 133
Rebeckah 13, 90
Redley 2
Redly 1, 2
Regdon 6
Reuben 62, 65
Richard 34
Rigdan 120
Rigdon 98
Rulany 126
S. E. 66
Salina H. 114
Sally 3, 5, 7, 34, 54,
  61, 74, 81, 82, 94
Samuel 65, 74, 75
Sarah 61, 74, 75, 78,
  126
Soloman 36
Solomon 65, 133
Stephen 25, 55, 65
Susan 26, 63
Thena 79
Tranquilla 67, 126
Uriah 111, 115
W. H. 13
Whitmell 128
William 35, 62, 64,
  78, 81, 105
William A. 15
William W. 63
Willie 61, 77, 131
Wilsy 62
Wily 40
Winefred 106
Winifred 58
Wm. 46, 82
Wm. P. 13
Zilpah 53
Johnston, Angeline 33
Budd 10
Delia 61
Kesiah 55
Lizzie 113
Mary 36
Moses 57, 90
Redden 107
Sarah 64
Staton 58
Susan 8, 79
Warren 58, 102
Winifred 126
Joiner, Betsey 30
Edith 6
Milly 110
Patience 42
Rhoda 119
Jonergan, Betsy 76
Jones, A. 50
Allen 56, 68
Alley Elizabeth 45
Amanda M. 38
Augustus G. 95

Jones (cont.)
Barbary 28
Benjamin 66, 67
Bethana 72
Bethaney 125
Bethany 88
Betsy 53
C. P. 43
Cally 29
Charles 48
Charllota 6
Creacy Ann 49
Darcas 45
Delia S. 57
Dianna 71
E. L. 79
E. S. 27, 58, 109
Edwin 19
Elihu N. 53
Elizabeth 40, 86, 88,
  109, 123, 133
Esther 44
Etheldread 67
Hardy 67
Henrietta 50
Isaac 14, 78
Isaac W. 66
James 20, 22, 79, 101
James A. 8
Jane C. 16
Jno. 86
John (Jr.) 10
John R. 9
Joseph 25, 111
Judith 6
Lemel 36
Leroy 76
Lotty 17
Louisa 93
Lucetta 6
Lusetto 22
Lydia 8
Margaret 56
Martha 59
Mary 14, 19, 91, 95
Mary J. 9, 14
Matthew 11, 52
Matthew (Jr.) 27
Mimme 103
Nancy 17, 21, 48
Nancy Ann 106
Nancy Ann Eliza 88
Nicy 68
P. A. 24
Patsey 99
Pency Villia 112
Penny H. 67
Phereby M. 68
Polly 29, 47, 56
Rachel 3
Rachell 60
Ray 67
Rebecca Ann 59
Rhoda 111
Ridley 25
Ritty 8
Sally 20
Samuel 95
Sarah 53
Sarah E. 52
Simon 67
Susan 8, 95
Sylvester 29
T. M. 8
Tempa Eliza 8
Thomas 21
Thos. 14
W. B. 51, 119, 124

149

Perry (cont.)
Mary 122
Pettis, Polly 100
Pew, Ceneth 68
Phililips, Dixon 105
Philips, Edith 47
Phillips, Augusta C. 92
Ben. 61
Edith 133
Elder Dixon 16
Elijah H. 22
Emma 132
F. 43
John 49
Mariah 40
N. L. 86, 115
Ray 18, 40, 48, 56,
109, 111, 121
Sarah 43
Susan 64
W. P. 110
William 96
Zilphea E. 77
Pike, J. T. 98
Pilkenton, Elizabeth 37
Hardy 90
Pilkinton, Betsy 90
Clinch 90
Hardy 23, 124
Morning 31
Patsy 69
Richard 93
Winny 69
Wm. H. 119
Pinks, Cynthea 75
Pinney, Lucy 63
Pipkin, Edith 40
Pitman, Betsy 66
Cherry 31
Elisha 12, 129
Joanah 12
Seney 18
Pitmon, Amanda 11
Elisha 11, 12
Joanah 12
Piety 74
Thomas 93
Pitmond, Charity 93
Pittes, Dorcas 68
Eliza 43
Sally 34
Pittman, Elisha 93
Pleasant, M. 113
Sarah 111
Pool, Celia 80
Elizabeth 84, 100
Fereby 106
Hardy 93, 94
John 32, 62
Johnathan 93
Martha 38
Mary Ann E. 28
Nancy 109
Patsy 13
Penny 38
Pherebee 84
Polly 34, 93
Sally 104
Sarry 25
Theo. 15
Wm. 68
Poole, Mary 31
Pattie 28
Pooll, Rhodes 42
Pope, Arthur 134
Delilah 115
Edith 124
Elizabeth 63, 112

Pope (cont.)
John 2, 115
Mourning 31
Nancy 127
Nicy 33
Patsy 131
Pherebee 110
Sally A. Q. 65
Simon 100
Temperance 54
Winny 70
Zachariah H. 60
Zelpha 33
Porch, Sarah 45
Winefred 96
Porter, Lotty 99
Mary 77
Nancy 50
Sarah 42
Potter, Wm. 41
Powel, Lydey 15
Martilly 105
Nancy 105
Powell, Adin 49, 105,
112
Ashley G. 75
Betsey 121
Cornelia A. 75
Cynthia 71
Edeth 25
Enos 94
Isbel 113
Jacob 4, 25
Jeremiah 91, 94, 95
Jno. S. 47
Kedar 58
Margaret 36
Martilly 105
Metildeth 64
Nancy 105
Nathan 27, 116
Patsy 38
Ruth 25
Rutha 25
Sally 7, 13, 21
Sarah 6
Sophia G. 120
Upton 101
Powells, Betsey 6
Powers, Thomas 35
William 84
Prett, Polly 11
Price, Ashley 122
B. 23, 48
Berry 122
Bud 96
Ceely 96
Culy 17
Cynthia 96
David H. 122
Dedemiah 33
Dixon 94, 96
Easter 23
Edward 61, 78, 95,
108, 120
Edy 91
Elizabeth 15
Esther 85
Evaline 117
Garry 124
George 128
Gideon 56
Gincy 33
Jane 35
John 13, 96
Julia 4
Martha 17, 106
Mary 18

Price (cont.)
Mary A. 72
Mary Ann 84
Maryan 13
Milly 82
Nancy 37, 42
Nelly 94
Patience 114
Patsy 123
Peguila 109
Penelopia 24
Penny 100
Piety 36
Polly 45
Priscilla 60
Quilly 96
Reley 114
Rhody 110
Richard 74
Riley 130
Rutha 122
Sally 133
Simon 85
Susan 77
Susanna 121
Temperance 96
Thomas 33, 37, 57, 78,
80, 95, 105, 106
Tranquilla 48
William 121
Willie 95
Willy 74
Winefred 33
Zella 11
Zilpha 23, 48
Zilphia 115
Pridgin, Willie N. 70
Pritchet, Alsey 116
Mary 69
Sarah 6
Privett, Penny 124
Wm. R. 77
Prker, Tempy 82
Proctor, Clarky 39
Gracy 15
Henry 72
Pugh, Elizabeth 80
Isabel 105
Orpah 93
Sally 46
Tignal 134
Zilpha 21
Pullen, Jonathan 94
Pulley, Bryant 97, 119,
126
Emiline 119
Purvis, Jesse 120
Radford, Anna 91
Rae, Betty 41
Raeford, Nancy 97
P. 123
Philip 31, 97
Ragan, Patsy 31
Raiford, Barsheba 84
Benja. W. 90
Civil 97
Harriet E. 105
James 4
Lotty 84
Mary Ann 103
Nancy 91, 97, 127
Philip 69, 70, 90, 97
Polly 69, 104
Robert 47
Robt. 42
Sarah 58
W. P. 22, 27, 46, 83
Wm. B. 113

Smith (cont.)
Caswell A. 93
Celia Ann 98
Christian 21
Cyntha 44
David 30, 123
Dorithy 72
Edith 115, 120
Edwin 24, 98
Elam 4
Eliza 20, 63
Elizabeth 17, 20, 44,
  67, 123
Ephraim A. 41
Esther 74
Etheldred 6, 123
Ether 68
F. E. 48
Felps 47
Henry 44, 70
Isaac 44
Isabella 16
J. Wesley 24
James A. 70, 88
Jane 18
Jno. 115
Jno. A. 70, 89
John 2, 6, 31, 106,
  107, 133
John (Jr.) 5, 32, 41,
  106
John A. 10, 41, 44,
  72, 113
Judith 66
Julia C. 19
Julius 107
Keran 104
L. 126
Larkin 106
Leathy 133
Lethey Ann 44
Leucy 83
Lewey 45
Lucinda 104
Ludom 41
Luvey 53
Martha 91
Mary 107
Mary B. 60
Mazallane 108
Meady 14
Minerva Ann 127
Olive 50
Peggy 32
Penellope 4
Pennina 126
Penny 41
Phereby 19, 63
Pinny 126
Polly 62, 105, 106,
  117
Purny Jane 116
Renda 108
Rober 127
Romeo 76
Ruth 121
S. A. 57
Sally 32, 66
Samuel 12, 19, 28, 41,
  130
Samuel (Jr.) 20
Samuel W. 128
Sarah Jane 15
Simon 8
Susey 92
Ursula 73
W. A. 15, 70, 106,
  118, 133

Smith (cont.)
W. G. 107
William 79, 101, 106
Winnefred 116
Smiths, Selah 98
Snead, Agnes 16
E. D. 14, 45, 54, 120
E. D. (Dr.) 124
Laura 77
Maria 54
Robert W. 21
Thos E. 77
Thos. D. 4, 27, 115,
  121
Sneed, Margaret 39
Robert W. 114
Stephen 90, 122
Thos. D. 74
Snipes, Ale 52
Bethaney 35
Betsey 95
Bridgers 36
Celie Elizabeth 36
Cherry 11
David 11, 36
Drewry 58
John (Jr.) 97
Lucy 95
Mindy 89
Polly 19, 101
Sally 37
Sindy 42
Solace, Eliza 59
Solomon, Aron 109
Rosey 7
Sowell, W. C. 100
Speed, Agatha H. 54
Mildred 132
Speight, Edy 9
Spence, Betsey A. 112
Elisha 109
Nancy E. 11
Spencer, Axcy 91
Betsey 42
Calley 67
Harriet 118
Jesse 91
Jno. 109
John 66
Polly 37, 91
Sally 17
William 78, 109
Spicer, Elizabeth 50
Joseph 109
Spiers, Martha 29
Spight, Thomas 62
Spights, Winifred 67
Spiur, William 32
Spivey, Charlotty 116
Edwin 5, 20
Jno. 51
Lovet 26
Spivy, Dixion 98
Edwin 51, 58, 75, 109,
  115
Lovet 86, 94
Nancy 116
Rindy 98
Stafford, Polly 117
Stallings, Betsy 34
Candice E. 104
Candis 3
Caroline 56
Collin 78
Edith 92
Elizabeth 18
Henry O. 101, 112
Isaac 40, 53, 109, 126

Stallings (cont.)
Isaac W. 23
Isac 84
Jacob 109
James 42
Judith 116
Kizia 104
Lydia 126
Mary Ann 20
Milly 18
Polly 64, 109
Richard 109
Sally 53, 54
Tadok 120
Ulrica 66
Zadak 76
Zadock 15
Zadok 13, 53, 116
Zelpha 78
Stallins, Zadok 67
Stallions, Elizabeth 47
Zadock 63
Stancell, Edith 129
Elisabeth 112
Elizabeth 110
Gaston 110
Hawkins 58
Martha 12
Mary 110
Morning 27
Nancy 96
Stephen H. 112
Stancill, Williams 109
Standen, Phereby 98
Standley, Elizabeth 122
James 122
Jesse 128
Polly 14
Sally 73
William (Sr.) 125
Wm. 7, 110
Standly, Jesse 13
Lewis 13
Sarah 13
Stanley, John 7
Mary 25
Mary Ann 129
Nancy 122
Ridly 34
William 129
Stanly, Barthsheba 110
Elizabeth 122
James 27, 110, 122
Jensey 110
Jesse 13, 110
Jno. W. 110
John 115
Lewis 13
Mariah 117
Nancy R. 7
Nannie 110
Patsey 69
Penny 65
Polly 7
Sally Ann 68
Sarah 13
Siorty 122
Susan 115
Susan Emily 110
William 110, 117
William (Sir) 110
Wm. (Sir) 114
Stansel, Aleaxnder 132
Elisabeth 80
Elizabeth 1
Godfrey 114
Lucinda 48
Luizer 50

157

Taltch, Elizabeth 94
Talton, Asa 122
  Cullen 109, 123
  Eliza 82
  Elizabeth 36, 120, 134
  Elsie 123
  Hasseltine 45
  Hawkins 22, 37
  Jess A. 125
  John D. 130
  Jonathan 116
  Julie Ann 90
  Lewis 22
  Louiza J. 122
  McC. 90
  Needham 116
  Nicy 100
  Olive 100
  Relcy 53
  Renda 82
  Rildy 109
  Sally 95, 116
  Sarah 106
  William 116
  Willy H. 11
Tant, Frances 80
Tarlor, Nancey 25
Tart, Betsey 131
  Henrietta 72
  James 131
  Jane E. 87
  Phebe 76
  Thomas 107
  W. B. 89
  William 87, 116
  Wm. Rilie 81
  Wm. T. 116
Tarts, Jane 10
Tartt, Nancy 76
Tarver, Betsy 58
  Elizabeth 124
  Polly 83
Taunt, Redden 66
Taver, Lolly 24
Taylor, A. J. 114
  Beneter 58
  Clary 111
  Mary J. 45
  Nancy 25
  Penny 90
  Phereby 89
  Polly 116
  Richard 127
  Sally 105
  Spency 30
  Susanna 66
  Thomas 108
Teal, William 30, 96
Tedder, Penny 87
Teel, Winifred 84
Tellington, Polly 26
Temple, Burwell 54
  Elizabeth 94
  Henry 78
  Lucy 78, 105
  Peter R. 81
  R. H. 78
  Sally 78
  Sarah A. 77
  Starling W. 14, 117
  Sterling 78, 85
  Sterling W. 78
  Susan 15
Temples, Polly 54
Terry, Julia M. 125
  Richard C. 18
  Sarrah Ann 83
Tew, Nancy 40

Thain, Alex 29
  Alexander 84, 133
  H. E. 3
  Jethro 3, 5, 103
Tharin, Thos. S. 5
Tharp, Celia 5
  Edith 75
  Patsey 94
  Rebeccah 5
Thaughn, Penelepy 43
Thawne, Nicholas 70
Thom, Sarah 6
Thomas, Betsy 79
  Cloe 62
  Cynthia 50
  David 47
  Elisha 84, 85, 117
  Elizabeth 47
  Gary W. 1
  Gray W. 17
  John 36, 107
  Joseph 117
  Louiza 54
  Lucy 75
  Nancy 127
  Nathan 95
  Rhoda 97
  Sally 10
  Temperance 46
  Winney 75
Thompsn, Edith 33
Thompson, Arthur 97
  Betsy 37
  Chilly 22
  Daniel 27
  David 19, 89
  Elijah 37, 118
  Elizabeth 70
  Jarrot 51
  Nicholas 19
  Nickolas 118
  Rebecca 29
  Sallie Ann 119
  Sally 115
  Sarah 27
  Sarah A. E. 118
  Stephen 118
  William 118
Thomson, Ann G. 13
  Asa 131
  David 20, 24, 27, 32,
    34, 115, 121
  Devereux D. 118
  Deverich D. 118
  Elijah 118
  Keran 112
  Lewis 58, 118
  Nicholas 28
  Rebecca 22
  Rebeccah 60
  Winefred 118
  Winnefred 28
Thorn, Polly 99
Thornton, A. G. 47
  Alexander H. 27, 113
  Allanson 35
  Alvin 74
  Eliza 62
  Elizabeth 41, 115
  Harrod 118
  Maledith 41
  Martha A. 81
  Mary M. 58
  Sally 43
  Sarah 120
  Sarah Ann 45
  Susan Caroline 56
  Thos. H. 50

Thornton (cont.)
  William 13
  Wm. 38
Thorp, Nancy 93
  Phebe 13
Thorton, Rebecca 18
Tillett, J. 103
Tiner, Adalne 119
  Catharine M. 62
  James 39, 84
  Jesse 119
  John 94
  Julia H. 84
  Mariah 133
  Mary 16
  Nancy 30
  Patience 47
  Rachel 59
  Sabry 36
  Sally 91
  Sarah 39
  Sarah J. 65
  Susan L. 84
  Willis 61
  Zachariah 81, 126
Tinor, Zachariah 46
Tisdale, Alcy 53
Tisdell, Aby 6
  Zady 36
Todd, Elijah 50
  George 105
  M. G. 58, 101, 127
  Tempe 33
  William 94
Tolar, Elizabeth 25
  Robrt 25
Toler, Caler(?) R. 3
  Charlotte 70
  Elizabeth 25
  Mary 61
  Mary W. 77
  N. B. 113
  Pherebe 4
  Robrt 25
  Sarah C. 3
  Thomas 41
  Thos. 45, 58, 81
  William H. 47
Tomkins, Easter 3
Tomlin, Sarah 88
Tomlinson, Allen 134
  Ann 88
  B. 8
  B. H. 134
  C. R. 74
  Cassandara 8
  Cazilla 24
  Drusilla 5
  Druzeilla 34
  Edmund 40, 108
  Harris 34, 113
  Harriss 106, 119
  James 26
  Martha 134
  Mary 132
  Pherebe 40
  Pheribee H. 8
  Polly 70
  Ruffin W. 9, 123
  Sally 62, 134
  Sarah 10
  Thomas 64, 85
  Violet 103
  William 119
Tompson, Phereby 100
Tomson, Nichols 50
Trawick, Emily 113
Trayway, Nancy 35

159